D1524693

American Indian Law Deskbook

FOURTH EDITION

Conference of Western Attorneys General

2011 Supplement

MONTGOMERY COLLEGE
TAKOMA PARK CAMPUS LIBRARY
TAKOMA PARK, MARYLAND

American Indian Law Deskbook

FOURTH EDITION
Conference of Western Attorneys General

2011 Supplement

UNIVERSITY PRESS OF COLORADO

1514826
APR 10 2012

© 2012 by the University Press of Colorado

Published by the University Press of Colorado
5589 Arapahoe Avenue, Suite 206C
Boulder, Colorado 80303

All rights reserved
Printed in the United States of America

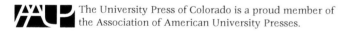 The University Press of Colorado is a proud member of
the Association of American University Presses.

The University Press of Colorado is a cooperative publishing enterprise supported, in part, by Adams State College, Colorado State University, Fort Lewis College, Mesa State College, Metropolitan State College of Denver, University of Colorado, University of Northern Colorado, and Western State College of Colorado.

∞ The paper used in this publication meets the minimum requirements of the American National Standard for Information Sciences—Permanence of Paper for Printed Library Materials. ANSI Z39.48-1992

Library of Congress Cataloging-in-Publication Data

American Indian law deskbook / Conference of Western Attorneys General ; chair, editing committee, Larry Long, chief editor, Clay Smith. — 4th ed.
       p. cm.
  ISBN 978-0-87081-925-4 (alk. paper)
 1. Indians of North America—Legal status, laws, etc. I. Myers, Hardy. II. Smith, Clay. III. Conference of Western Attorneys General.
  KF8205.A76 2008
  342.7308'72—dc22
                                                                    2008041532

The barcode on the back cover, 978-1-60732-188-0, is a control number only.

Typeset by Daniel Pratt

21   20   19   18   17   16   15   14   13   12   10   9   8   7   6   5   4   3   2   1

Contents

Preface

When the *American Indian Law Deskbook* was conceived, the Conference of Western Attorneys General recognized that any Indian law treatise would soon become outdated unless supplemented regularly. The absence of supplementation is a major drawback in other treatises in this area. As with the main volume, the 2011 Supplement represents a collaborative effort in which many CWAG member states participated. In particular, I would like to thank Jas. Jeffrey Adams and Stephanie Striffler of Oregon, Fronda Woods and Rob Costello of Washington, Jennifer Henderson of California, Dawn Williams of Arizona, Charlie McGuigan and John Guhin of South Dakota, and Charles Carvell of North Dakota for their assistance in drafting and reviewing various parts of this 2011 Supplement. A special thank you goes to Clay Smith of Idaho, our long-time editor, who has kept this project going for many years.

In preparing the 2011 Supplement, an effort was made to review all decisions contained in reporters and advance sheets issued prior to July 2011. Federal statutes, administrative regulations and law review articles, often are quite helpful in Indian law, were also updated.

CHRIS COPPIN
Legal Director
Conference of Western Attorneys General

American Indian Law Deskbook

FOURTH EDITION

Conference of Western Attorneys General

2011 Supplement

Chapter 1
Federal Indian Law Policy: Origins and Legal Development

P.2, n.9. **Add the following to line 1 of the footnote after "*See generally*":**

Michael D. Oeser, *Tribal Citizen Participation in State and National Politics: Welcome Wagon or Trojan Horse?*, 36 Wm. Mitchell L. Rev. 793, 825–26 (2010) ("[A] person with tribal ancestry is not necessarily politically 'Indian.' Such a person is genetically Indian, might be culturally 'Indian,' and might even be entitled to tribal citizenship, but until enrollment, he or she forms no part of the tribal body politic. A person merely ancestrally or culturally 'Indian' who lives off-reservation deserves all the civil rights protections state and federal citizenship afford, including protection from racial discrimination in voting. On the other hand, individuals that are politically 'Indian'—i.e. enrolled tribal 'members'—are citizens of another sovereign"); Matthew L.M. Fletcher, *Factbound and Splitless: The Certiorari Process as Barrier to Justice for Indian Tribes*, 51 Ariz. L. Rev. 933, 980 (2009) (examining 163 "preliminary memoranda" prepared by Supreme Court law clerks concerning certiorari petitions during the 1986–1993 period, and concluding that "[t]he modern certiorari process, with its dependence on law clerks applying the Court's Rule 10, virtually guarantees that the cert pool will denigrate petitions filed by tribal interests" because "[t]ribal petitions, often involving the interpretation of Indian treaties or complicated and narrow common law questions of federal Indian law, are readily deemed 'factbound' and 'splitless[]'" and because "the cert pool values and perhaps better understands the interests of state and state agency petitions");

P.4, n.14. **Add the following to the beginning of the footnote:**

Tonya Kowalski, *The Forgotten Sovereigns*, 36 Fla. St. U. L. Rev. 765, 771–72 (2009) ("At the heart of today's tribal-federal relations is the colonial doctrine of discovery. . . . Whether one agrees about the extent to which the cognitive model of the Conqueror is embedded within key Supreme Court cases like *Johnson v. M'Intosh*, there can be no doubt that the central method of classifying Native American people as 'subhuman' and 'heathens' dominated large portions of U.S. law and policy during the assimilation era");

P.5, n.23.   **Add the following to line 3 of the footnote after "*e.g.,*":**

Nicholas A. Fromherz & Joseph W. Mead, *Equal Standing with States: Tribal Sovereignty and Standing After Massachusetts v. EPA*, 29 Stan. Envtl. L.J. 130, 155, 159 (2010) (observing that "[m]any of the fundamental principles underlying Indian law were framed by Chief Justice John Marshall" in the trilogy, and arguing that "*Worcester* recognized that states have no power to regulate Indian tribes, essentially placing them at an equal mark on the sovereignty scale" and that, "[i]n placing tribes and states on a more or less equal footing in terms of sovereignty, *Worcester* supports the claim that tribes should be entitled to the same 'special solicitude' as states" for standing purposes in environmental law-related controversies);

P.7, n.29.   **Add the following to the end of the footnote:**

but see Fife v. Moore, No. CIV-11-133-RAW, 2011 WL 1533147, at *3 (E.D. Okla. 2011) (enjoining tribal prosecution because "crimes committed by Native Americans outside the territorial boundaries of Indian country are subject to state [not tribal] prosecution[,]" and "the definition of Indian country is provided by federal statute, not the tribe.").

P.11, n.51.   **Add the following to the end of the footnote before the period:**

, *rev'd*, 559 F.3d 1228 (Fed. Cir. 2009), *cert. denied*, 130 S. Ct. 2090 (2010)

P.14, n.71.   **Delete that portion of the footnote from "On remand" in line 8 through the period at the end of line 21.**

P.14.   **Add the following to the text after footnote 71:**

The Supreme Court applied the same analytical approach in reversing the Federal Circuit's determination following remand proceedings in the *Navajo* litigation that a combination of federal statutes, other than the IMLA, created a money-mandating trust obligation.[71.1]

[71.1]   *United States v. Navajo Nation*, 129 S. Ct. 1547 (2009). On remand, the tribe had been permitted to pursue another breach of trust theory premised on a "network" of treaties, statutes and regulations other than those before the Supreme Court. Its theory was rejected by the Federal Claims court but accepted by the Court of Appeals for the Federal Circuit. *Navajo Nation v. United States*, 68 Fed. Cl. 805 (2005), *rev'd*, 501 F.3d 1327 (Fed. Cir. 2007), *rev'd*, 129 S. Ct. (2009). The "network" claim was predicated on two treaties, an Executive Order and several statutes including the 1950 Navajo-Hopi Rehabilitation Act, the 1977 Surface Mining Control and Reclamation Act, the 1983 Federal Oil and Gas Royalty Management Act, and regulations implementing the latter two laws. The Federal Circuit found the "network" to be money-mandating on the basis of five considerations: the existence of a trust relationship and trust language; federal control of coal resource planning; federal control of coal mining operations; federal control of the management and collection of coal mining royalties; and federal control of coal leasing and liabilities arising from the leasing arrangements. 501 F.3d at 1340–45; *see generally* Kimberly C. Perdue, Comment, *The Changing Scope of the United States' Trust Duties to American Indian Tribes: Navajo Nation v. United States*, 80 U. Colo. L. Rev. 487, 520–21 (2009) (reasoning that "the Federal Circuit evaluated the network as an aggregate, considering the manner in which the network's elements worked together to assign to the Secretary of the Interior control over coal resource planning, coal mining operations, the management and collection of coal mining royalties, and coal leasing" and that, in contrast to the Court of Federal Claims, "the Federal Circuit concluded that the network collectively established the Secretary of the Interior's comprehensive control over all aspects of the Nation's coal resources, and, according to the doctrine that the greater includes the lesser, likewise established the Secretary's control over the renegotiation of . . . [the] royalty rate"). It thus held that assigning money-mandating status to the "network" was consistent with the involved laws' purposes and rejected the United States' argument that the tribe "must allege a violation of a specific rights-creating or duly-imposing statute or regulation and the common law of trusts cannot be applied." 501 F.3d at 1345. Although the Supreme Court agreed as a "[t]hreshold [m]atter" (129 S. Ct. at 1554) that the earlier decision had not analyzed the breach of trust claim under any statute other than the IMLA and thus was unable to "say that our mandate completely foreclosed the possibility that [another] statute might allow for the Tribe to succeed on remand[,]" the Court could say "that our reasoning in [the first *Navajo* decision]—in particular, our emphasis on the need for courts to 'train on specific rights-creating or duty-imposing statutory or regulatory prescriptions[]'—left no room for that result based upon the sources of law that the Court of Appeals relied upon." *Id.* at 1555. It then addressed each of the non-IMLA statutes relied upon by the lower court and found none of them contained a rights-creating or duty-imposing prescription. *Id.* at 1557–58. The Supreme Court also rejected the Federal Circuit's more generalized reliance on federal governmental control over Indian-land coal development as a basis for implying a compensable trust obligation, reiterating that the complainant must identify the requisite statutory prescription and explained that if such "prescription bears the hallmarks of a 'conventional fiduciary relationship,' . . . *then* trust principles (including any such principles premised on 'control') could play a role in 'inferring that the trust obligation [is] enforceable by damages.'" *Id* at 1558 (citation omitted). "Control" under this formulation constitutes "the second step of the analysis, not (as the Federal Circuit made it) the starting point." *Id.* The second *Navajo* decision appears fatal to the "network" theory because it examined the money-mandating requirement on a statute-by-statute basis; *i.e.*, complainants must be able to point to provisions in the relied-upon statute that give rise to a money-mandating trust obligation.

P.16, n.83.   Add the following to line 1 of the footnote after "*See*":

United States v. Navajo Nation, 129 S. Ct. 1547 (2009) (reversing as inconsistent with the standards described in *Navajo* application of a "network" approach to determining existence of a money-mandating trust obligation adopted on remand in *Navajo Nation v. United States*, 501 F.3d 1327 (Fed. Cir. 2007));

Add the following to line 7 of the footnote before the semi-colon:

, and 85 Fed. Cl. 525, 530–31 (2009) (declining to enter partial final judgment where the two claims involve "the same legal frameworks but invoke different liability theories" with the attendant possibility of multiple appeals over "interrelated issues"), and 90 Fed. Cl. 122, 148 (2009) (dismissing action for failure to establish money-mandating trust obligation under various statutes and programs in the event of governmental default or even a common-law trust *res* in "funds that plaintiff might have received if it [had been] treated as a federally recognized tribe" during period at issue;

Add the following to the sixth-to-last line before the semi-colon:

, *rev'd*, 559 F.3d 1228, 1238 (Fed. Cir. 2009) (declining to read 1888, 1889 and 1890 appropriations acts as creating a trust relationship; "[a]lthough the Appropriations Acts impose some limited restrictions as to how the appropriated funds are to be spent, those restrictions are consistent with the kinds of directions that are routinely contained in appropriations statutes dictating that the appropriated funds are to be spent for a particular purpose"), *cert. denied*, 130 S. Ct. 2090 (2010)

P.16, n.84.   Add the following to line 4 of the footnote after the semi-colon:

Oenga v. United States, 83 Fed. Cl. 594, 621–22 (2008) (BIA possessed money-mandating duty under 25 C.F.R. § 162 to investigate landowner claims of lease breach and to give the landowner notice of any violation found), and 91 Fed. Cl. 629, 646–47 (2010) (present fair annual rental value constituted measure of damages for six-year period preceding filing of amended complaint that asserted claim);

P.17, n.85.   Add the following to line 8 of the footnote before the semi-colon:

, *rev'd on other grounds*, 559 F.3d 1228 (Fed. Cir. 2009), *cert. denied*, 130 S. Ct. 2090 (2010)

P.17, n.86.　　**Add the following to line 1 of the footnote after "*See, e.g.,*":**

Yankton Sioux Tribe v. USDHHS, 533 F.3d 634, 644 (8th Cir. 2008) (applying *Mitchell I*, and rejecting challenge to closure of a clinic's emergency room where "[t]he Tribe has not identified any assets taken over by the government such as tribally owned land, timber, or funds which would give rise to a special trust duty");

Add the following to line 22 of the footnote after the semi-colon:

Miami Tribe v. United States, 679 F. Supp. 2d 1269, 1285 (D. Kan. 2010) ("[w]hile *Mitchell I* and *Mitchell II* involved a tribe's claim for money damages under Tucker Act and the Indian Tucker Act, other courts have permitted breach of trust causes of action against the federal government in cases where an Indian tribe sought non-monetary relief under the APA");

P.18, n.88.　　**Delete the portion of the footnote between the period on line 8 and the period on line 13 and replace with the following:**

In *United States v. Tohono O'Odham Nation*, the Court construed a jurisdictional bar provision in the Tucker Act, 28 U.S.C. § 1500, to preclude the Court of Federal Claims from exercising jurisdiction over a claim for damages when a suit for relief based on "substantially the same operative facts" is already pending in district court, regardless of the relief sought in each suit. 563 U.S. ___, 131 U.S. 1723, 1731 (2011). The Court did not foreclose the possibility of concurrent claims with significant factual overlap, however, when a Court of Federal Claims suit is filed first. *Id.* at 1730–1731.

Add the following to the end of the footnote:

See id. at 1291 ("§ 1500 does not actually prevent a plaintiff from filing two actions seeking the same relief for the same claims" but, instead, "merely requires that the plaintiff file its action in the Court of Federal Claims *before* it files its district court complaint"); *United Keetoowah Band of Cherokee Indians v. United States*, 86 Fed. Cl. 183, 191 (2009) (adopting the "majority view" that the jurisdiction bar in § 1500 should be measured, as to filing sequence, with reference to the actual time and not merely the date of filing); *Nez Perce Tribe v. United States*, 83 Fed. Cl. 186, 191 (2008) (same).

P.18, n.90.　　**Add the following to line 2 of the footnote after the semi-colon:**

Miami Tribe v. United States, 679 F. Supp. 2d 1269, 1284 (D. Kan. 2010);

Add the following to the end of the footnote:

At least in one instance, however, a substantial monetary judgment—$455.6 million—was entered by a district court as equitable relief in the form of restitution or disgorgement where a "failure properly to allocate and pay trust funds to beneficiaries" had been established and the amount awarded equaled "the very money that has been withheld." *Cobell v. Kempthorne*, 569 F. Supp. 2d 223, 243 (D.D.C. 2008). The court distinguished this restitution relief from damages for the United States' failure to provide a proper accounting for the involved trust funds because the latter would be an "alternative remedy" intended to assign a value to the accounting failure and thus would fall outside the remedial authority contained in 5 U.S.C. § 702. 569 F. Supp. 2d at 243. On interlocutory appeal, however, the District of Columbia Circuit Court of Appeals vacated the order and remanded for further proceedings to conduct an accounting for the trust funds—which the district court had concluded could not occur "given inadequate present and (likely) future funding from Congress"—because the plaintiffs were entitled to one under Public Law No. 103-412, 108 Stat. 4239 (1994). *Cobell v. Salazar*, 573 F.3d 808, 810 (D.C. Cir. 2009).

P.19, n.94.   **Add the following at the end of the footnote before the period:**

, and 590 F. Supp. 2d 15, 18 (D.D.C. 2008) (declining to issue permanent injunction to plaintiffs, and clarifying that the statute's unambiguous language "establishes . . . the preference applies to 'positions' and not to 'organizational units[]' . . . that directly and primarily relate to the provision of services to Indians")

P.20, n.98.   **Add the following to the fifth-to-last line of the footnote after "*See generally*":**

Lincoln T. Davies, *2009 Skull Valley Crossroads: Reconciling Native Sovereignty and the Federal Trust*, 68 Md. L. Rev. 290, 367 (2009) (discussing the tension between the traditional trust doctrine and tribal self-governance in the context of one tribe's efforts to enter into a lease for nuclear waste storage on its lands and the Bureau of Indian Affairs' refusal to approve the proposed lease, and suggesting a "new model" of tribal self-determination under which tribes would have the option "to accept additional levels of governmental power and responsibility up to the same level that states hold today");

P.21, n.100.   **Add the following to line 20 of the footnote after the semi-colon:**

Miami Tribe v. United States, 679 F. Supp. 2d 1269, 1286, 1287 (D. Kan. 2010) (citing *Morongo Band* for principle that "the Ninth Circuit . . . limited the government's duty so that unless a specific duty has been placed on the government with respect to the Indian tribe, the government's responsibility is discharged by the agency's compliance with general regulations and statutes not specifically aimed at protecting Indian tribes[;]" and concluding that "the actions or inactions of an administrative agency in carrying out its agency duties do not constitute a valid basis for Miami Tribe's breach of trust claim" because, "[w]hile the administrative agency's duties may be statutorily required, they are not duties the breach of which would necessarily give rise to a breach of trust claim");

Add the following to the sixth-to-last line of the footnote after "*See generally*":

Sean Hill, Note, *Sunshine in Indian Country: A Pro-FOIA View of Klamath Water Users*, 32 Am. Indian L. Rev. 463, 484 (2007–2008) ("The decision by the Court not to read into FOIA an Indian-trust exemption seems to have followed congressional intent while also signaling who to turn to for relief. This was a wise decision, as Congress has twice considered legislation that would achieve this purpose, with both proposals failing") (footnote omitted);

P.22, n.102.   **Add the following to line 1 of the footnote after "*see*":**

In re United States, 590 F.3d 1305, 1313 (Fed. Cir. 2009) ("The United States' relationship with the Indian tribes is sufficiently similar to a private trust to justify applying the fiduciary exception" to the attorney-client privilege doctrine);

Add the following to line 13 of the footnote before the semi-colon:

rev'd, 559 F.3d 1228, 1238 (Fed. Cir. 2009) (relying on the *Restatement* to conclude, contrary to the trial court, that several appropriations acts did not reflect the requisite intent to create a trust relationship), *cert. denied*, 130 S. Ct. 2090 (2010)

P.23, n.107.   **Add the following to the end of the footnote:**

The district court subsequently awarded $455.6 million to the plaintiff class—an amount that the United States argued could be identified with 99 percent confidence as missing from individual Indian money trust accounts—but its order was vacated on appeal with a direction to conduct the accounting requested by plaintiffs and mandated by 25 U.S.C. § 4011(a). *Cobell v. Kempthorne*, 569 F. Supp. 2d 223, 252 (D.D.C. 2008), *vacated*, 573 F.3d 808, 813, 815 (D.C. Cir. 2009).

P.23, n.108.   **Add the following to the third-to-last line of the footnote before the semi-colon:**

, *rev'd on other grounds*, 559 F.3d 1228 (Fed. Cir. 2009), *cert. denied*, 130 S. Ct. 2090 (2010); *Chippewa Cree Tribe v. United States*, 85 Fed. Cl. 646, 654–56 (2009) (intervention of right denied, *inter alia*, for lack of a legally protectable interest in a judgment fund where the proposed intervenors' ancestors were not included on the tribal membership roll selected by the Secretary of the Interior from congressionally-identified alternatives to be used in determining eligibility to share in the fund)

P.23, n.109.   **Add the following to line nine of the footnote after "*see*":**

Ute Distrib. Corp. v. Secretary, 584 F.3d 1275, 1283 (10th Cir. 2009) (continuing violation doctrine did not apply to save suit from dismissal under 28 U.S.C. § 2401 to asset distribution plan adopted by Secretary in 1961 where complaint did not allege mismanagement of assets and the alleged injury had been "'definite and discoverable'" and "'nothing prevented plaintiff from coming forward to seek redress'"), *cert. denied*, 130 S. Ct. 3285 (2010); *Shoshone Indian Tribe of the Wind River Reservation, Wyoming v. United States*, 93 Fed. Cl. 449, 462 (2010) (breach-of-trust suits initiated in 1979 were barred by six-year limitation period in 28 U.S.C. § 2501 where tribe's attorney wrote letter in 1959 expressing concerns over not converting oil-and-gas leases from coverage under 1916 statute to coverage under 1938 Indian Mineral Leasing Act; suits not saved by accounting requirement in Public Law No. 108-7, 117 Stat. 11, 234 (2003), since, *inter alia*, claim was "more readily characterized as mismanagement of an asset" rather than as mismanagement of a trust fund); *Felter v. Salazar*, 679 F. Supp. 2d 1, 6–7, 10–11 (D.D.C. 2010) (Public Law No. 108-7 applied retroactively to preclude running of six-year limitation period in 28 U.S.C. § 2501 until accounting prepared in action alleging trust fund mismanagement and pending as of statute's effective date, but action nevertheless barred by collateral estoppel); *Rosales v. United States*, 89 Fed. Cl. 565, 578 (2009) (six-year limitation period in 28 U.S.C. § 2501 barred breach-of-trust claim in 2008 suit arising under 1982 Secretarial determination to recognize tribal village, rather than the plaintiffs, as parcel's beneficial owner); *Oenga v. United States*, 83 Fed. Cl. 594, 609 (2008) (applying 28 U.S.C. § 2501 in light of the Indian Trust Accounting Statute, Pub. L. No. 109-54, Tit. I, 119 Stat. 499, 519 (2005), which bars the limitation period from commencing to run "on any claim . . . concerning losses to or mismanagement of trust funds, until the affected tribe or individual Indian has been furnished with an accounting of such funds from which the beneficiary can determine whether there has been a loss"), and 91 Fed. Cl. 629, 646–47 (2010) (present fair annual rental value constituted measure of damages for six-year period preceding filing of amended complaint that asserted claim);

P.25, n.117.   **Add the following to line 16 of the footnote after the semi-colon:**

but see Cachil Dehe Band of Wintun Indians of Colusa Indian Community v. California, 629 F. Supp. 2d 1091, 1107 n.13 (E.D. Cal. 2009), *aff'd in part and rev'd in part*, 618 F.3d 1066 (9th Cir. 2010) (in dispute over tribal-state gaming compact entered into under the Indian Gaming Regulatory Act, the court declined to extend the *Blackfeet* canon of liberal construction of statutes in favor of tribes to contracts, absent any issue of statutory interpretation raised in the contract claims);

P.25, n.118.   **Add the following to line 3 of the footnote after "*see also*":**

Carcieri v. Salazar, 129 S. Ct. 1058, 1078 (2009) (Stevens, J., dissenting) (arguing that the majority, which deemed the term "now" in 25 U.S.C. § 479 unambiguous without discussion of the Indian canons, "adopt[ed] a cramped reading of a statute that Congress intended to be 'sweeping' in scope" and "ignore[d] the 'principle deeply rooted in [our] Indian jurisprudence' that 'statutes are to be construed liberally in favor of the Indians'") (some internal quotation marks omitted);

P.26, n.124.   **Add the following to line 7 of the footnote after the semi-colon:**

Tunica-Biloxi Tribe v. United States, 577 F. Supp. 2d 382, 421 (D.D.C. 2008) (Indian canons and not ordinary *Chevron* standards control), *recons. denied*, 655 F. Supp. 2d 62 (D.D.C. 2009);

P.27, n.129.   **Add the following to line 1 of the footnote after "*Compare*":**

Menominee Tribal Enters. v. Solis, 601 F.3d 669, 674 (7th Cir. 2010) (following, *inter alia, Coeur d'Alene Tribal Farm* to find Occupational Safety and Health Act applicable to tribal sawmill operated as commercial enterprise; *i.e.*, it "is not part of the Menominee's governance structure; it is just a sawmill"); *In re Shinnecock Smoke Shop*, 571 F.3d 1171 (2d Cir. 2009) (tribe constitutes "institution" under 15 U.S.C. § 1052(a) of Trademark Act), *cert. denied*, 130 S. Ct. 1156 (2010); *Solis v. Matheson*, 563 F.3d 425, 429–37 (9th Cir. 2009) (applying *Coeur d'Alene Tribal Farm*, and finding overtime provisions of the Fair Labor Standards Act applicable to tribal member-owned reservation business that sells tobacco products to the general public and employs both members and nonmembers);

Add the following to line 17 of the footnote after the semi-colon:

Pearson v. Chugach Gov't Servs., Inc., 669 F. Supp. 2d 467, 473–74 (D. Del. 2009) (Alaskan Native corporation entitled to exemption from "employer" status under Title VII of 1964 Civil Rights Act for Indian tribes, at least to the extent "the burden of employer liability under federal antidiscrimination laws impinge on a tribe's self-governance by interfering with the Native American employment preference" but constituted "covered entity" under the Americans With Disabilities Act and Family Medical Leave Act);

Add the following to the eighth-to-last line after *cf.*:

Dobbs v. Anthem Blue Cross and Blue Shield, 600 F.3d 1275, 1284 (10th Cir. 2010) (2006 amendments to Employee Retirement Income Security Act's exclusion of "governmental plan[s]" from coverage to apply retroactively to tribal plans because, in part, "[a]pplying certain federal regulatory schemes to Indian tribes would impinge upon their sovereignty by preventing tribal governments from freely exercising their powers, including the 'sovereign authority to regulate economic activity within their own territory' ");

Add the following to the fifth-to-last line of the footnote on page 28 after *"see generally"*:

Ezekiel J.N. Fletcher, *De Facto Judicial Preemption of Tribal Labor and Preemption Law*, 2008 Mich. St. L. Rev. 435, 465 (analyzing major federal employment-related statutes with reference to their applicability to tribal governments and enterprises, and arguing that some recent cases, rather than using *Tuscarora* principles to fill tribal regulatory gaps with federal law, use them to supersede "positive tribal law"); Vicki J. Limas, *The Tuscagornization of the Tribal Workforce*, 2008 Mich. St. L. Rev. 467, 485 (criticizing the distinction between governmental and commercial tribal activity drawn in *San Manuel* and other decisions because it "leave[s] Indian nations in a state of confusion, not knowing which of their activities will trigger federal regulation and oversight . . . [or] precisely what factors will be used to make this determination" and because "the determination of whether activities trigger regulation will always be made by federal courts or agencies"); Wenona T. Singel, *The Institutional Economics of Tribal Labor Relations*, 2008 Mich. St. L. Rev. 487, 503 (presenting an "economic analysis" of factors that affect the choice of "paths" in Indian country labor relations, and recommending adoption of strategies that will promote "new, alternative organizations of employees . . . for collective representation . . . within the rubric of tribal law" and, thereby, will create "a stake in looking to tribal law to address labor concerns"); Kaighn Smith Jr., *Tribal Self-Determination and Judicial Restraint: The Problem of Labor and Employment Relations Within the Reservation*, 2008 Mich. St. L. Rev. 505, 536 (arguing that *Coeur d'Alene Tribal Farm*'s three-part test improperly diminishes tribal self-governance and that the Tenth Circuit's approach is proper; the latter "first . . . consider[s] whether the imposition of a federal labor or employment law of general application would interfere with attributes of tribal sovereignty established by treaty or common law" and "[i]f it would, . . . holds the law inapplicable absent a clear directive from Congress"); Bryan H. Wildenthal, *How the Ninth Circuit Overruled a Century of Supreme Court Indian Jurisprudence—And So Far Has Gotten Away with It*, 2008 Mich. St. L. Rev. 547, 586 (discussing the federal circuits' varying approaches to the statute-of-general-applicability issue; challenging the analysis in *Coeur d'Alene Tribal Farm* on various grounds; but observing that "the fact remains that the Supreme Court—for more than a generation now—has not chosen, or perhaps has not been given an opportunity, to directly rein in the Ninth Circuit or those that have followed it down the trail of *Tuscarora-Coeur d'Alene*"); Alex Tallchief Skibine, *Tribal Sovereign Interests Beyond the Reservation Borders*, 12 Lewis & Clark L. Rev. 1003, 1013–14 (2008) (contrasting *Coeur d'Alene Tribal Farm*-based analysis with the "very different vision of tribal sovereignty when [the Tenth Circuit] decided not to apply some provisions of the NLRA to the Pueblo of San Juan[,]" and deeming the latter "more coherent" and consistent with Supreme Court tribal sovereignty decisions; courts therefore should "ask whether the tribe has any inherent jurisdiction to regulate the type of activity that is being regulated by the federal law of general applicability" and, "[i]f the answer is yes, . . . should look for a clear indication of congressional intent to interfere with such tribal sovereignty");

P.32, n.153.   **Add the following to the end of the footnote:**

But see Brian Pierson, *Resolving a Perilous Uncertainty: The Right of Tribes to Convey Fee Simple Lands*, 57-APR Fed. Law. 49, 50 (2010) (arguing that Congress did not intend prohibition on alienation in 25 U.S.C. § 177 to apply to lands held by tribes in fee simple absolute, and that a formal statement from the Department of Interior is necessary to "remove a cloud over numerous transactions" arising from confusion over the scope of § 177).

P.32, n.158.   **Add the following to line 2 of the footnote after *"see generally"*:**

Ethan Davis, *An Administrative Trail of Tears: Indian Removal*, 50 Am. J. Legal Hist. 49, 98 (2010) (discussing formulation and implementation of the Removal Policy and concluding that it embodied a "failure of multiple levels of guidance and control[;]" *i.e.*, although "[b]road, external guidance came from Congress in the form of the Removal Act of 1830 and constant pressure to economize[] and from the executive in the form of the removal treaties[,]" actual implementation was left largely to one Commissary General because "[w]hen the time came to hammer out the technical details of the removal and to ensure the integrity of the treaty making process, Congress faded into the background[,]" with judicial oversight "nowhere to be seen" and relevant treaties providing "no guidance");

P.39, n.194.   **Add the following to line 1 of the footnote after *"see generally"*:**

Michael D. Oeser, *Tribal Citizen Participation in State and National Politics: Welcome Wagon or Trojan Horse?*, 36 Wm. Mitchell L. Rev. 793, 856 (2010) (arguing that tribal member participation in federal and state electoral processes, and particularly the latter, necessarily diminishes tribal sovereignty interests given the "consent of the governed" principle: "If consent by participation represents a subtext to the sovereign struggle between tribes and states, and the Founders' fears regarding dual sovereignty have any validity, continued participation by tribes will eventually hollow out tribal sovereignty. The general downward trajectory of tribal sovereignty suggests these concepts are indeed at play");

P.40, n.199.   **Add the following to the end of the footnote before the period:**

; *see Carcieri v. Salazar*, 555 U.S. 379, 129 S. Ct. 1058, 1061 (2009) (phrase "now under Federal jurisdiction" in 25 U.S.C. § 479 limits tribes for which the Secretary of Interior can take land into trust to those recognized by the federal government at the time the IRA was enacted in 1934)

P.41, n.202.   **Add the following to the end of the footnote before the period:**

; *see generally* Keith Richotte, Jr., *Legal Pluralism and Tribal Constitutions*, 36 Wm. Mitchell L. Rev. 447, 500 (2010) (discussing events preceding and following IRA-exclusion vote by the Turtle Mountain Band of Chippewa Indians and the tribe's adoption of a pre-IRA constitution; and drawing the conclusion that "[r]ather than suffering under the imposition of an IRA constitution, the people of Turtle Mountain were actively seeking a constitution as a way to initiate a claim against the United States, to reaffirm their status as a tribal nation, and to reclaim political authority from their superintendents")

P.45, n.228.   **Add the following to the end of the footnote before the period:**

; *see MacArthur v. San Juan County*, 566 F. Supp. 2d 1239, 1248 (D. Utah 2008) (rejecting contention that ISDEAA contract for judicial services extended tribal jurisdiction to nonmembers because "[t]his assertion misses a subtle but critically important distinction: contracts *make law* between the parties in the sense that they create promissory obligations and corresponding rights to performance that are legally enforceable in the courts in the event of a breach" but "do not have any *legislative* effect, in the sense of making new legal rules of general application or altering the substantive fabric of the law itself"), *aff'd*, 355 Fed. Appx. 243 (10th Cir. 2009), *cert. denied*, 130 S. Ct. 2378 (2010)

P.46, n.235.   **Add the following to the third-to-last line of the footnote before the period:**

; *Boney v. Valline*, 597 F. Supp. 2d 1167, 1181 (D. Nev. 2009) (tribal officer was not "investigative or law enforcement officer of the United States Government" for FTCA purposes, notwithstanding the existence of an ISDEAA contract funding the tribe's law enforcement functions, where the officer was not certified or commissioned by the Bureau of Indian Affairs and the alleged tort arose when the officer was enforcing tribal law against a tribal member); *see generally* Thomas W. Christie, *An Introduction to the Federal Tort Claims Act in Indian Self-Determination Act Contracting*, 71 Mont. L. Rev. 115, 130 (2010) (discussing difficulties that have arisen with respect to FTCA application to tribal law enforcement officers, including Special Law Enforcement Commission deputation agreement under which "the BIA forces tribes to agree that the tribal law enforcement officer will only have FTCA protections when enforcing Federal law" and thereby "excludes enforcement of tribal law and state law"); Blake R. Bertagna, *Reservations About Extending Bivens to Reservations: Seeking Monetary Relief Against Tribal Law Enforcement Officers for Constitutional Violations*, 29 Pace L. Rev. 585, 614–18 (2009) (precedent relevant to FTCA's application to tribal officers establishes that FTCA coverage applies only when tribal officer enforces federal law pursuant to Special Law Enforcement Commission under Indian Law Enforcement Reform Act);

P.46, n.237.   Add the following to line 1 of the footnote after "*See, e.g.,*":

Arctic Slope Native Ass'n v. Sebelius, 583 F.3d 785, 799 (Fed. Cir. 2009) (Contract Disputes Act's six-year "presentment" requirement subject to equitable tolling doctrine since "[t]he language of the time limitation in section 605(a) is anything but emphatic; it simply states that the claim 'shall be submitted' within six years"); *S. Ute Indian Tribe v. Leavitt*, 564 F.3d 1198 (10th Cir. 2009) (dismissing on jurisdictional grounds an appeal under 28 U.S.C. § 1292(a)(1) by a tribe from a district court order that was entered in the wake of an earlier determination that the Secretary of the Interior had improperly declined to enter into an ISDEAA contract with the plaintiff tribe and that directed the parties to complete negotiations over and to include certain language in the contract and that required the Secretary to place the tribe on its "shortfall list");

Add the following to line 3 of the footnote after "*see also*":

Council of Athabascan Tribal Gov'ts v. United States, 693 F. Supp. 2d 116, 120–21 (D.D.C. 2010) (declining to dismiss suit over alleged breach of ISDEEA contract with respect to indirect payment of contract support costs and calculation of indirect cost rate, and citing precedent for principle that indirect costs must be funded to the greatest extent possible); *Boye v. United States*, 90 Fed. Cl. 392, 416 (2009) (although ISDEAA-based contracts are "money-mandating" for Tucker Act purposes, tribal law enforcement officers lacked third party beneficiary status to sue the United States for alleged violation of self-determination contracts related to their compensation; evidence "demonstrating that the relevant statutes, regulations, and contracts required them to be paid at the same rate as their BIA counterparts" was insufficient to establish "the plaintiffs can recover their unpaid wages and benefits from United States as third-party beneficiaries of the relevant 638 contracts"—as opposed to recovering against their tribal employer "for failure to pay them the salaries and provide them with the benefits required by statute"); *Three Affiliated Tribes v. United States*, 637 F. Supp. 2d 25, 34 (D.D.C. 2009) (25 U.S.C. § 450m-1(a) deemed "broad waiver of sovereign immunity" over any claim arising under ISDEAA, including Secretary of the Interior's refusal to include contract provision that would have extended health clinic services to non-Indians pursuant to the Indian Health Care Improvement Act; ongoing tribal contractors held not required to be joined under Fed. R. Civ. P. 19 since, *inter alia*, Secretary adequately represented absent tribes' interests); *Tunica-Biloxi Tribe v. United States*, 577 F. Supp. 2d 382, 399–413 (D.D.C. 2008) (rejecting, *inter alia*, mootness and administrative-remedy-exhaustion defenses in action over contract support costs where injunctive relief could prove appropriate and where exhaustion would have offered the Secretary of the Interior no opportunity to correct any error or make an adequate record for judicial review purposes), *recons. denied*, 655 F. Supp. 2d 62 (D.D.C. 2010);

P.47, n.239.   **Add the following to line 1 of the footnote after "*see generally*":**

Gavin Clarkson, *Wall Street Indians: Information Asymmetry and Barriers to Tribal Capital Market Access*, 12 Lewis & Clark L. Rev. 943 (2008) (discussing informational and regulatory disadvantages under which tribes operate in gaining access to the capital market);

Add the following to the end of the footnote:

The American Recovery and Reinvestment Act of 2009 ("ARRA"), Pub. L. No. 111-5, 123 Stat. 115 (2009), augmented the ability of tribes to issue tax-exempt and tax-credit bonds. *See generally* James F. Hayden *et al.*, *New Bonds Available to Tribes to Finance Hotels and Other Amenities*, 13 Gaming L. Rev. & Econ. 217, 220 (2009) (discussing provisions in American Recovery and Reinvestment Act of 2009, that allow tribes in the aggregate to issue up to $2 billion in Tribal Economic Development Bonds and Build America Bonds for various non-gaming commercial activities on Indian reservations; and concluding that while "[p]rior to the Act's passage, tribes could offer tax-exempt bonds only to finance 'essential government functions'—a term the Internal Revenue Service interpreted very narrowly—and certain manufacturing activities[,] . . . [n]ow, with the exception of casinos, tribes will be able to offer tax-exempt bonds and tax credit to finance hotels, convention centers, and other related developments). ARRA also encourages alternative energy development that may facilitate reservation economic growth. *See* Elizabeth Ann Kronk, *Alternative Energy Development in Indian Country: Lighting the Way for the Seventh Generation*, 46 Idaho L. Rev. 449, 460–61 (2010); *but see* Kathleen R. Unger, Note, *Change Is in the Wind: Self-Determination and Wind Power Through Tribal Energy Resources Agreements*, 43 Loy. L.A. L. Rev. 329 (2009) (criticizing 2005 Energy Policy Act as insufficiently protective of tribal self-government: "[t]he TERA framework allows the federal government to retain control over resource development by imposing stringent environmental review requirements, by using the trust responsibility to justify federal power, by withholding authority for 'inherently Federal functions,' and by dictating the terms of tribal energy development projects pursuant to TERAs").

Chapter 2
Indian, Indian Tribe, and Indian Country

P.48.   **Delete the last five lines of the text and the associated footnotes, and replace the deletion with the following:**

2010 Census, 2,932,248 persons identified themselves as one-race Indians, while 5,220,579 persons identified themselves as either one-race or multiple-race Indians.[3] In the prior Census, 7,876,568 persons claimed American Indian "ancestry or ethnic origin"[4] but this question was not asked on the 2010 census. The 2010 Census data indicated that 43.8 percent of persons identifying themselves as American Indian or Alaska Native reported such status in combination with one or more other races.[5]

[3]   U.S. Census Bureau, Overview of Race and Hispanic Origin: 2010, 2010 Census Briefs, at 7 (March 2011).

[4]   U.S. Census Bureau, Ancestry: 2000, Census 2000, Census 2000 Brief at 3 (June 2004).

[5]   U.S. Census Bureau, Overview of Race and Hispanic Origin: 2010, 2010 Census Briefs, at 7 (March 2011).

P.49.   **Delete the text of the first incomplete sentence and the text of n.5.**

P.49, n.6.   **Delete *"see also"* in line 3 of the footnote and add the following after semi-colon:**

Kirsty Gover, *Genealogy as Continuity: Explaining the Growing Tribal Preference for Descent Rules in Membership Governance in the United States*, 33 Am. Indian L. Rev. 243, 247, 263 (2008–2009) (examination of 322 tribal constitutions indicates, *inter alia*, that (1) "[t]ribes are increasingly likely to use lineal descent and blood-quantum rules after 1970, in place of the parental-enrollment or residency rules that were dominant in constitutions adopted in the 1930s" and thus "increasingly use tribe-specific measures of blood quantum, in contrast to the pan-tribal concept of Indian blood quantum used in federal policy[;]" and (2) quoting from Circular No. 3123 (Nov. 18, 1935) issued by

Commissioner for Indian Affairs John Collier to Bureau of Indian Affairs field personnel which observed that the Department of the Interior historically had sought to exclude in its review of tribal constitutions "'a large number of applicants of small degree of Indian blood'" from tribal membership);

Add the following to line 7 of the footnote after "*see also*":

Bethany R. Berger, *Red: Racism and the American Indian*, 56 UCLA L. Rev. 591, 633, 636 (2009) (contrasting forms of racism experienced by American Indians and African-Americans; during the Assimilation Era, for example, "[d]espite the color prejudice many Indians experienced, individual Indian integration was publicly celebrated as another symbol of the triumph of European-American civilization over savagery" and "[p]olicymakers . . . explicitly support[ed] intermarriage with Indians as an assimilation tool");

P.49, n.7.   **Add the following to line 8 of the footnote following the semi-colon:**

Timbisha Shoshone Tribe v. Kennedy, 687 F. Supp. 2d 1171, 1185 (E.D. Cal. 2009) (federal court refuses to intervene in dispute between tribal factions over legitimacy of disenrollment because it is "without authority" to "interfere in the internal affairs of the Tribe");

Add the following to the end of the footnote:

See also, Kirsty Gover, *Comparative Tribal Constitutionalism: Membership Governance in Australia, Canada, New Zealand, and the United States*, 35 Law &. Soc. Inquiry 689 (2010) (comparing approaches to the selection of tribal membership within four nations; concluding that tribes in the United States are "moving away from a race-based tribal membership" toward a "sui generis construction of membership, in the form of 'genealogic' tribalism'"); Brian L. Lewis, *So Close, Yet So Far Away: A Comparative Analysis of Indian Status in Canada and the United States*, 18 Willamette J. Int'l. L. & Disp. Resol. 38, 39 (2010) (addressing "[w]ho is politically an Indian in Canada and the United States").

P.51, n. 14.   **Add the following to the end of the footnote before the period:**

see generally, Katharine C. Oakley, *Defining Indian Status for the Purpose of Federal Criminal Jurisdiction*, 35 Am. Indian L. Rev. 177, 193 (2010)("Each court applies the [*Rogers*] test differently, leading to inconsistent holdings"); *cf. Eagle v. Yerington Paiute Tribe*, 603 F.3d 1161, 1164 (9th Cir. 2010) (although Indian Civil Rights Act sets affirmative limits on tribal criminal jurisdiction by defining the term "Indian" by reference to 18 U.S.C. §1153, tribe possessed the "inherent power of self-government to define its child abuse offense without an Indian status element and to create a procedural rule requiring defendants to raise the jurisdictional issue of Indian status before the Tribe must prove it at trial")

Add the following to line 7 of the text after the period:

The Ninth Circuit has added that the bloodline must "be derived from a federally recognized tribe."[16.1]

[16.1]   *United States v. Maggi*, 598 F.3d 1073, 1080 (9th Cir. 2010).

P.51, n.18.   **Add the following to the end of the footnote before the period:**

; *but see United States v. Stymiest*, 581 F.3d 759, 762 (8th Cir. 2009), *cert. denied*, 130 S. Ct. 2364 (2010) ("parties agree" that blood quantum requirement is met because defendant had "three thirty-seconds Indian blood")

P. 51, n.20.   **Add the following to the end of the footnote:**

The requisite degree of "Indian blood," as Justice Breyer's observation suggests, appears indefinite but, in any event, demands some measure of particularized attention not always given. In *United States v. Ramirez*, 537 F.3d 1075 (9th Cir. 2008), the panel deemed "'some' Indian blood" to be "generally sufficient" at least when conjoined with evidence that a "'parent, grandparent, or great-grandparent'" is "'clearly identified as an Indian.'" *Id.* at 1082. However, a great-grandparent could have possessed—as an illustration—1/4 "Indian blood" and thus conferred, in the absence of any intervening new "Indian blood," only a 1/32 quantum upon the descendant.

P. 52, n.23.   **Add the following at the end of the footnote before the period:**

; *cf.* Paul Spruhan, *The Canadian Indian Free Passage Right: The Last Stronghold of Explicit Race Restriction in United States Immigration Law*, 85 N.D. L. Rev 301 (2009) (discussing "50 per centum of blood of the American Indian race" requirement imposed on Canadian Indians under 8 U.S.C. § 1359 to qualify them for the statutory right of free passage between the United States and Canada)

P.52, n. 24.   **Add the following to the footnotes before the period:**

; *In re Garviais*, 402 F. Supp.2d 1219 (E.D. Wash. 2004) (refusing to find person of 3/16 Indian blood and limited integration with tribal community to be an "Indian" so as to allow prosecution as "Indian" by a tribe

P. 52, n.28.   **Add the following to line 6 of the footnote before "*see generally*":**

; *compare United States v. Stymiest*, 581 F.3d 759, 764 (8th Cir. 2009) ("*St Cloud* factors may prove useful . . . but they should not be considered exhaustive" and should not "be tied to an order of importance, unless the defendant is an enrolled tribal member, in which case that factor becomes dispositive"), *cert. denied*, 130 S. Ct. 2364 (2010), *with United States v. Cruz*, 554 F.3d 840, 851 n.17, 852 (9th Cir. 2009) (majority opinion, relying on *Bruce,* applied the four factors "'in declining order of importance[,]'" while dissenting panel member argued that the majority had inaccurately turned the four factor test into a "rigid multipart balancing test"); *United States v. Ramirez,* 537 F.3d 1075, 1082 (9th Cir. 2008);

P. 53.   Delete the first sentence of second full paragraph and the associated footnote, and replace the deletion with the following:

In *Carcieri v. Salazar,*[33] the Supreme Court interpreted the phrase "tribe now under Federal jurisdiction" as in section 19 to encompass tribes under such jurisdiction at the date of the IRA's enactment.[33.1] The term "Indian" includes, under the first definitional prong, only those individuals who were members of tribes federally recognized as of the IRA's effective date—June 18, 1934.

[33]   555 U.S. 379 (2009).

[33.1]   *Id.* at 1068; *see generally* Scott A. Taylor, *Taxation in Indian Country After Carcieri v. Salazar,* 36 Wm. Mitchell L. Rev. 590, 596, 599 (2010) (criticizing opinion's focus on "now" rather than on "include" that is "used pervasively in federal legislation to provide partial definitions of things that are specifically included, but without explicit limitation[,]" but deeming as the "biggest, and most obvious mistake in its interpretation of section § 19[] was to ignore the definition of the word 'tribe' contained in the same text that defines 'Indian[]'"—a term that is not subject to "[t]he temporal limitation of 'now'"); G. William Rice, *The Indian Reorganization Act, the Declaration on the Rights of Indigenous Peoples, and a Proposed Carcieri "Fix": Updating the Trust Land Acquisition Process,* 45 Idaho L. Rev. 575, 594–608 (2009) (contending that *Carcieri* "will create a cloud upon the trust title of every tribe first recognized by Congress or the executive branch after 1934, every tribe terminated in the termination era that has since been restored, and every tribe that adopted the IRA or [Oklahoma Indian Welfare Act] and changed its name or organizational structure since 1934[,]" and proposing statutory amendments that not only would modify the IRA's definition of "Indian" and add definitions of "Indian tribe" and "Indian reservation" but also would alter various aspects of trust land acquisition, management and taxability). Legislation has been introduced to address *Carcieri* by altering the language "tribe now under Federal jurisdiction" to "any federally recognized Indian tribe." S. 676, 112th Cong. (2011); H.R. 1291, 112th Cong. (2011); H.R. 1234, 112th Cong. (2011);

P.53, n.34.   Delete the text of the footnote and replace it with the following:

Although the First Circuit's decision in *Carcieri* indicated in dictum that the second prong of the "Indian" definition "covered those people of Indian descent then [in 1934] living on a reservation, that phrase more likely refers not to "descendants" but to the immediately antecedent "members." *Carcieri v. Kempthorne,* 497 F.3d 15, 30 (1st Cir. 2007) (*en banc*), *rev'd on other grounds,*

129 S. Ct. 1058 (2009). The First Circuit's construction, if accepted, creates an apparent conflict with the definition's first prong unless the term "members" means only those persons possessing membership in an otherwise qualifying tribe as of the IRA's effective date; *i.e.*, it would be impossible for an individual to be a "descendant[]" residing on a reservation in June 1934 unless "members" refer only to individuals who had such status when the statute was adopted.

P.55, n.45. **Add the following at the end of the footnote:**

The regulation classifies those eligible for preferences for vacancies in the BIA as "members of any recognized Indian tribe now under Federal Jurisdiction." The Supreme Court in *Carcieri v. Salazar*, 129 S. Ct. 1058 (2009), however, held that the first prong of the IRA's "Indian" definition in 25 U.S.C. § 479 applies only to individuals who were "members of tribes that were under federal jurisdiction at the time the IRA was enacted." *Id.* at 1065. This aspect of the regulation is thus inconsistent with the Court's construction of "now" as referring to the IRA's enactment date and not the present time.

P.55, n.48. **Add the following to the end of the footnote:**

Considerations other than political affiliation with a tribe also may affect the appropriate level of equal protection scrutiny. *E.g., Pyke v. Cuomo*, 567 F.3d 74, 77 (2d Cir. 2009) (roadblock placed at edge of a reservation in an attempt to contain impact of violence was "saved by the fact that it was aimed at an area, not a racial class" where state officials "explained that they were attempting to respect the sovereignty of the reservation, and only set up border checkpoints to keep out *non-residents*, not non–Native Americans"), *cert. denied*, 130 S. Ct. 741 (2010).

P.56, n.49. **Add the following to line 7 of the footnote after the semi-colon:**

Greene v. Comm'r, 755 N.W.2d 713, 726–727 (Minn. 2008) (state statute requiring tribal members off reservation to utilize tribal employment services rather than state services upheld under rational basis, rather than strict scrutiny, analysis since (1) the classification was political, not racial, and (2) it was "'not simply another state law'" but was adopted in direct response to federal enactments);

P.58, n.57. **Add the following to the end of the footnote before the period:**

; *see generally* David Alan Ezra, *Doe v. Kamehameha Schools: A "Discrete and Insular Minority" in Hawai'i Seventy Years After Carolene Products?*, 30 U. Haw. L. Rev. 295, 316–17 (2008) (discussing the several opinions in the *Kamehameha* litigation, and concluding that "[t]he three *Doe* [*en banc*] opinions differ in result but share two assumptions: (1) the term 'Native Hawaiian' is, at least for purposes of judicial review, strictly a racial classification, and (2) Title VII standards, which are rooted in employment law, apply to race-based section 1981 challenges" and that "[e]ven though the [*en banc*] majority . . . made no mention of the 'discrete and insular' terminology made famous by footnote four [in *United States v. Carolene Products, Inc.*, 304 U.S. 144 (1938)], it recognized that the context of the relationship between Native Hawaiians and the United States was critical to formulating the standard by which the Policy should be reviewed"); Angela (Riya) Kuo, *Let Her Will Be Done: The Role of the Kamehameha Policy in Promoting Native Hawaiian Self-Determination*, 13 Asian Pac. Am. L.J. 72, 88 (2008) (arguing that the Kamehameha preferential admissions policy "is an appropriate and balanced remedial measure" given not only "the founding circumstances and the stated purpose of the school, as well as federal and state governmental policy on Native Hawaiian entitlement programs" but also "the decline of the Native Hawaiian population and its continued and severe socioeconomic disadvantages")

P.59, n.58.   Delete the text of the footnote after the period in the third-to-last line and replace the deletion with the following:

S. 675, 112th Cong. (2011); H.R. 1250, 112th Cong. (2011). Hawaii's unique history has been posited by at least one commentator as a basis for pursuing a route toward increased sovereignty for Native Hawaiians other than one derived from traditional Indian law principles. David Keanu Sai, *A Slippery Path Towards Hawaiian Indigeneity: An Analysis and Comparison Between Hawaiian State Sovereignty and Hawaiian Indigeneity and Its Use and Practice in Hawai'i Today*, 10 J. L. & Soc. Challenges 68, 70 (2008) ("providing an analysis of Hawaiian sovereignty under international law since the nineteenth century[,] and discussing "the current erroneous identification of native Hawaiians as an indigenous group of people within the United States, rather than nationals of an extant sovereign, but occupied, State"). *See also*, Ryan William Nohea Garcia, *Who is Hawaiian, What Begets Federal Recognition, and How Much Blood Matters*, 11 Asian-Pac. L. & Policy J. 85, 162 (2008) (analyzing recent proposed Hawaiian recognition legislation and concluding that "political history, not indigeneity, begets federal recognition").

P.61.   Delete the text following the period in the seventh line from the bottom, and the text in the sixth line from the bottom up to the period, along with the accompanying footnote and insert the following:

In 2010, there were 565 federally recognized tribes, of which 336 are within the continental United States.[82]

[82]   75 Fed. Reg. 60810 (October 1, 2010), as supplemented by 75 Fed. Reg. 66124 (October 27, 2010).

P. 61, n. 84.   Add the following to the end of the footnote after the period:

See Winnemum Wintu Tribe v. United States Department of the Interior, 725 F. Supp. 2d 1119, 1133 (E. D. Cal. 2010) (claims asserting "tribal interests" may not be brought by entity lacking federal recognition).

P.65, n.101.   **Add the following to the text on line 2 after *"cf."*:**

Schaghticoke Tribal Nation v. Kempthorne, 587 F.3d 132, 134 (2d Cir. 2009) (rejecting claim that improper political influence affected decision to deny tribal recognition application even though governor, attorney general and congressional delegation had communicated adamant opposition to the application to the agency given lack of evidence that the submissions actually influenced the outcome

P.69, n.128.   **Add the following to the end of the footnote:**

See also, United States v. Tony, 637 F.3d 1153 (10th Cir. 2011) (Tenth Circuit finds that claim that crime did not occur in "Indian Country" does not affect subject matter jurisdiction of federal court; claim is actually an "insufficiency of evidence argument and was waived when he failed to raises it on direct appeal").

P.71, n.148.   **Add the following to the end of the footnote:**

The involved statute, the Alaska Native Claims Settlement Act ("ANCSA"), 43 U.S.C. §§ 1601–1629h, had been in place for almost 30 years at the time of *Venetie*'s issuance. *See generally* Eric C. Chaffee, *Business Organizations and Tribal Self-Determination: A Critical Reexamination of the Alaska Native Claims Settlement Act,* 25 Alaska L. Rev. 107, 136 (2008) (discussing the advantages and disadvantages attendant to ANCSA, and observing that, in view of *Venetie,* "[t]he Act debatably diminished sovereignty by ending the protections and powers of Indian Country, denying Alaska Natives the ability to choose their own governance structures, and providing limited opportunities for self-determination").

P.71, n.149.   **Replace *"Id."* with "522 U.S.".**

P.72, n. 154.   **Add the following to the end of the footnote:**

The Eighth Circuit found the absence of a federal set-aside of land conveyed by a town to a tribal housing authority by way of a 99 year lease with minimal payment, in that the town had retained its fee title to the land. *Owen v. Weber,* __F.3d __, 2011 WL 3112004 (8th Cir. 2011).

P.73, n.159.   **Add the following to the end of the footnote:**

An *en banc,* closely divided Tenth Circuit, however, overruled prior three-judge panels' use of the "community of reference" doctrine to include lands that are neither set-aside nor superintended by the United States as part of a "dependent Indian community." *Hydro-Res., Inc. v. USEPA,* 608 F.3d 1131 (10th Cir. 2010) (*en banc*). The *en banc* court found that use of the "community of reference" test would be inconsistent with *Venetie* which "rejected the idea that the boundaries of a federally dependent Indian community should be determined by a sort of judicially administered census study of the nature of 'the Indian tribe inhabiting' the area" and instead identified as "[t]he right question . . . whether Congress has taken some action to designate and maintain the land in question for Indian use." *Id.* at 1150. The dissenters deemed *Venetie* not dispositive because, in their view, "the Supreme Court did not address a separate, antecedent question: to what area of land should this two-part test be applied" and argued that "[o]ver the last twenty years in this circuit, we have held that a 'community-of-reference' test must be employed to determine the appropriate community, before determining whether that community is both 'dependent' and 'Indian.'" *Id.* at 1168 (Ebel, J., dissenting).

P.74, n.166.   Add the following to the end of the footnote before the period:

; *cf. Magnan v. State,* 207 P.3d 397, 405 (Okla. Crim. App. 2009), *cert. denied,* 130 S. Ct. 276 (2009) ("allotted" status of Indian lands terminated upon surface estate's transfer to non-Indians; retention of 4/5 restricted interest in mineral estate did not change the result)

P. 74, n. 166.   Add the following to the end of the footnote:

A pair of decisions by the Eighth Circuit Court of Appeals has put the status of allotted and former allotted lands within the 1858 boundaries of the Yankton Reservation in doubt. In *Yankton Sioux Tribe v. Podhradsky,* 606 F.3d 994, 1007–1010 (8th Cir. 2010), the Court found that allotments retained "reservation" status after opening of the reservation in 1894 but, up to enactment 18 USC 1151 in 1948, lost both allotted and "reservation" status when transferred to non-Indians. The Court found, however, that after enactment of 18 USC 1151, allotments achieved permanent "reservation" status. Such lands, it could be argued, do not lose "reservation" status when transferred to non-Indians. In a companion case, a different panel of the same Court ignored any question of the relevance of 18 USC 1151 and its enactment in 1948. It adopted a prior decision to the effect that the "transfer of lands from Indian ownership diminished the Reservation." *Yankton Sioux Tribe v. U.S. Army Corps of Eng'rs,,* 606 F.3d 895, 900 (8th Cir. 2010), *cert. denied,* __ S. Ct. __ (2011).

P.76, n.179.   Add the following to line 11 after the period:

The Eighth Circuit, more recently, held that all lands taken into trust under 25 U.S.C. § 465 within the former boundaries of the Yankton Sioux Reservation are themselves reservation under 18 USC § 1151(a) and so, arguably, would retain "reservation" status even if later taken out of trust. *Yankton Sioux Tribe v. Podhradsky,* 606 F.3d 994 (8th Cir. 2010). The panel distinguished *Stands* where, in its view, the issue was "whether a particular parcel of land was or was not an allotment" and prompted "no argument regarding the Indian country status of trust lands since that issue was irrelevant" and which, in any event, "acknowledged that '[i]n some circumstances, off-reservation tribal trust land may be considered Indian country.'" *Id.* at 1011 n.12.

Chapter 3
Indian Land and Property: Title and Use

P.83, n.28.   **Add the following to the end of the footnote before the period:**

; *see also Oglala Sioux Tribe v. United States Corps of Eng'rs*, 570 F.3d 327, 331 (D.C. Cir. 2009) ("Congress deliberately used broad terminology in the Act in order to permit tribes to bring all potential historical claims and to thereby prevent them from returning to Congress to lobby for further redress"), *cert. denied*, 130 S. Ct. 3503 (2010)

P.83, n.34.   **Add the following to line 3 of the footnote after the period:**

But the Act does, of course, preclude litigation of some claims. *E.g., Oglala Sioux Tribe v. United States Corps of Eng'rs*, 570 F.3d 327, 331–33 (D.C. Cir. 2009), *cert. denied*, 130 S. Ct. 3503 (2010).

Add the following to the end of the footnote:

See also Michelle Smith & Janet C. Neuman, *Keeping Indian Claims Commission Decisions in Their Place: Assessing the Preclusive Effect of ICC Decisions in Litigation Over Off-Reservation Treaty Fishing Rights*, 31 U. Haw. L. Rev. 475 (2009)

P.86, n.52.   **Replace "*id*" in line 1 with the following:**

Oneida Indian Nation v. County of Oneida, 617 F.3d 114, 118 (2nd Cir. 2010) (disruptive possessory and nonpossessory claims to ancestral lands are subject to equitable defenses); *Cayuga Indian Nation*, 413 F.3d

P.87, n.58.   **Add the following to line 3 of the footnote after the semi-colon:**

Unalachtigo Band of Nanticoke-Lanape Indians v. New Jersey, Civ. No. 05-5170, 2008 WL 2165191, at *15–16 (D.N.J. May 20, 2008) (dismissing on standing grounds Nonintercourse Act claim by group absent showing of successorship status to original tribe), *vacated in part on other grounds*, 606 F.3d 126 (3d Cir. 2010);

Add the following to line 1 of the footnote after "*E.g.,*":

Paiute-Shoshone Indians v. City of Los Angeles, 637 F.3d. 993, 998–99 (9th Cir. 2011) (court lacked jurisdiction over claim that a 1941 land conveyance from the United States to Los Angeles was illegal because the claim was not filed within the Indian Claims Commission Act's statute of limitations);

P.89, n.76. ### Add the following to line 7 of the footnote before the period:

; *cf. Crow Creek Sioux Tribal Farms, Inc. v. IRS*, 684 F. Supp. 2d 1152, 1159 (D.S.D. 2010) (expressing, in preliminary injunction context, uncertainty as to "whether a levy and seizure by the IRS [on tribally owned fee land] constitutes express consent of the United States to extinguish title, or whether this land is protected by the [Nonintercourse Act]"); *see generally* Brian Pierson, *Resolving a Perilous Uncertainty: The Right of Tribes to Convey Fee Simple Lands*, 57-APR Fed. Law. 49, 52 (2010) ("[f]ederal courts that have addressed the issue have overwhelmingly rejected any [25 U.S.C.] § 177 limitation on tribal authority over land owned in fee simple absolute title")

P.89, n.77. ### Add the following to the end of the footnote:

A section of the Act, 25 U.S.C. § 479, defines "Indian" to include "members of any recognized Indian tribe now under Federal jurisdiction." Thus, to be entitled to the Secretary's land acquisition authority a tribe had to be under federal jurisdiction when the IRA was enacted, that is, 1934. *Carcieri v. Salazar*, 129 S. Ct. 1058, 1064–65 (2009). Bills introduced in Congress to amend the IRA seek to overturn *Carcieri*. S. 676, 112th Cong. (2011); H.R. 1291, 112th Cong. (2010); H.R. 1234, 112th Cong. (2011).

P.90, n.82. ### Add the following after "*E.g.*":

, *Iowa Tribe v. Salazar*, 607 F.3d 1225 (10th Cir. 2010);

P.91, n.89. ### Add the following to line 1 of the footnote after "(*en banc*)":

, *rev'd on other grounds*, 129 S. Ct. 1058 (2009)

Add the following to line 4 of the footnote after the period:

Mich. Gambling Opposition v. Kempthorne, 525 F.3d 23, 30–33 (D.C. Cir. 2008), *cert. denied*, 129 S. Ct. 1002 (2009);

Delete the following from line 6 of the footnote:

Mich. Gambling Opposition v. Norton, 477 F. Supp. 2d 1, 2–22 (D.D.C. 2007);

Add the following to line 15 of the footnote after the period:

E.g., County of Charles Mix v. USDOI, 2011 WL 1303125, **5–7 (D.S.D. Mar. 31, 2011);

Add the following to the end of the footnote:

Claims of institutional bias on the part of the BIA have also failed. *South Dakota v. USDOI*, 2011 WL 382744, *9 (D.S.D. Feb. 3, 2011).

P.91, n.90.   ## Add the following to line 1 of the footnote after "*see*":

Iowa Tribe v. Salazar, 607 F.3d 1225, 1237 (10th Cir. 2010) (Quiet Title Act's sovereign immunity exception with respect to Indian tribes applies where the Secretary put the land at issue into trust *after* suit had commenced);

Add the following to the end of the footnote before the period:

; *cf. Robinson v. United States*, 586 F.3d 685, 688 (9th Cir. 2009) (holding Quiet Title Act inapplicable in dispute over easement encroachment, since "a suit that does not challenge title but instead concerns the use of land as to which title is not disputed can sound in tort or contract and not come within the scope of the QTA"). Another impediment to challenging the Secretary's trust land acquisitions can be standing requirements. *See, e.g., Patchak v. Salazar*, 632 F.3d 702, 704 (D.C. Cir. 2011) (reversing district court by finding all Article III standing requirements met in challenge by a neighboring landowner to the Secretary's decision to take tribal land into trust, thereby allowing the tribe to proceed with plans to construct a gambling facility); *Preservation of Los Olivos v. USDOI*, 635 F. Supp. 2d 1076 (C.D. Cal. 2008) (Indian Board of Land Appeals erred in applying judicial standing principles to dismiss an appeal by private parties challenging the Secretary's land acquisition).

P.93, n.101.   ## Add the following to line 6 of the footnote after "*see also*":

Plains Commerce Bank v. Long Family Land & Cattle Co., 554 U.S. 316, 328 (2008) (general rule limiting tribal authority over non-members "is particularly strong when the nonmember's activity occurs on land owned in fee simple by non-Indians");

P.94, n.106.   ## Add the following to the end of the footnote:

Lower courts provide useful summaries of the Supreme Court's reservation diminishment and disestablishment jurisprudence. *E.g., Osage Nation v. Irby*, 597 F.3d 1117, 1121–28 (10th Cir. 2010), *cert. denied*, __ S. Ct. __, 2011 WL 2518867 (2011); *Yellowbear v. State*, 174 P.3d 1270, 1273–84 (Wyo. 2008), *on habeas corpus review sub nom. Yellowbear v. Wyoming Att'y General*, 636 F. Supp. 2d 1254, 1262–71 (D. Wyo. 2009), *aff'd*, 380 Fed.App'x 740 (10th Cir. 2010), *cert. denied sub nom., Yellowstone v. Salzburg*, 131 S. Ct 1488 (2011); *cf. N. Arapaho Tribe v. Harnsberger*, 660 F. Supp. 2d 1264, 1271 (D. Wyo. 2009) (finding *Yellowbear* dispositive of Wyoming Supreme Court's view on the diminished status of the Wind River Indian Reservation).

P.95, n.112.   Add the following to line 2 of the footnote following the semicolon:

Osage Nation v. Irby, 597 F.3d 1117, 1125 (10th Cir. 2010), *cert. denied*, __ S. Ct. __, 2011 WL 2518867 (2011) (examining the "legislative history and negotiation process");

P.96, n.118.   Add the following to line 5 after "also":

Osage Nation v. Irby, 597 F.3d 1117, 1127 (10th Cir. 2010), *cert. denied*, __ S. Ct. __, 2011 WL 2518867 (2011) (relying, in part, on shifts in demographics and land ownership to find disestablishment);

Add the following to the end of the footnote before the period:

; *see generally*, Comment, *The Legacy of Solem v. Bartlett: How Courts Have Used Demographics to Bypass Congress and Erode the Basic Principles of Indian Law*, 84 Wash. L. Rev. 723, 762 (2009) (arguing that "[i]t is difficult to think of a more attenuated measure of congressional intent than the changing racial composition of a particular piece of land over the last century" and that "[w]hen courts apply such an elusive tool to help decide whether an Indian tribe retains its reservation—despite canons assigning Congress sole authority over a reservation's borders and demanding that courts interpret ambiguities in favor of the Indians—they undermine democratic values and goals, and the canons designed to guard them")

P.96.   Add the following new footnote at the end of the second sentence in the first full paragraph:

[119.1] *E.g., Osage Nation v. Irby*, 597 F.3d 1117, 1126–27 (10th Cir. 2010), *cert. denied*, __ S. Ct. __, 2011 WL 2518867 (2011).

P.97, n.126.   Delete lines 2, 3, and 4 of the footnote and replace with:

606 F.3d 994 (8th Cir. 2010), *cert. denied sub nom., Daugaard v. Yankton Sioux Tribe*, __ S. Ct. __, 2011 WL 196308 (2011) (determining what lands within a diminished reservation retain reservation status).

P.100, n.147.   Add the following to the end of the footnote before the period:

; *see United States v. Milner*, 583 F.3d 1174, 1185–86 (9th Cir. 2009) (relying on ratified treaty's delegation of authority to modify reservation and statehood disclaimer provision as adequate basis to find state divested of title to navigable waters within executive order-created reservation) , *cert. denied*, 130 S. Ct. 3273 (2010)

P.104. **Add the following new footnote 176.1 in the text at the end of the sentence in line 3 in Section "IV. LEASING INDIAN NATURAL RESOURCES":**

[176.1] Alternative energy, particularly wind and solar, creates new economic possibilities for tribes. *See generally* Elizabeth Ann Kronk, *Alternative Energy Development in Indian Country: Lighting the Way for the Seventh Generation*, 46 Idaho L. Rev. 449, 452 (2010) ("[s]tudies increasingly show that Indian country may be uniquely positioned to develop alternative energy"); Tracey A. LeBeau, *The Green Road Ahead: Renewable Energy Takes a Stumble But Is on the Right Path, Possibly Right Through Indian Country*, 56-APR Fed. Law. 38 (2009); Patrick M. Garry, Candice J. Spurlin, and Derek A. Nelsen, *Wind Energy in Indian Country: A Study of the Challenges and Opportunities Facing South Dakota Tribes*, 54 S.D. L. Rev. 448 (2009); Kevin L. Shaw & Richard D. Deutsch, *Wind Power and Other Renewable Energy Projects: The New Wave of Power Project Development on Indian Lands*, 5 Rky. Mtn. Min. L. Inst 9-1 (2005). "[S]olar electricity prospects on tribal land are estimated to be four and a half times the annual total electricity needs of the United States." Ryan David Dreveskracht, *Native Nation Economic Development via the Implementation of Solar Projects: How to Make it Work*, 68 Wash. & Lee L. Rev. 27, 30 (2011).

P.104, n.177. **Add the following to line 2 of the footnote before the period:**

; *see generally* Brian Pierson, *Resolving a Perilous Uncertainty: The Right of Tribes to Convey Fee Simple Lands*, 57-APR Fed. Law 49 (2010) (arguing that § 177 was not intended to apply to lands held by tribes in fee simple)

Add the following to the end of the footnote:

Congress has removed the Act's restriction for some lands of some tribes. *E.g.*, Pub. L. No. 102-497, § 4, 106 Stat. 3255 (1992) (Mississippi Choctaw Indians); Pub. L. No. 101-630, § 102, 104 Stat. 4531 (1990) (Rumsey Indians).

P.105, n.180. **Add the following to the end of the footnote before the period:**

; *Grondal v. United States*, 682 F. Supp. 2d 1203, 1221 (E.D. Wash. 2010) ("[t]he Government holds the allotment in trust for allottees and has the power to control occupancy on the property and to protect it from trespass")

p.105, n.181. **Add the following to the end of the footnote:**

At least one tribe unsuccessfully sought to expand the resources under tribal control by asserting that the United States owns, in trust for the tribe, the electromagnetic spectrum, or radio spectrum, over the reservation. *Alltell Commc'ns., LLC v. Oglala Sioux Tribe*, Civ. No. 10-5011 JLV, 2011 WL 796409, **1–2 (D.S.D., Feb. 28, 2011).

P.105.   **Add the following to the text after the second line:**

Control, however, does not necessarily mean effective and economic use, particularly for developing energy resources, where tribal efforts are hampered by outdated laws, cumbersome regulations, lack of access to the transmission grid, and difficulty in obtaining financing and investment for projects.[181.1]

> [181.1]   U.S. Sen. Comm. on Indian Affairs, *Indian Energy and Energy Efficiency Concept Paper* at 1, attached to Letter from Sen. Byron L. Dorgan, Chrm., U.S. Sen. Comm. on Indian Affairs, and Sen. John Barrasso, Vice Chrm., U.S. Sen. Comm. on Indian Affairs, to "Tribal Leader" (Sept. 10, 2009) (*"Indian Energy Concept Paper"*), *available at* http://www.indian.senate.gov/public/_files/IndianEnergy.pdf. One of these problems, access to capital, is the subject of provisions in the American Recovery and Reinvestment Act of 2009 that enhance tribal ability to finance energy and conservation projects and authorize the issuance of $2,000,000 in tax-exempt Tribal Economic Development Bonds. Pub. L. No. 111-5, § 1402, 123 Stat. 115 (2009) (codified at 26 U.S.C. § 7871(f)). Tribes also are eligible under the Energy Improvement and Extension Act of 2008 for "new clean renewable energy bonds" and "qualified energy conservation bonds." Pub. L. No. 110-343, §§ 107, 301, 122 Stat. 3807 (2008) (codified at 26 U.S.C. §§ 54C, 54D).

P.108, n.218.   **Add the following to line 6 of the footnote after the period:**

> Tribes, however, have not taken advantage of Tribal Energy Resource Agreements, probably because exercising rights under them releases the United States from liability for any contract term or loss resulting from the Agreements. Elizabeth Ann Kronk, *Alternative Energy Development in Indian Country: Lighting the Way for the Seventh Generation*, 46 Idaho L. Rev. 449, 470 (2010); *Indian Energy Concept Paper, supra* note 181.1 at 4 (no tribe had entered into a Tribal Energy Resource Agreement as of 2009). Rules have been adopted to describe procedures for obtaining and implementing a Tribal Energy Resource Agreement. 25 C.F.R. pt. 224.

P.109, n.224.   **Add the following to the end of the footnote before the period:**

> , *repealed by* Indian Land Consolidation Act Amendments of 2000, Pub. L. No. 106-462, § 106(a)(1), 114 Stat. 1991 (2000)

P.111.   **Add the following to the end of the first full paragraph in the text:**

More recent legislation allows owners of trust and restricted land to apply to the Secretary for owner-manager status.[241.1] With this status, owners are allowed to issue leases for "agricultural purposes" for up to ten years and to do so without Secretarial approval.[241.2]

> [241.1]   25 U.S.C. § 2220.

> [241.2]   *Id.*

P.111, n.241.   **Add the following to the end of the footnote before the period:**

; *see O'Bryan v. United States*, 93 Fed. Cl. 57, 63 (2010) (rejecting breach of trust claim for alleged improper cancellation of lease issued pursuant to AIARMA "[b]ecause the authority for the issuance of the permits rests in the first instance with the Indian landowners, the permits are properly regarded as contracts with the landowners" and not the federal government)

P.112, n.246.   **Add the following to the end of the footnote:**

If owners of trust or restricted land receive from the Secretary owner-manager status, they then have authority to issue grazing lease up to a term of ten years. 25 U.S.C. § 2220.

P.112, n.252.   **Add the following to the end of the footnote:**

"Section 415(a) protects the ability of owners of restricted Indian lands to lease those lands," *Bullcreek v. USDOI*, 426 F. Supp. 2d 1221, 1230 (D. Utah 2006); protects Indian "interests by insuring that their land transactions with third parties are advantageous," *Utah v. U.S. Dep't of Interior*, 45 F. Supp. 2d 1279, 1283 (D. Utah 1999); and "encourage[s] and enable[s] Indian landowners to handle their own affairs," *Brown v. United States*, 42 Fed.Cl. 538, 553 (1998), *aff'd on other grounds*, 195 F.3d 1334 (Fed. Cir. 1999).

P.113, n.253.   **Add the following to line 6 after "for":**

lease interpretation purposes and

Add the following to line 6 after the sentence ending period:

Wapato Heritage. L.L.C. v. United States, 637 F.3d 1033, 1037–39 (9th Cir. 2011);

P.114.   **Add the following new footnote at the end of the fourth sentence in the first paragraph:**

[261.1] The Secretary's role as trustee and fiduciary does not trump the Secretary's duty to comply with section 415(a)'s implementing regulations even when the Secretary believes a proposed lease compromises the tribe's long-term future. *Skull Valley Band of Goshute Indians v. Davis*, 728 F. Supp. 2d 1287, 1299–1302 (D. Utah. 2010) (Secretary's refusal to approve a lease to store spent nuclear fuel remanded to Secretary for reconsideration).

P.114, n.262.   **Add the following to the end of the footnote:**

As this section suggests, breach of trust liability may exist in connection with lease administration prior to termination of the land's trust status. *See Confederated Tribes and Bands of Yakama Nation v. United States*, 89 Fed. Cl. 589, 593–94 (2009) (denying motion to dismiss on ripeness grounds suit by tribe and certain members that alleged failure to enforce lease agreement); *United*

States v. Duro, 625 F. Supp. 2d 938, 942 (C.D. Cal. 2009) (fiduciary duty exists under § 415)

P.114, n.267.   Add the following to the end of the footnote:

Water Wheel Camp Recreational Area, Inc. v. LaRance, 642 F.3d 802, 808–09 (9th Cir. 2011) ("acknowledge[ing] the long-standing rule that Indian tribes possess inherent sovereign powers, including the power to exclude" from which "flow lesser powers, including the power to regulate non-Indians on tribal land.").

P.115, n. 269.   Add the following to the end of the footnote:

A contract falling under 25 U.S.C. § 81 that lacks Secretarial approval is "null and void." *E.g., A.K. Mgmt. Co. v. San Manuel Band*, 789 F.2d 785, 788 (9th Cir. 1986).

P.115, n. 270.   Add the following to the end of the footnote:

; *see also A.K. Mgmt. Co. v. San Manuel Band*, 789 F.2d 785, 787 (9th Cir. 1986) ("The broad language of section 81 expresses congressional intent to cover almost all Indian land transactions.").

P.119, n.308.   Add the following to the end of the footnote before the period:

; *see also* Act of Mar 4, 1911, 36 Stat. 1253, and Act of May 27, 1952, 66 Stat. 95 (1911) (codified at 43 U.S.C. § 961) (authorizing agency heads to grant easements not exceeding fifty years over "public lands and reservations" for telecommunication and electrical power purposes)

P.119, n.309.   Replace the semi-colon in line 1 of the footnote with the following:

, amended by

**   Add the following to line two of the footnote after "§ 169.25":**

(regulations for oil and gas pipeline rights-of-way on Indian lands);

P.120, n.323.   Add the following to the end of the footnote before the period:

; *see generally* Brian Sawers, *Tribal Land Corporations: Using Incorporation to Combat Fractionation*, 88 Neb. L. Rev. 385, 397 (2009) (Department of the Interior "began exploring strategies to reverse fractionation" in 1938)

P. 121.   Delete from the last line of the second full paragraph "is still ongoing" and replace with the following:

was resolved

P.121, n.332.   Delete in line 4 of the footnote everything following "litigation" and replace with the following:

was exceedingly contentious. The last decision by the Court of Appeals in the case summarized the thirteen years of litigation and the many district and appellate court decisions issued in the lawsuit, *Cobell v. Salazar*, 573 F.3d 808, 809–11 (D.C. Cir. 2009), which the Court described as a "complicated legal morass." *Id.* at 812; *see generally*, Armen H. Merjian, *An Unbroken Chain of Injustice: The Dawes Act, Native American Trusts, and Cobell v. Salazar*, 46 Gonzaga L. Rev. 609 (2010–11). The dispute was resolved by legislation. Claims Resolution Act of 2010, Pub. L. No. 111-291, 124 Stat. 3064 (2010).

P.124, n.351.   Add the following to the end of the footnote before the period:

; *see generally* Brian Sawers, *Tribal Land Corporations: Using Incorporation to Combat Fractionation*, 88 Neb. L. Rev. 385, 402–03 (2009) (reviewing the pilot program and stating that by 2006 $97 million had been spent on it and interests in 243,000 parcels acquired, but "[u]fortunately, the number of interests is increasing so rapidly that it would cost $135 million each year just to maintain the current level of fractionation."). The settlement in the *Cobell* litigation includes $1.9 billion to acquire individual interests in Indian lands, with the goal to consolidate fractionated lands. Pub. L. No. 111–291, § 101(d), 124 Stat. 3064 (2010). The Food, Conservation, and Energy Act of 2008 authorizes of the Secretary of Agriculture to make and insure loans to tribes so that they can purchase highly fractionated land. Pub. L. No. 110-246, § 5501, 122 Stat. 1651 (2008) (codified at 25 U.S.C. § 488)

P.124, n.357.   Add the following to the end of the footnote before the period:

; *see generally* Brian Sawers, *Tribal Land Corporations: Using Incorporation to Combat Fractionation*, 88 Neb. L. Rev. 385, 408–09, 421–22 (2009) (arguing that because Congress has been unwilling to address fractionation, tribes must take the lead, and proposing as a solution tribal land corporations with eminent domain powers)

P.124, n.362.   Add the following to line 1 in the footnote after "*see generally*":

Brian Sawers, *Tribal Land Corporations: Using Incorporation to Combat Fractionation*, 88 Neb. L. Rev. 385, 405 (2009) ("[p]erhaps it is too soon to judge AIPRA; but because the changes to inheritance laws are hardly radical it appears that fractionation will decline only slowly");

P.125.   Add the following after the period to line 9 of the text:

To avoid some land management problems caused by fractionated ownership, the Act allows the Secretary to approve "any lease or agreement that affects" allotted, trust, or restricted land provided that a certain percentage of the owners consent, with the percentage dropping with the more owners there are.[368.1]

[368.1]   25 U.S.C. § 2218.

Add the following to the last line of the text:

Recently Congress, as part of the settlement of the *Cobell* litigation—involving the government's mismanagement of individual Indian money accounts—established a Trust Land Consolidation Fund, allocating $1.9 billion for a Land Consolidation Program under which the Secretary may purchase fractional interests in trust and restricted land.[373.1] The Secretary must consult with tribes to identify fractional interests.[373.2]

[373.1]   Pub. L. No. 111-291, § 101(d), 124 Stat. 3064 (2010).

[373.2]   *Id.*

P.127, n.384.   Add the following to line 1 after "see generally":

Steven J. Gunn, *The Native American Graves Protection and Repatriation Act at Twenty: Reaching the Limits of Our National Consensus*, 36 Wm. Mitchell L. Rev. 503, 526–31 (2010); Julia A. Cryne, Comment, *NAGPRA Revisited: A Twenty-Year Review of Repatriation Efforts*, 34 Am. Indian. L. Rev. 99 (2010);

P.128, n.393.   Add the following to the end of the footnote:

And it does not apply to remains and objects excavated or discovered before November 16, 1990. 25 U.S.C. § 3002(a).

P.130, n.411.   Add the following to line 1 of the footnote after "*See generally*":

Steven J. Gunn, *The Native American Graves Protection and Repatriation Act at Twenty: Reaching the Limits of Our National Consensus*, 36 Wm. Mitchell L. Rev. 503, 526–31 (2010);

Add the following to the end of the footnote:

Another problem with NAGPRA is the challenge identifying a tribe affiliated with Indian remains and cultural items still held by museums and federal agencies, and that number over 100,000 remains, over 800,000 funerary objects, and hundreds of thousands if not millions of sacred and cultural objects. Gunn, *supra*, at 524.

P.132, n.438.   Replace "are being considered on" in line 1 with the following:

define

Replace "72 Fed. Reg. 58582 (proposed Oct. 16, 2007) (to be codified at 43 C.F.R. pt.10)" in lines 4 and 5 of the footnote with the following:

43 C.F.R. pt. 10

P. 133, n.439.   Add the following to the end of the footnote before the period:

; Steven J. Gunn, *The Native American Graves Protection and Repatriation Act at Twenty: Reaching the Limits of Our National Consensus*, 36 Wm. Mitchell L. Rev. 503, 503–04, 523 (2010) (NAGPRA "provides far-reaching protections" and has "encouraged cooperative arrangements between scientists and American Indians" that in turn "have increased good will between scientists and tribes and led to productive synergies"); Julia A. Cryne, Comment, *NAGPRA Revisited: A Twenty-Year Review of Repatriation Efforts*, 36 Am. Indian L. Rev. 99, 108–09, 122 (2010) (discussing, *inter alia*, 2008 National Association of Tribal Historic Preservation Officers report "rais[ing] serious concerns about agencies failing to carry out the primary requirement of NAGPRA: repatriating the remains of Native Americans currently held in government collections to their tribes[,]" and concluding that while "[s]cience and religion do not have to be mutually exclusive, . . . each should respect the other" and that "[w]hen remains are discovered that have potential religious significance and also potentially important scientific value, NAGPRA stands at the intersection of these two public values but has not sufficiently established as a national policy how these values should be compared and preserved while giving priority to the claims of American Indians having an affiliation with the remains")

P.136, n.475.   Add the following to line 6 the footnote after "*see generally*":

; Joshua A. Edwards, *Yellow Snow on Sacred Sites: A Failed Application of the Religious Freedom Restoration Act*, 34 Am. Indian L. Rev. 151, 166 (2010) (disagreeing with the *Navajo Nation* majority opinion because "[i]nterpreting the definition of 'substantial burden' to apply only to government actions that criminalize behavior or deny government benefits offers minimal additional protection for the exercise of religion"—an "interpretation [that] is directly against the will of Congress" because, "[i]mmediately after the Supreme Court decided *Smith*, both parties in Congress began working on legislation that would ultimately become RFRA"); Jessica M. Erickson, Comment, *Live and Letting Die: The Biopolitical Effect of Navajo Nation v. U.S. Forest Service*, 33 Seattle U. L. Rev. 463, 488 (2010) (arguing that *Navajo Nation* majority erred because " '[g]reater weight should be assigned because the character of native religion is inherently different from the Western-based religions on which the RFRA precedent is founded" and, therefore, existing Supreme Court "precedent is insufficient for an adequate RFRA sacred site test"); Ruth Stoner Muzzin, *Seeing the Free Exercise Forest for the Trees: NEPA, RFRA and Navajo Nation*, 16 Hastings W.-N.W. J.Envtl. L. & Pol'y 277, 295 (2010) (the *Navajo Nation* majority "opinion acknowledges that *Lyng* was decided before

RFRA and that RFRA restored the compelling interest test where there is a 'substantial burden[,]" but "RFRA does not require 'coercion' in order to find that a burden is substantial"); Jonathan Knapp, *Making Snow in the Desert: Defining a Substantial Burden Under RFRA*, 36 Ecology L. Q. 259, 283–84, 314 (2009) (agreeing with the *Navajo Nation* majority insofar as "the Act's legislative history indicates that RFRA's codification of the substantial burden requirement was merely intended to restore the Court's treatment of burden analysis and 'did not purport to change the law' as it stood prior to *Smith*[;]" arguing, however, that majority opinion failed to apply pre-*Smith* decisional authority properly by, *inter alia*, interpreting *Yoder* to prohibit only laws that compel conduct in violation of religious beliefs given the fact that "the attendance law at issue in *Yoder* did not compel violation of any particular religious beliefs or practices because the Amish religion does not expressly proscribe secondary public school education")

P.137, n.480   Add the following to the end of the footnote:

One recent commentator thus has argued that "RFRA has no bearing on how the government makes use of public land" given legislative "history [that] suggests Congress did not intend the Act to have any effect on the pre-*Smith* decisions of *Lyng* and [*Bowen v. Roy*, 476 U.S. 693 (1986)]" and that "[t]he use of RFRA in public land use cases likely reflects perceived shortcomings in two other legal arenas: the inadequacy of current environmental laws in protecting non-economic uses of public lands and the absence of legislation favoring religious sites." James E. Key, *This Land Is My Land: The Tension Between Federal Law and the Religious Freedom Restoration Act*, 65 Air Force L. Rev. 51, 88, 105 (2010).

P.137.   ERRATA: The reference to "law" in the third-to-last line of the text should read "land."

P.137, n.484.   Add the following to the end of the footnote:

The Executive Order, however, may have more legal significance than its terms suggest. *See S. Fork Band Council of W. Shoshone v. USDOI*, 588 F.3d 718, 724 (9th Cir. 2009) (analyzing the Order as if the obligations it imposes on the BLM are judicially enforceable obligations).

P. 138, n.496.   Add the following to line 1 in the footnote after "E.g.,":

Te-Moak Tribe v. USDOI, 608 F.3d 592, 595–96 (9th Cir. 2010);

Add the following to the end of the footnote before the period:

; *Quechan Tribe v. USDOI*, 755 F. Supp. 2d 1104, 1107 (S.D. Cal. 2010);

P.139, n.504.   Add the following to the beginning of the footnote:

Te-Moak Tribe v. USDOI, 608 F.3d 592 (9th Cir. 2010) (FLPMA); *S. Fork Band Council of W. Shoshone v. USDOI*, 588 F.3d 718, 723–25 (9th Cir. 2009) (FLPMA);

P.139, n.505.   Add the following to the end of the footnote:

In 2008 Congress enacted a law of general applicability making lands in the National Forest System available to tribes and individual Indians for reburial of certain human remains and cultural items and also providing access to the lands for "traditional and cultural purposes" and providing for free certain forest products for the same purposes. The Food, Conservation, and Energy Act of 2008, Pub. L. No. 110-246, §§ 8101–8106, 122 Stat. 1651 (2008) (codified at 25 U.S.C. §§ 3051–3057).

Chapter 4
Criminal Law

P.143, n.8.   **Add the following to line 1 of the footnote after "*see also*":**

United States v. Fox, 573 F.3d 1050 (10th Cir. 2009) (statute prohibiting a felon from possessing a firearm is a law of general applicability and the Navajo Nation's Treaty of 1868's right to hunt did not insulate a tribal member from prosecution for possession of firearm by a felon), *cert. denied*, 130 S. Ct. 813 (2009); *United States v. Fiander*, 547 F.3d 1036 (9th Cir. 2008) (tribal member can be prosecuted for Racketeer Influenced and Corrupt Organization Act violation for conspiring to violate Contraband Cigarette Trafficking Act even though he cannot be convicted of violating the CCTA itself);

Add the following to the tenth-to-last line of the footnote after the semi-colon:

cf. United States v. Gallaher, 608 F.3d 1109 (9th Cir. 2010) (tribe's failure to authorize imposition of death penalty for violations under 18 U.S.C. §§ 1152 and 1153, as provided under 18 U.S.C. § 3598, crime remained "punishable by death" and a "capital offense" for purposes of exclusion from five-year limitation period in 18 U.S.C. § 3282; "'whether a crime is "punishable by death" under [18 U.S.C.] § 3281 or "capital" under § 3282 depends on whether the death penalty may be imposed for the crime under the enabling statute, not "on whether the death penalty is in fact available for defendants in a particular case"'"); *United States v. Newell*, 578 F. Supp. 2d 207 (D. Me. 2008) (Maine Indian Claims Settlement Act did not remove federal criminal jurisdiction over prosecution for conspiracy to defraud the United States);

P.144, n.13.   **Add the following to the end of the footnote:**

See generally Virginia Davis & Kevin Washburn, *Sex Offender Registration in Indian Country*, 6 Ohio St. J. Crim.L. 3 (2008) (urging Congress to revisit the Sex Offender Registration and Notification Act so that it can be tailored to the unique problems of Indian reservations and allow each tribe to develop the system that works best for that particular tribe); Brian P. Dimmer, *How Tribe and State Cooperative Agreements Can Save the Adam Walsh Act from Encroaching Upon Tribal Sovereignty*, 92 Marq. L. Rev. 385 (2008) (suggesting a compact process similar to the process used by the Indian Gaming Regulatory Act and limit the possibility that the delegation to state authority under the Adam Walsh Act will infringe on tribal sovereignty); *cf.* Amber Halldin, *Restoring the Victim and the Community: A Look at the Tribal Response to Sexual Violence Committed by Non-Indians in Indian Country Through Non-Criminal Approaches*, 84 N.D. L. Rev. 1, 14 (2008) (arguing that tribes should resist simply replicating state laws in their tribal codes with respect to sexual violence-related offenses; instead, "[t]ribal governments must also implement new tactics in order to solve the severe problem of sexual violence against Native American women" including use of traditional values, restorative justice and civil protection orders).

P.145.   **Delete the third sentence of the text up to, but not including, the footnote, and insert in its place:**

Consonant with this holding, a federal court of appeals and several state courts have found that the federal government lacks, and the states possess, jurisdiction over victimless crimes committed by non-Indians in Indian country.

P.145, n.18.   **Add the following to the beginning of the footnote:**

United States v. Langford, 641 F.3d 1195 (10th Cir. 2011) (no federal jurisdiction under the Assimilative Crimes Act over the victimless crime of a non-Indian being a spectator at a cockfight);

P.145, n.19.   **Add the following to the footnote after "*E.g.,*":**

United States v. Ramirez, 537 F.3d 1075 (9th Cir. 2008);

Add the following to the end of the footnote before the period:

;*United States v. Graham*, 585 F. Supp. 2d 1144, 1147–48 (D.S.D. 2008) (failure of superseding indictment to allege defendant's Indian status required dismissal; although dismissal would not be required "[i]f the elements are clearly set forth in the indictment in the words of the statute itself, . . . [s]imply citing the charging statute . . . does not cure the omission of an essential element of the charge because that citation does not ensure that the grand jury has considered and found all essential elements of the crime"), *aff'd United States v. Graham*, 572 F.3d 954, 957 (8th Cir. 2009) (also finding the aiding and abetting murder count deficient because 18 U.S.C. § 2 "does not extend federal jurisdiction to an accomplice charged under § 1153")

P.147.   **In the block quote of the Major Crimes Act, replace (a) with the following:**

(a) Any Indian who commits against the person or property of another Indian or other person any of the following offenses, namely, murder, manslaughter, kidnapping, maiming, a felony under chapter 109A, incest, assault with intent to commit murder, assault with a dangerous weapon, assault resulting in serious bodily injury (as defined in section 1365 of this title), an assault against an individual who has not attained the age of 16 years, felony child abuse or neglect, arson, burglary, robbery, and a felony under section 661 of this title within the Indian country, shall be subject to the same law and penalties as all other persons committing any of the above offenses, within the exclusive jurisdiction of the United States.

P.147, n.29.   Add the following to the end of the footnote before the period:

; *United States v. Other Medicine*, 596 F.3d 677, 681–82 (9th Cir. 2010) (rejecting "'federal law first' rule that would require prosecutors to charge a crime defined and punished by federal law when a defendant's conduct fits such a crime, even if the defendant's conduct also fits a separate Major Crimes Act crime defined and punished by state law" because § 1153(b) refers to "offenses"—a term that means "the legally defined crime, not the underlying criminal conduct—and "does not prevent prosecutors from charging that crime in instances [where a § 1153(a) offense] . . . rise[s] to the level of a state-defined felony")

P.147, n.30.   Add the following to line 6 of the footnote after the period:

United States v. Doe, 572 F.3d 1162, 1170–71 (10th Cir. 2009) (juvenile can be adjudicated a delinquent under the arson provision of the Major Crime Act for setting fire to a church owned by a non-profit corporation; "§ 1153's use of 'person' applies to living individuals and corporations, but does not apply to unincorporated associations"), *cert. denied*, 130 S. Ct. 1687 (2010);

Add the following to line 5 of the footnote before the period:

; *cf. United States v. Other Medicine*, 596 F.3d 677, 682 (9th Cir. 2009) (provision of Major Crime Act prohibiting felony child abuse was not unconstitutionally vague and using state criminal statutes to define felony child abuse provided "appropriate notice of what was condemned by law.")

P.148, n.31.   Add the following to line 1 of the footnote after "See":

United States v. Maggi, 598 F.3d 1073 (9th Cir. 2010) (convictions reversed because defendants were not Indians within the meaning of the Major Crimes Act even though they had Indian blood and one defendant was an enrolled member of a state but not federally recognized tribe); *United States v. Stymiest*, 581 F.3d 759, 762 (8th Cir. 2009) (whether defendant is an Indian for Major Crime Act purposes is a jury question using the generally accepted two-part *Rogers* test of "whether the defendant (1) has some Indian blood, and (2) is recognized as an Indian by a tribe or the federal government or both"), *cert. denied*, 130 S. Ct. 2364 (2010); *United States v. Cruz*, 554 F.3d 840, 850–51 (9th Cir. 2009) (Indian status is an element of a Major Crimes Act prosecution but an affirmative defense under the General Crimes Act);

P.150, n.50. Add the following to the end of the footnote before the period:

; *see also, United States v. I.L.*, 614 F.3d 817 (8th Cir. 2010) (tribal approval to transfer juvenile to adult court only required if the juvenile is 13 or 14 years of age, no tribal consent required when juvenile is 17 years old)

P.151, n.54. Add the following to the end of the footnote before the period:

; *see generally* Matthew Handler, *Tribal Law and Disorder: A Look At a System of Broken Justice in Indian Country and the Steps Needed to Fix It*, 75 Brook L. Rev. 261 (2009) (arguing for tribal criminal jurisdiction over non-Indians and analyzing the Tribal Law and Order Act of 2008); Samuel E. Ennis, *Reaffirming Indian Tribal Court Criminal Jurisdiction Over Non-Indians: An Argument for Statutory Abrogation of Oliphant*, 57 UCLA L. Rev. 553 (2009) (urging Congress to authorize tribal court prosecution of non-Indians and arguing that reaffirming tribal court jurisdiction over non-Indians would not amount to a delegation of federal prosecutorial power but would rather recognize inherent tribal authority); Benjamin J. Cordiano, *Unspoken Assumptions: Examining Tribal Jurisdiction Over Nonmembers Nearly Two Decades After Duro v. Reina*, 41 Conn. L. Rev. 265 (2008) (examining the effect of the decisions in *Oliphant*, *Duro* and *Lara*, and concluding that criminal jurisdiction over nonmember Indians is crucial to tribal self-governance);

P.152, n.64. Add the following to the beginning of the footnote:

United States v. Antelope, 548 F.3d 1155, 1157 (8th Cir. 2008);

Add the following to the end of the footnote:

The existence of separate sovereign status, however, does not mean that convictions valid under one sovereign's law must be accorded the same status as a valid conviction in a second sovereign's prosecution. *See United States v. Cavanaugh*, 680 F. Supp. 2d 1062, 1070–77 (D.N.D. 2009) (federal domestic violence prosecution cannot be based upon the use of tribal court domestic violence prosecutions where the defendant did not have a right to legal counsel); *see generally* Alex M. Hagen, *From Formal Separation to Functional Equivalence: Tribal-Federal Dual Sovereignty and the Sixth-Amendment Right to Counsel*, 54 S.D. L. Rev. 129 (2009); David L. Lane, Comment, *Twice Bitten: Denial of the Right to Counsel in Successive Prosecutions by Separate Sovereigns*, 45 Hous. L. Rev. 1869, 1871, 1880 (2009) (analyzing *Wheeler* in the overall context of "separate or dual sovereign[]" double jeopardy jurisprudence).

P.153, n.69.   **Add the following to line 3 of the footnote after "*see generally*":**

Marie Quasius, Note, *Native American Rape Victims: Desperately Seeking an Oliphant-Fix*, 93 Minn. L. Rev. 1902, 1927 (2009) (recommending adoption of ICRA and Major Crime Act amendments that would allow tribes to opt into jurisdiction over reservation sexual assault crimes by any person; although accepting the proposition that "Congress must consider certain factors in order to reinvest inherent sovereignty with regard to criminal jurisdiction" by virtue of perceived constitutional requirement, arguing that "ICRA already imposes nearly all of those requirements on tribal courts, and with additional funding, it would be easy for tribal courts to meet the single remaining requirement that defendants in a criminal trial have the opportunity to have legal counsel provided by the court") (footnotes omitted);

P.153.   **Add the following to the text after the first full paragraph:**

In response to the escalating levels of crime in Indian country and especially the high levels of violence against women, Congress adopted the Tribal Law and Order Act of 2010.[69.1] The Tribal Law and Order Act attempts to address a wide range of criminal justice and resource issues within Indian country. The Tribal Law and Order Act allows tribes to impose a three year maximum sentence and a $15,000 fine if certain due process requirements are met such as the appointment of adequate legal counsel and the use of judges with legal training.[69.2] It allows for the designation of tribal prosecuting attorneys as Special Assistant United States Attorneys and the designation of tribal liaisons by the United States Attorney.[69.3] The Tribal Law and Order Act also allows for the possible extension of concurrent federal jurisdiction to those areas subject to Public Law 280.[69.4]

[69.1]   Pub. L. No. 111-211, 124 Stat. 2258. *Contrast* Gideon M. Hart, Crisis in Indian Country: An Analysis of the Tribal Law and Order Act of 2010, 23 Regent U. L. Rev. 139 (2010–2011) (arguing for an expansion of the Act on the basis of reports of the Department of Justice that most rape and violent crime against Indian women in Indian country is committed by non-Indians) with Larry Long, et al., Understanding Contextual Differences in American Indian Criminal Justice, 32 Am. Indian Culture & Res. J. 41 (2008) (concluding, on the basis of state and federal records, that the DOJ is "wrong" to assert that most of the perpetrators of homicide and rape against Indian women in Indian country are non-Indians, at least in the context of South Dakota and, likely, other rural areas).

[69.2]   Tribal Law and Order Act of 2010, Pub. L. No. 111-211,

[69.3]   §234, 124 Stat. 2258, 2280.

[69.4]   Pub. L. No. 111-211, §401, 124 Stat. 2258, 2272 (2010)

P.155, n. 77.   **Add the following to line 4 of the footnote after *"see also"*:**

State v. Beasley, 199 P.3d 771 (Idaho Ct. App. 2008) (extradition was not necessary for a tribal member stopped by tribal police and subsequently arrested for traffic offense by state highway patrol trooper when state exercises Public Law 280 jurisdiction over the federal highway within the reservation);

P.158, n.91.   **Add the following to line 1 of the footnote after "*E.g.,*":**

State v. Losh, 755 N.W.2d 736, 744 (Minn. 2008) (offense of driving after revocation held criminal-prohibitory where the basis for revocation was driving with a blood-alcohol concentration of 0.15; "[t]he policy of protecting the public from drunk drivers is implicated when a person who has had his or her driving privileges revoked for driving while impaired continues to drive");

Add the following to the end of the footnote before the period:

; *but see Morgan v. 2000 Volkswagen*, 754 N.W.2d 587, 594 (Minn. Ct. App. 2008) (vehicle forfeiture deemed civil-regulatory even though underlying offenses arose from driving while impaired and thereafter refusing to submit to chemical test given that, *inter alia*, the vehicle owner "need not be the person who commits the conduct on which forfeiture is based" and the absence of any criminal sanctions under the forfeiture statute)

P.158, n.92.   **Add the following to the beginning of the footnote:**

State v. Roy, 761 N.W.2d 883 (Minn. Ct. App. 2009) (prohibition against a felon in possession of a firearm constitutes a criminal-prohibitory offense, and its application to a tribal member did not infringe on treaty hunting rights), *cert. denied*, 130 S. Ct. 1022 (2009);

P.159, n.101.   **Add the following to the end of the footnote:**

See also Confederated Tribes of the Colville Reservation v. Anderson, 761 F.Supp.2d 1101 (E.D. Wash. 2011) (state can regulate "in common" off-reservation hunting rights if the regulations are for public-safety purposes).

P.167, n. 131.   **Add the following to line 7 of the footnote after the semi-colon:**

Bressi v. Ford, 575 F.3d 891 (9th Cir. 2009) (tribal roadblock on state highway may stop all drivers long enough to determine if they are Indian or non-Indian; tribal officers with state authority can issue citations to non-Indians to state court; because tribal officers were operating under color of state law the plaintiff may proceed with his civil rights action under §1983);

P.168, n.132.   **Add the following to line 4 of the footnote after the semi-colon:**

Colyer v. State, 203 P.3d 1104 (Wyo. 2009) (BIA officer could lawfully detain traffic-offense suspect until deputy sheriff arrives to make actual arrest); *State v. Eriksen*, 241 P.3d 399 (Wash. 2010) (tribal officers have authority, under fresh pursuit doctrine, to continue chase beyond reservation boundaries and to detain non-Indian offender until authorities with jurisdiction arrive); *State v. Kurtz*, 249 P.3d 1271 (Or. 2011) (tribal officer could pursue offender off reservation because he was a "peace officer" under Oregon law for purposes of fleeing, eluding and resisting arrest offenses);

Add the following to line 5 of the footnote after the semi-colon:

but see State v. Hiester, 796 N.W.2d 328 (Minn. 2011) (tribal police officer not a "peace officer" under Minnesota law authorized to invoke implied consent law to require DWI suspect to take chemical test due to the tribe's lack of full compliance with state liability insurance requirement);

Add the following to line 9 of the footnote after the semi-colon:

State v. Madsen, 760 N.W.2d 370, 377, 381 (S.D. 2009) (where security guards were employed by tribe and therefore "government actors" subject to the Indian Civil Rights Act, ordinary Fourth Amendment standards, including the Exclusionary Rule, must be applied in a subsequent state court prosecution to determine the admissibility of evidence seized by them during a warrantless search; citing *Ramirez* favorably); *United States v. Wilson*, 754 F.Supp.2d 450 (N.D.N.Y. 2010) (tribal officer's off reservation stop for illegal border crossing and marijuana possession invalid because officer did not receive prior approval as required by Memorandum of Understanding between the Immigration Customs Enforcement Agency and the tribe),

Chapter 5
General Civil Regulatory Jurisdiction

P.180, n.89.   **Add the following to the end of the footnote:**

Another commentator, however, has suggested that "Congress should care-fully deliberate" over proposed legislation that would extend tribal criminal jurisdiction to non-Indians and cited Justice Kennedy's concurrence inso-far as it stressed the importance of the "federal structure." Patience Drake Roggensack, *Plains Commerce Bank's Potential Collision with the Expansion of Tribal Court Jurisdiction by Senate Bill 3320*, 38 U. Balt. L. Rev. 29, 41 (2008); *see also* Ann E. Tweedy, *Connecting the Dots Between the Constitution, the Marshall Trilogy, and United States v. Lara: Notes Toward a Blueprint for the Next Legisla-tive Restoration of Tribal Sovereignty*, 42 U. Mich. J.L. Reform 651, 700 (2009) (although questioning analytical legitimacy of Justice Kennedy's concerns, concluding that "his opinion unequivocally suggests that to decrease its vul-nerability, any restoration statute should, to the extent possible, provide for protection of individual constitutional rights").

P.183, n. 115.   **Add the following to line 2 after "E.g.,":**

Ann E. Tweedy, *Connecting the Dots Between the Constitution, the Marshall Trilogy, and United States v. Lara: Notes Toward a Blueprint for the Next Legisla-tive Restoration of Tribal Sovereignty*, 42 U. Mich. J.L. Reform 651, 717 (2009) (under *Lara* "[t]he scope of possible restoration, based on constitutional provisions as well as the Court's earliest Indian law jurisprudence, is quite broad[,]" but "because of the danger that the Court's distrust of tribes and increasing enforcement of constitutional norms will influence its evaluation of any legislative restoration, a legislative restoration should include protec-tions for individual rights and extensive findings supporting restoration" and be "optional for tribes");

P.186, n.126.   **Add the following to the end of the footnote before the period:**

; *see MacArthur v. San Juan County*, 566 F. Supp. 2d 1239, 1245 (D. Utah 2008) (rejecting contention that scope of inherent tribal authority constituted a nonjusticiable political question committed to Congress and the Executive Branch, since "much of the existing legal authority defining the subject-matter jurisdiction of Indian tribal courts over non-Indian litigants consists of judicially made federal Indian law, that is, federal case law precedent representing a species of federal common law—which common law federal courts develop as a necessary expedient when Congress has not spoken to a particular issue") (internal quotation marks omitted), *aff'd without published op.*, 355 F. App'x 243 (10th Cir. 2009), *cert. denied*, 130 S. Ct. 2378 (2010)

P.186, n.134.   Add the following to the end of the footnote before the period:

; *see generally* Katherine J. Florey, *Indian Country's Borders: Territoriality, Immunity, and the Construction of Tribal Sovereignty*, 51 B.C. L. Rev. 595, 609 (2010) (arguing that "[i]n a series of cases, the Court has limited the geographical dimension of tribal sovereignty still further by relying primarily on membership status within a tribe rather than the ownership status of land in determining who tribes can regulate[,]" and identifying *Oliphant* as where "[t]his progression began")

P.200, n.221.   Add the following to the end of the footnote before the period:

; *see Philip Morris USA, Inc. v. King Mountain Tobacco Co.*, 569 F.3d 932, 942 (9th Cir. 2009) (that the tribal court defendant had a consensual relationship with reservation tribal retailers as to sale of its cigarettes did not constitute the consent contemplated under the first *Montana* exception with respect to a suit by a rival tribal tobacco manufacturer over a trademark dispute; "[t]he mere fact that a nonmember has some consensual commercial contacts with a tribe does not mean that the tribe has jurisdiction over all suits involving that nonmember, or even over all such suits that arise within the reservation; the suit must also arise out of those consensual contacts")

P.200, n.222.   Replace "*Id.*" with "532 U.S.".

P.208, n.267.   Add the following to the end of the footnote before the period:

; *see Attorney's Process and Investigation Servs., Inc. v. Sac & Fox Tribe*, 609 F.3d 927, 939, 940–41 (8th Cir. 2010), *cert. denied*, 131 S. Ct. 1003 (2011) (second *Montana* exception applied where tribal court defendant's employees "organiz[ed] a physical attack by thirty or more outsiders armed with batons and at least one firearm against the Tribe's facilities and the tribal members inside, including the duly elected council" and thereby "directly threatened the tribal community and its institution[;] exception did not apply to alleged conversion of tribal funds paid defendant prior to the raid where it was not claimed that (1) the payments were for planning and executing the raid, (2) their receipt or retention occurred within the reservation).

P.206, n.257.   Add the following to the end of the footnote:

The need to focus on the factual basis of the claim presented to the tribal court in resolving application of the consent exception is reflected in *Attor-*

ney's Process and Investigation Servs., Inc. v. Sac & Fox Tribe, 609 F.3d 927 (8th Cir. 2010), *cert. denied*, 131 S. Ct. 1003 (2011), where the court of appeals held open the possibility of the exception's applicability to a conversion claim even if a contract between the tribal court parties was invalid. *Id.* at 941 ("the operative question for jurisdictional purposes is whether the conversion claim has a sufficient nexus to the consensual relationship"); *see also Water Wheel Camp Recreational Area, Inc. v. Larance*, 642 F.3d 802, 812, 818 (9th Cir. 2011) ("For purposes of determining whether a consensual relationship exists under *Montana's* first exception, consent may be established 'expressly or by [the nonmember's] actions.' . . . There is no requirement that [the nonmember's] commercial dealings with the [tribe] be a matter of written contract or lease actually signed by [the nonmember]").

P.208, n.266.   Add the following to the end of the footnote before the period:

; *but see Water Wheel Camp Recreational Area, Inc. v. Larance*, 642 F.3d 802, 812, 819 (9th Cir. 2011) (trespass claim satisfied second *Montana* exception where "unpaid rent and percentages of the business's gross receipts here totaled $1,486,146.42 at the time of the tribal court's judgment" and "unlawful occupancy and use of tribal land not only deprived the [tribe] of its power to govern and regulate its own land, but also of its right to manage and control an asset capable of producing significant income")

P.209, n.274.   Add the following to the end of the footnote:

The commentary since *Plains Commerce*'s issuance generally recognizes the uncertain nature of the opinion's future application. *Compare* Douglas B. L. Endreson, *Reconciling the Sovereignty of Indian Tribes in Civil Matters with the Montana Line of Cases*, 55 Vill. L. Rev. 863, 892 (2010) ("[I]n *Plains Commerce Bank*, as in *Hicks* and *Strate*, the Court avoided ruling on the fundamental question of tribal court jurisdiction over non-Indian defendants. In all of these cases, the Court limited the decision to the jurisdictional issue presented, which it resolved by using the *Montana* decision to provide a fact-specific standard of review. While all of these decisions are unfavorable, at the same time, they are narrow rulings. . . . This approach may reflect the Court's awareness that tribal jurisdiction is being used to address an increasingly wide variety of subjects—legislative and adjudicative—as it expands and matures under the Self-Determination Policy, and a disinclination to interfere with that progress except to the degree necessary to resolve the case before it"); Ann E. Tweedy, *Connecting the Dots Between the Constitution, the Marshall Trilogy, and United States v. Lara: Notes Toward a Blueprint for the Next Legislative Restoration of Tribal Sovereignty*, 42 U. Mich. J.L. Reform 651, 681 (2009) ("[g]iven that the *Long Family Land & Cattle Co.* Court's holding is primarily based on its reading of the consensual relationship exception but that its analysis of that exception is only cursory, it is difficult to know precisely how the Court will construe the majority opinion in future cases"); Lisa M. Slepnikoff, Student Article, *More Questions Than Answers: Plains*

Commerce Bank v. Long Family Land and Cattle Company, Inc. and the U.S. Supreme Court's Failure to Define the Extent of Tribal Civil Authority Over Non-members on Non-Indian Land, 54 S.D. L. Rev. 460, 491–92 (2009) (discussing uncertainty and potential implications as to distinctions between contract and tort actions and as to the need for express or implied consent to tribal civil authority), *with* Samuel E. Ennis, *Implicit Divestiture and the Supreme Court's (Re)Construction of the Indian Canons*, 35 Vt. L. Rev. 623, 649 (2011) ("Although the future of tribal civil jurisdiction over non-members is still undetermined, *Hicks* and *Plains Commerce Bank* stand as twin pincers ready to decapitate civil jurisdiction in an *Oliphant*-esque bright line divestiture of sovereignty: *Hicks* to apply *Montana* to the entirety of Indian reservations, and *Plains Commerce Bank* holding tribes to an impossible standard under *Montana*"), and Katherine J. Florey, *Indian Country's Borders: Territoriality, Immunity, and the Construction of Tribal Sovereignty*, 51 B.C. L. Rev. 595, 612–13 (2010) ("where previous cases had suggested that only nonmember activities on nonmember land were presumptively exempt from tribal regulation, *Plains Commerce Bank* now indicates that nonmember activities are exempt, period, where nonmember land is involved").

P.210, n.278.   Add the following to line 12 of the footnote after the semi-colon:

Judicial Standards Comm'n v. Not Afraid, 245 P.3d 1116, 1121 (Mont. 2010) (a judicial officer's "actions, in filing and running for state office, involved much more than 'significant contacts with the state[,]' since "[h]e became a state official and took a constitutional oath of office to support, protect, and defend the Montana Constitution"); *Paquin v. Mack*, 788 N.W.2d 899, 905 (Minn. 2010) ("Running for state legislative office and signing a nominating petition for state legislative office are activities 'going beyond reservation boundaries.' In seeking to become a candidate for state legislative office, and in signing the nominating petition, petitioner and his supporters are subject to state election laws"); *State ex rel. Edmondson v. Native Wholesale Supply*, 237 P.3d 199, 216 (Okla. 2010), *cert. denied*, 131 S. Ct. 2150 (2011) (where tribal tobacco wholesaler's "transactions . . . "extend beyond the boundaries of any single 'reservation[,]'" court deemed them "not on-reservation conduct for purposes of Indian Commerce Clause jurisprudence, but rather off-reservation conduct by members of different tribes" not subject to *Bracker* interest-balancing); *Dep't of Health & Human Servs. v. Maybee*, 965 A.2d 55, 57 (Me. 2009) (retailer of cigarettes doing business from the out-of-state reservation of his tribe subject to tobacco-retailer-license requirement by virtue of Internet and mail-order sales to state residents; "the balancing test [applied generally in Indian law preemption disputes] . . . is inapplicable to the present case because [the retailer's] interactions with consumers in Maine extend beyond the boundaries of the reservation" and because "[a]ctivity of tribal members that takes place within the reservation but has an impact outside the reservation may be regulated by the states");

Add the following to line 17 of the footnote before the period:

; *cf. State v. Grand River Enters., Inc.,* 757 N.W.2d 305, 319 (S.D. 2008) (personal jurisdiction did not exist over cigarette manufacturer doing business from Canadian reserve and selling its product to tribal member-owned businesses located on a New York reservation; that the latter business eventually marketed the cigarettes to a Nebraska distributor, also located on an Indian reservation, which then introduced them for retailing, primarily on Indian reservations, in South Dakota and other states did not establish the requisite "minimum contacts" absent proof of "a more significant relationship with or knowledge of [the] distribution chain suggesting that [the manufacturer] expected or should have expected its manufacturing activities to be directed at the South Dakota market")

P.215, n.306. **Add the following to the end of the footnote before the period:**

; *Karcz v. Klewin Bldg. Co.,* 926 N.Y.S.2d 227, 228 (App. Div. 2011) (state labor law vicarious liability provisions applied to action by injured non-Indian construction worker against non-Indian companies related to accident at tribal casino, since "[t]his action is between non-Indians . . . and does not implicate the internal affairs of the [tribe]")

P.218, n.323. **Add the following to line 11 of the footnote after the semi-colon:**

; *Swenson v. Nickaboine,* 793 N.W.2d 738, 744 (Minn. 2011) (state workers' compensation statute applicable to on-reservation injury while worker employed by tribal member given express authorization in 40 U.S.C. § 3172, since "[t]he federal government clearly 'owns or holds' land it holds in trust for the [tribe], and it is a basic principle of trust law that a trustee holds legal title to trust property");

P.220, n.332. **Add the following to the fifth-to-last line of the footnote after the semi-colon:**

cf. Ho-Cak Fed. v. Herrell (In re DeCora), 396 B.R. 222, 225 (W.D. Wis. 2008) (*Bracker* and *Mescalero Apache* interest-balancing standard applied to select tribal, rather than state, law as determinative of lien-holder priority in bankruptcy proceeding with respect to debtor's per capita entitlement; "[a]ny creditor taking a security interest or lien in tribal per capita payments should reasonable [*sic*] anticipate that its rights may be affected by tribal law[,]" and here the tribe's "interest in controlling the distribution of its revenue far outweighs [the State's] interest in enforcing its commercial code");

**P.224, n.363.   Add the following to the end of the footnote before
the period:**

; *see generally* Alex Tallchief Skibine, *Tribal Sovereign Interests Beyond the Reservation Border*, 12 Lewis & Clark L. Rev. 1003, 1030 (2008) (observing that
"the Tenth Circuit on remand was able to conveniently abdicate from its original position while still being able to reach the same result," but suggesting
further that it "left unanswered . . . whether the Indian preemption test can
ever be applied to situations involving tribal immunity from state regulation
for conduct or issues arising off the reservation")

Chapter 6
Civil Adjudicatory Jurisdiction

P.225, n.2.   **Add the following to line 1 of the footnote after "*See*":**

Cook v. Avi Casino Enters., Inc., 548 F.3d 718, 722 (9th Cir. 2008), *cert. denied*, 129 S. Ct. 2159 (2009);

P.231, n.34.   **Add the following to the eleventh-to-last line of the footnote before the semi-colon:**

, *vacated in part & remanded*, 569 F.3d 589, 596 (6th Cir. 2009) (§ 1983 claim remanded for determination of "whether the [tribe] was entitled to the federal funds (a) only as a result of its sovereignty, or (b) simply because it provides certain social services" since, under any "plausible" reading of *Inyo County*, "[i]f it is the latter, then [the tribe's] § 1983 suit would not be in any way dependent on its status as a sovereign, and it should be considered a 'person' within the meaning of that statute, so long as other private, nonsovereign entities could likewise sue under § 1983")

P.233, n.48.   **Add the following to the end of the footnote:**

As would appear implicit from *National Farmers*—where exhaustion had not occurred—appellate review is available of a stay or dismissal order. *See Philip Morris USA, Inc. v. King Mountain Tobacco Co.*, 569 F.3d 932, 936 (9th Cir. 2009) (order staying action to allow for tribal court exhaustion deemed appealable under 28 U.S.C. § 1292(a)(1)); *Elliott v. White Mountain Apache Tribal Ct.*, 566 F.3d 842, 845–46 (9th Cir. 2009) (order dismissing action without prejudice to allow for tribal court exhaustion deemed final for appeal purposes under 28 U.S.C. § 1291), *cert. denied*, 130 S. Ct. 624 (2009). Also implicit is the absence of tribal immunity from suit where its courts are alleged to be acting in contravention of federal law-imposed limitations. *See Attorney's Process and Investigation Servs., Inc. v. Sac & Fox Tribe of Miss. in Iowa*, No. 05-CV-168-LRR, 2009 WL 1783497, at *6 (N.D. Iowa June 18, 2009) ("[t]he wealth of federal case law concerning tribal court civil jurisdiction over non-members demonstrates that sovereign immunity does not bar a district court from considering this matter"), *aff'd in part and vacated in part*, 609 F.3d 927 (8th Cir. 2010), *cert. denied*, 131 S. Ct. 1003 (2011).

P.234, n.54.   **Add the following to the end of the footnote before the period:**

; *see Miner v. Standing Rock Sioux Tribe*, 619 F. Supp. 2d 715, 726 (D.S.D. 2009) (declining to consider merits of contract claim by former tribal court judge against tribe which was resolved against the federal court plaintiff by tribal courts and where no claim existed that the latter lacked jurisdiction; complaint dismissed for lack of subject matter jurisdiction since neither diversity nor federal question jurisdiction existed)

P.234, n.55.   **Delete "*Id.*" and replace the deletion with "480 U.S.".**

P.238, n.68.   **Add the following to the end of the footnote before the period:**

; *see also QEP Field Servs. Co. v. Ute Indian Tribe*, 740 F. Supp. 2d 1274, 1280 (D. Utah 2010) (analyzing, and relying upon, arbitration provision in surface use and access agreement to conclude that exhaustion of tribal court remedies not required; "because there was a clear and unambiguous waiver of Tribal Court jurisdiction in the Agreement, the litigation in Tribal Court is patently violative of the parties' written agreement and exhaustion is unnecessary")

P.238, n.73.   **Add the following to line 1 of the footnote after "*E.g.*,":**

Philip Morris USA, Inc. v. King Mountain Tobacco Co., 569 F.3d 932, 935 (9th Cir. 2009) (engaging in detailed analysis of the merits to determine whether the defendant's claim of tribal court jurisdiction is "colorable"); *Elliott v. White Mountain Apache Tribal Ct.*, 566 F.3d 842, 848 (9th Cir. 2009) ("plainly lacking" exception identified in *Strate* footnote 14 resolved on the basis of whether assertion of tribal adjudicatory authority over nonmember was "plausible" or "colorable"), *cert. denied*, 130 S. Ct. 624 (2009);

P.245, n.115.   **Add the following to the beginning of the footnote:**

Philip Morris USA, Inc. v. King Mountain Tobacco Co., 569 F.3d 932, 944 (9th Cir. 2009) (rejecting contention that "*Hicks* . . . stand[s] for a rule that tribes have no jurisdiction over federal statutory claims absent an explicit statutory grant[,]" but holding further that "where Congress is silent—as in the Lanham Act—tribal jurisdiction rests on inherent sovereignty, and its scope is prescribed by *Montana*");

Add the following to the end of the footnote before the period:

; *but see Graham v. Applied Geo Techs., Inc.*, 593 F. Supp. 2d 915, 919–21 (S.D. Miss. 2008) (exhaustion of tribal remedies required with respect to employment discrimination claim under Title VII of the Civil Rights Act of 1964, where the action was against a for-profit corporation chartered by tribe, not a non-Indian, and was predicated upon conduct occurring on reservation out of a consensual relationship)

P.255, n.168.   Add the following to line 13 of the footnote after the semi-colon:

Philip Morris USA, Inc. v. King Mountain Tobacco Co., 569 F.3d 932, 934 (9th Cir. 2009) (rejecting reliance on the *Montana* consent exception in part because "this is a suit by the holder of a federally-registered trademark for trademark infringement, unfair competition, and passing off through worldwide Internet sales and off-reservation sales to tribes in New York" with the complaint's "focus" on "the passing off, which occurs beyond the reservation boundaries and . . . beyond tribal jurisdiction");

Add the following to the end of the footnote:

The necessary focus of the tribal authority issue on the relationship between the nonmember's activity and tribal lands would appear to obviate the need for a separate personal jurisdiction analysis in most instances, but the Ninth Circuit discretely analyzed the issue and found such jurisdiction on the basis of the nonmember's residence on tribal land, the service of process upon him on tribal land. *Water Wheel Camp Recreational Area, Inc. v. Larance*, 642 F.3d 802, 819 (9th Cir. 2011). Under these circumstances, "it was reasonable to anticipate that he could be haled into tribal court." *Id.* at 820.

P.256, n.169.   Add the following to the second-to-last line of the footnote after the semi-colon:

Crowe & Dunlevy P.C. v. Stidham, 609 F. Supp. 2d 1211, 1226 (N.D. Okla. 2009) (probability-of-success element of preliminary injunction standard satisfied where law firm challenged tribal court jurisdiction to direct return of fees in action by a tribal faction against the nominal tribal government which had retained and paid the firm; although the firm's client possessed a "historical relationship" with the tribe maintaining the court system and many of its members possessed dual membership, the firm "had not entered into an explicit contractual relationship with the [latter tribe] or its citizens"), *aff'd*, 640 F.3d 1140, 1153 (10th Cir. 2011) ("[w]hile Crowe attorneys submitted themselves to the Muscogee (Creek) Nation tribal court when they brought the [tribal court] litigation, there is no basis on which to conclude they or the firm submitted themselves to the general subject matter jurisdiction of the tribal court for all purposes, especially not for the purpose of voiding their contractual relationship with the [tribal court plaintiff], when that contract is not, directly or indirectly, part of the . . . defendant's claims before the court");

P.257, n.177.   Add the following to the first line of the footnote after "See":

Attorney's Process and Investigation Servs., Inc. v. Sac & Fox Tribe, 609 F.3d 927, 940–41 (8th Cir. 2010), *cert. denied*, 131 S. Ct. 1003 (2011) (declining to find second *Montana* exception applicable to alleged conversion of tribal funds because, in part, no facts established that the funds' receipt and retention occurred on reservation);

Add the following to the seventh-to-last line of the footnote after *"but see"*:

Qwest Corp. v. Bailey, 2009 Indian L. Rep. 6020 (Nez Perce Tr. Ct. App. Oct. 7, 2008) (tribal court lacked adjudicatory authority over trespass claim filed by tribal member property owners against telecommunications carriers for trespass; *Montana* consent exception held inapplicable where the only contractual relationship related to communications services with "no nexus to a claim of trespass, which is a tort[,]" while the second exception was deemed unavailable in part because "allowing telephone service providers to service the Tribe by maintaining their service lines and underground 'drop lines' mostly on or directly adjacent to the State Highway, stemming from telephone poles with proper easements and rights-of-way, is most likely a benefit to the Tribe");

P.260, n.199.   Add the following to the end of the footnote before the period:

; *but see Water Wheel Camp Recreational Area, Inc. v. Larance*, 642 F.3d 802, 812, 814 (9th Cir. 2011) (concluding that "[a]s a general rule, both the Supreme Court and the Ninth Circuit have recognized that *Montana* does not affect [the principle that the right exclude includes the right to regulate] as it relates to regulatory jurisdiction over non-Indians on Indian land ... unless Congress has said otherwise[] or unless the Supreme Court has recognized that such power conflicts with federal interests promoting tribal self government[,]" and holding that tribe possessed "regulatory jurisdiction over Water Wheel and Johnson for claims arising from their activities on tribal land, independent of *Montana*")

P.263, n.212.   Add the following to the end of the footnote before the period:

; *see Elliott v. White Mountain Apache Tribal Ct.*, 566 F.3d 842, 850 (9th Cir.), *cert. denied*, 130 S. Ct. 624 (2009) (holding, without discussion or citation to *Plains Commerce*, tribal adjudicatory authority not "plainly lacking" for exhaustion purposes under the second exception with respect to tribe's damages claim against nonmember for fire within reservation that affected 400,000 acres; "the tribe makes a compelling argument that the regulations at issue are intended to secure the tribe's political and economic well-being, particularly in light of the result of the alleged violations of those regulations in this very case: the destruction of millions of dollars of the tribe's natural resources")

P.263, n.213.   Add the following to the end of the footnote before the period:

; *but see Water Wheel Camp Recreational Area, Inc. v. Larance*, 642 F.3d 802, 812, 816 (9th Cir. 2011) (holding that *Montana* had no application to the scope of tribal regulatory authority with respect to access to tribal lands and that, "[w]hile it is an open question as to whether a tribe's adjudicative jurisdiction is equal to its regulatory jurisdiction, the important sovereign interests at stake, the existence of regulatory jurisdiction, and long-standing Indian law principles recognizing tribal sovereignty all support finding adjudicative jurisdiction here[,]" since "[a]ny other conclusion would impermissibly interfere with the tribe's inherent sovereignty, contradict long-standing principles the Supreme Court has repeatedly recognized, and conflict with Congress's interest in promoting tribal self-government")

P.267, n.233. Add the following to the fifth-to-last line after *"contra see generally"*:

Jackie Gardina, *Federal Preemption: A Roadmap for the Application of Tribal Law in State Courts*, 35 Am. Indian L. Rev. 1, 29 (2010–2011) ("[S]tate courts assume concurrent adjudicative jurisdiction in a significant number of circumstances. In these instances, both the tribal and state courts have authority to enter binding judgments against the parties. Because a tribe's adjudicative and legislative jurisdiction are essentially coextensive, tribal law would also be applicable to the underlying dispute. But the converse is not necessarily true; state courts cannot assume that if they have adjudicative jurisdiction, they automatically have legislative jurisdiction") (footnote omitted);

P.268, n.237. Add the following to line 7 of the footnote after the semi-colon:

Luger v. Luger, 765 N.W.2d 523, 527 (N.D. 2009) (state court jurisdiction existed over reservation-based partnership dispute where none of the parties was a member of the resident tribe although all were members of another tribe; neither of the *Montana* exceptions applied since "[t]here is no evidence that the partnership or the partners have entered into any relationships with the tribe or its members pertinent to this lawsuit" and "the subject matter of this lawsuit does not involve conduct that threatens or has some direct effect on the political integrity, the economic security, or the health or welfare of the . . . Reservation");

P.269, n.238. Add the following to line 1 of the footnote after *"See"*:

Oglala Sioux Tribe v. C & W Enters., Inc., 542 F.3d 224, 232 (8th Cir. 2008) (notwithstanding absence of a choice-of-law provision, state court possessed jurisdiction to enforce arbitration award against a tribe under commercial contract adopting American Arbitration Rules which, in relevant part, authorized the award's entry as a judgment by any state or federal court with jurisdiction; "[w]hen it agreed to arbitrate disputes and incorporated the AAA's claim resolution procedures into the contracts, and when it participated in the South Dakota arbitration, the Tribe acquiesced in the arbitrator's decision, placing jurisdiction over the award in South Dakota's courts");

Add the following to line 5 of the footnote after "*cf.*":

Cossey v. Cherokee Nation Enters., LLC, 212 P.3d 447, 454–56 (Okla. 2009) (tribal-state gaming compact allowing suits over claims in a "court of competent jurisdiction" deemed not dispositive in itself of state court jurisdiction in casino patron's tort action, but such jurisdiction existed where application of *Montana* standards established the lack of tribal adjudicatory authority);

P.269, n.239.   Add the following to the first line of the footnote after "*E.g.,*":

Judicial Standards Comm'n v. Not Afraid, 245 P.3d 1116, 1121 (Mont. 2010) (state court possessed jurisdiction over complaint seeking to enforce constitutional provision that prohibits holder of judicial position from seeking elective public office against tribal member county justice of the peace who had entered race for tribal chairperson; the judicial officer's "actions, in filing and running for state office, involved much more than 'significant contacts with the state[,]' since "[h]e became a state official and took a constitutional oath of office to support, protect, and defend the Montana Constitution");

P.270, n.241.   Add the following to the first paragraph of the footnote after "*E.g.,*":

C.L. v. Z.M.F.H., 18 A.3d 1175, 1180 (Pa. Super. Ct. 2011) (state court properly applied the Uniform Child Custody and Jurisdiction Enforcement Act in declining to exercise jurisdiction over custody petition where prior tribal court proceeding existed); *Schirado v. Foote*, 785 N.W.2d 235, 239 (N.D. 2010) (remanding for "home state" determination under the Uniform Child Custody and Jurisdiction Enforcement Act after holding that an Indian reservation "is a state under UCCJEA"); *Duwyenie v. Moran*, 207 P.3d 754, 757–58 (Ariz. Ct. App. 2009) (state court possessed jurisdiction over child custody dispute under the Uniform Child Custody Jurisdiction and Enforcement Act as the "home State" notwithstanding the fact where the child had been residing on a South Dakota Indian reservation for more than six months in whose tribal court the father had commenced a custody proceeding; the father removed the child from Arizona during a one-week visitation without the mother's consent and had initiated the tribal court proceeding at a time when Arizona was the "home State"); *Kelly v. Kelly*, 759 N.W.2d 721 (N.D. 2009) (state court possessed jurisdiction over non-child custody issues in divorce proceeding in view of the significant off-reservation contacts to marriage and the commencement of the state proceeding prior to the tribal court action, but matter remanded to trial court for determination of "home state" status of tribal court under the Uniform Child Custody Jurisdiction and Enforcement Act and, if such status exists, whether convenient-forum considerations warrant deferring exercise of jurisdiction over the other incidents of the marital relationship to the tribal court);

Add the following to third paragraph of the footnote after "*E.g.,*":

Mendoza v. Tamaya Enters., Inc., 2011-NMSC-030, 2011 WL 3111922, at *1 (June 27, 2011) (tribe consent to state court suit for personal injury claims by casino patrons under gaming compact); *Lozeau v. Geico Indem. Co.*, 207 P.3d 316, 319 (Mont. 2009) (applying common-law equitable-tolling principles in personal injury suit against tribal member by a nonmember where the latter had commenced a tribal court action within the applicable state limitation period which had been dismissed on jurisdictional grounds; "[w]hile [the defendant] characterizes exclusive state jurisdiction for [the plaintiff's] claim as virtually certain, we recognize that the issue of state and tribal jurisdiction can present a procedural quandary for litigants"); *Griffith v. Choctaw Casino of Pocola*, 230 P.3 488, 497, 498 (Okla. 2009) (applying canons of statutory construction, state court deemed "court of competent jurisdiction" under voter-approved statute, which prescribed terms of "model" gaming compact, since such term "as used in federal statutes has long been construed to mean federal and state courts[;]" disclaiming any intent that anything in opinion "should be taken as a holding that a tribal court is not a 'court of competent jurisdiction' or should be taken as eliminating the tribal court as a forum available to a tort claimant if the claimant chooses to file suit in tribal court"); *Dye v. Choctaw Casino of Pocola*, 230 P.3d 507, 510 (Okla. 2009) (following *Griffith*); *Cossey v. Cherokee Nation Enters., LLC*, 212 P.3d 447, 454–56 (Okla. 2009) (state court deemed "court of competent jurisdiction" over patron's personal injury suit given such court's status under federal common law as one of general jurisdiction and the absence of tribal adjudicatory authority under *Montana* exceptions); *Francis v. Dana-Cummings*, 962 A.2d 944, 949 (Me. 2008) (applying "internal tribal matters" exception to state jurisdiction under the Maine Implementing Act, as construed in prior decisions, to preclude suit between tribal members over tort and other claims arising from eviction from tribal housing);

Add the following to fourth paragraph of the footnote after "*E.g.,*":

In re Estate of Big Spring, 255 P.3d 121, 134–35 (Mont. 2011) (state court lacked subject matter jurisdiction over probate dispute arising from on-reservation property in tribal member's estate);

P.272, n.245.   Add the following to line 4 of the footnote before the semi-colon:

, *rev'd*, 992 So. 2d 446, 451–52 (La. 2008) (finding a valid waiver of sovereign immunity expressly subjecting tribe to state court jurisdiction; reasoning further that "the tribal exhaustion doctrine is one based in comity, a discretionary policy" and that several considerations supported the trial court's exercise of such discretion, including a choice-of-law provision selecting Louisiana law, the state's "major interest in contractual disputes involving its corporations[,]" the fact that "the dispute does not involve tribal governance or political integrity[,]" and the fact that the trial court "carefully considered the arguments of both parties in reaching its decision")

P.275, n.261. **Add the following to the end of the footnote before the period:**

; *see generally* Terry L. Anderson & Dominic P. Parker, *Sovereignty, Credible Commitments, and Economic Development on American Indian Reservations*, 51 J.L. & Econ. 641, 658–59 (2008) (concluding that per capita income on Public Law 280 reservations grew 30 percent more than on non–Public Law 280 reservations between 1969 and 1999, and attributing the greater growth in part to "a more stable contracting environment" created by the "greater degree of credible commitment available under PL 280")

P.281, n.295. **Add the following to the second-to-last line of the footnote after the semi-colon:**

but see Beltran v. Harrah's Ariz. Corp., 202 P.3d 494, 497 (Ariz. Ct. App. 2008) (declining, in part, to apply procedural rule that tribal judgments sought to be enforced be filed with the clerk of court because nothing indicated that the rules were intended to be the exclusive mechanism for enforcing such judgments and "[t]raditionally, Arizona courts have recognized tribal court judgments as a matter of comity[,]" and citing *Tracy* as authority for the latter proposition);

P.283, n.300. **Add the following to line 1 of the footnote after "*compare*":**

Duwyenie v. Moran, 207 P.3d 754, 757–58 (Ariz. Ct. App. 2009) (state court possessed "home State" jurisdiction over child custody dispute where the father had removed the child from Arizona during a one-week visitation without the mother's consent and had initiated a tribal court proceeding at a time when Arizona was the "home State");

Chapter 7
Tribal Sovereign Immunity and the Indian Civil Rights Act

P.288, n.8.   **Add the following to line 6 of the footnote after the semi-colon:**

NLRB v. Fortune Bay Resort Casino, 688 F. Supp. 2d 858, 871 (D. Minn. 2010) (rejecting sovereign immunity claim with respect to subpoena issued by the National Labor Relations Board's General Counsel because "the underlying proceeding" was a "prosecution" in which the General Counsel was "responsible for enforcing the public interest, not for enforcing the rights of private litigants");

Replace ", *with*" in line 9 of the footnote with a period.

Replace "*but see*" in the second-to-last line of the footnote with a period and the following:

A contrary conclusion, however, was reached in *Gristede's Foods, Inc. v. Unkechuage Nation*, 660 F. Supp. 2d 442 (E.D.N.Y. 2009), where the district court held that federal recognition was not a prerequisite and that common law-based tribal status sufficed. *Id.* at 465 ("[p]ursuant to federal law, a group of Indians is a tribe—and therefore enjoys sovereign immunity—if it either 1) has been federally recognized by Congress or the BIA, or 2) meets the federal common law definition"); *cf.*

Add the following to the end of the footnote:

A tribe's immunity from suit also has been held inapplicable to *in rem* actions that may affect its property interests. *E.g., Smale v. Noretep*, 208 P.3d 1180, 1181 (Wash. Ct. App. 2009) (applying *Anderson & Middleton Lumber Co. v. Quinault Indian Nation*, 929 P.2d 379 (Wash. 1996), and holding that tribal immunity from suit did not preclude an *in rem* action to quiet title under an adverse possession claim without regard to whether land was within or without the tribe's reservation).

P.294, n.50.   **Add the following to line 1 of the footnote after *"see also"*:**

Oneida Indian Nation v. Madison County, 605 F.3d 149, 157 (2d Cir. 2010); *vacated*, 131 S. Ct. 704 (2011) (tribe possessed immunity from property foreclosure action based upon tax delinquencies; outcome was not controlled by *City of Sherrill v. Oneida Indian Nation*, 544 U.S. 197 (2005), which upheld involved counties' right to impose taxes, because "[w]hile the tax exemption of reservation land arises from a tribe's exercise of sovereignty over such land, and is therefore closely tied to the question of whether the specific parcel at issue is 'Indian reservation land,' . . . a tribe's immunity from suit is independent of its lands");

Add the following to line 4 of the footnote after the semi-colon:

Ameriloan v. Superior Ct., 86 Cal. Rptr. 3d 572, 579 (Cal. Ct. App. 2008) (noting state agency's contention that *Manufacturing Technologies* "is inapposite because it involved a private action, not a government-initiated enforcement action," and responding that the agency "misapprehends the relevant case law and confuses principles of preemption with those governing tribal sovereign immunity");

Add the following to the end of the footnote before the period:

; *see generally* Nathaniel T. Haskins, Note, *Framing Current Jurisdiction Issues in the Self-Determination Era: Accepting the First Circuit's Analysis but Rejecting Its Application to Preserve Tribal Sovereignty*, 32 Am. Indian L. Rev. 441, 458 (2007–2008) (characterizing the *Narragansett* majority opinion's analysis as "a work of fiction" to the extent it reasoned "that tribal sovereign immunity was an incident of its sovereignty, and therefore, when the tribe subjugated its autonomy by consenting to concurrent jurisdiction, it did the same to its sovereign immunity")

P.295, n.51.   **Add the following to line 2 of the footnote after "*E.g.,*":**

Vann v. Kempthorne, 534 F.3d 741, 756 (D.C. Cir. 2008) (concluding that *Ex parte Young* relief is available against tribal officers, but remanding for a determination of "whether 'in equity and good conscience' the suit can proceed with the [tribe's] officers but without the [tribe] itself");

Add the following to line 26 of the footnote after the semi-colon:

Oklahoma v. Tyson Foods, Inc., 258 F.R.D. 472, 482 (N.D. Okla. 2009) (dismissing action under Rule 19 as to damages claim related to poultry operation's allegedly adverse impact on watershed for failure to join tribe as party, and reasoning in part that "[b]ecause the State's claims involve allegations of harm to natural resources in which the [the tribe] claims an interest, a judgment for damages in this case would either impinge on the [tribe's] sovereign and statutory rights or leave defendants exposed to subsequent suit by the [tribe], or both");

Add the following to the eleventh-to-last line of the footnote after *"see generally"*:

Katherine Florey, *Sovereign Immunity's Penumbras: Common Law, "Accident," and Policy in the Development of Sovereign Immunity Doctrine*, 43 Wake Forest L. Rev. 765, 767, 826, 829 (2008) (contending that courts, other than the United States Supreme Court, "have gone from strictly construing the doctrine to creating a sort of common law, 'penumbral' sovereign immunity that extends well beyond what are normally considered to be the doctrine's boundaries[;]" identifying several such penumbral areas including derivative sovereign immunity, indispensable party decision-making, and *res judicata*; and suggesting four principles for resolving "marginal sovereign immunity" cases among which is treating different types of sovereigns discretely in penumbral areas, with tribes having "strong and unique policy justifications . . . for a vigorous doctrine of tribal immunity");

P.297, n.61. **Add the following to the beginning of the footnote:**

Ingrassia v. Chicken Ranch Bingo and Casino, 676 F. Supp. 2d 953, 958 (E.D. Cal. 2009) (no abrogation under Copyright Act or Indian Gaming Regulatory Act with respect to claim related to marketing of products with "MiWuk Indian riding on a chicken" image); *Freemanville Water Sys., Inc. v. Poarch Band of Creek Indians*, 563 F.3d 1205, 1209 (11th Cir. 2009) (no abrogation under Consolidated Farm and Rural Development Act with respect to "anti-curtailment" lawsuits; reasoning in part clear-and-unequivocal standard was not satisfied given the fact that "Indian tribes are explicitly included within the scope of seven provisions of the Rural Development Act, but they are not mentioned in [the] anti-curtailment provision" and the settled canon that "'it is generally presumed that Congress acts intentionally and purposely in the disparate inclusion or exclusion'");

Add the following to line 11 of the footnote after the semi-colon:

Bales v. Chickasaw Nation Indus., 606 F. Supp. 2d 1299, 1308 (D.N.M. 2009) (even if secretarially-chartered corporation did not partake of the coverage exemption accorded tribes themselves under Title VII of the Equal Employment Opportunity Act, "Plaintiff has failed to convince the Court that Congress has unequivocally abrogated tribal sovereign immunity" as to claims under the statute; corporation also immune from suit under the Age Discrimination in Employment Act, notwithstanding law's general applicability, given the lack of congressional abrogation); *cf. United States v. Menominee Tribal Enters.*, 601 F. Supp. 2d 1061, 1068 (E.D. Wis. 2009) (tribe is not a "person" under the False Claims Act, but tribal employees sued in their individual capacity are; as to the former, "the existence of immunity is what drives a key statutory interpretation *presumption* . . . that the term 'person' does not include the sovereign, the upshot of which is that before a sovereign can be sued there must be some 'affirmative indications' of Congress' intent to abrogate immunity), *recons. denied*, No. 07-C-316, 2009 WL 1373952 (E.D. Wis. May 15, 2009);

Add the following to line 12 of the footnote after *"see generally"*:

Jeremiah A. Bryar, Comment, *What Goes Around, Comes Around: How Indian Tribes Can Profit in the Aftermath of Seminole Tribe and Florida Prepaid*, 13 Marq. Intell. Prop. L. Rev. 229, 248 (2009) (suggesting that tribes, like state universities and research organizations, can use their sovereign immunity as a shield against patent infringement suits and create "sovereign chartered research groups [which] will drive additional funding into the tribes, create jobs for tribal members, and bring hope into the lives of a people who desperately need it");

P.298, n.62. Add the following to line 9 of the footnote before the semi-colon:

, *rev'd in part*, 534 F.3d 741, 747–48 (D.C. Cir. 2008) ("[t]he district court [wa]s mistaken to treat every imposition upon tribal sovereignty as an abrogation of tribal sovereign immunity" because, while "[s]overeignty and immunity are related, . . . Congress can impose substantive constraints upon a tribe without subjecting the tribe to suit in federal court to enforce those constraints[;]" here, the court could "find no express and unequivocal abrogation of the [tribe's] sovereign immunity in the texts upon which the [plaintiffs] rely"); *Ameriloan v. Superior Ct.*, 86 Cal. Rptr. 3d 572, 581 (Ct. App. 2008) (distinguishing *Agua Caliente*, and rejecting broad assertion that "the state's right to enforce its consumer protection laws is derived from the Tenth Amendment and leaving the state without the right to enforce its own laws violates the Constitution")

Add the following to line 9 of the footnote after *"see generally"*:

Mary Beth Moylan, *Sovereign Rules of the Game: Requiring Campaign Finance Disclosure in the Face of Tribal Sovereign Immunity*, 20 B.U. Pub. Int. L. J. 1 (2010) (based on the interests that the federal government has articulated concerning the sources and uses of tribal casino money and the disclosure of campaign finance spending, Congress should enact legislation expressly abrogating tribal sovereign immunity for enforcement actions by states seeking to uphold their campaign finance laws against American Indian tribes);

P.299, n.70. Add the following to the sixth-to-last line of the footnote after *"see generally"*:

Merritt Schnipper, Note, *Ambiguous Abrogation: The First Circuit Strips the Narragansett Indian Tribe of Its Sovereign Immunity*, 31 W. New Eng. L. Rev.

243, 286 (2009) (the *en banc* decision in *Narragansett* misconstrued not only the Settlement Act provision that granted the state civil and criminal jurisdiction over settlement lands but also relevant preemption standards by assuming that the statutory conferral of authority would be superfluous absent an attendant waiver of sovereign immunity; such assumption ignored *Manufacturing Technologies* which "forcefully drew a distinction between the applicability of state law and the availability of state law enforcement means" against a tribe itself);

P.302, n.81.   Add the following to line 7 of the footnote after "*with*":

Attorney's Process and Investigation Servs., Inc. v. Sac & Fox of Miss. in Iowa, No. 05-CV-168-LRR, 2009 WL 1783497, at *7 (N.D. Iowa June 18, 2009) (challenge to contract's validity calls into question all provisions in the agreement, including purported sovereign immunity waiver in arbitration clause), *aff'd in part & rev'd in part*, 609 F.3d 927 (8th Cir. 2010), *cert. denied* 131 S. Ct. 1003 (2011);

P.302, n.81: Add the following to the end of the footnote before the period:

; *Storevisions, Inc. v. Omaha Tribe of Neb.*, 795 N.W. 2d 271, 289 (Neb. 2011) (without deciding whether tribal officials had actual authority to waive the tribe's sovereign immunity the court concluded that the tribal officials had apparent authority to do so)

P.304, n.91.   Add the following to line 5 of the footnote after the semi-colon:

Hunt Constr. Group, Inc. v. Oneida Indian Nation, 862 N.Y.S.2d 423, 424 (App. Div. 2008) (where contract limited tribe's waiver of immunity from suit to particular forum location, suit in different location fell outside the waiver's scope; "a sovereign may place geographic limits on its waiver of sovereign immunity");

P.305, n.98.   Add the following to the end of the footnote before the period:

; *Ingrassia v. Chicken Ranch Bingo and Casino*, 676 F. Supp. 2d 953, 958 (E.D. Cal. 2009) (plaintiffs required to "show an affirmative waiver in the contract" and failed to do so); *Oneida Indian Nation v. Hunt Constr. Group, Inc.*, 888 N.Y.S.2d 828, 829 (App. Div. 2009) (tribal consent to suit as to "'[a]ll claims, disputes and other matters . . . arising out of, or relating to, [the contract], the Project, the Work, the Contract Documents or the breach thereof'" did not extend to suit brought by contractor alleging claims for breach of implied warranty, quantum meruit and account stated); *State ex rel. Cooper v. Seneca-Cayuga Tobacco Co.*, 676 S.E.2d 579, 584 (N.C.Ct. App. 2009) (escrow agreement waiver of immunity from suit for "'amounts that are held in or previously have been held'" in a particular account did not encompass suit "to impose obligations on Defendants with respect to funds that never have been placed in escrow")

P.305, n.99.   **Add the following to line 3 of the footnote after the semi-colon:**

Ameriloan v. Superior Ct., 86 Cal. Rptr. 3d 572, 584 (Cal. Ct. App. 2008) (waiver provision in "pay day loan" consumer contract inapplicable in action brought by state agency to enforce deferred deposit transaction statute; where "at most the arbitration clause effects a waiver of immunity in a suit brought in an arbitral forum by a party to the contract[,] . . . even if the [state agency] could advance a compelling argument that it somehow stood in the shoes of the consumer in bringing this action and could be considered a party to the loan contract, and entitled to enforce its arbitration provision, the waiver itself would encompass only a consent to be sued in an arbitral forum or in a forum to enforce an arbitration award, not in an enforcement action filed in state court");

P.306, n.100.   **Add the following to line 1 of the footnote after "*Compare*":**

Hoffman v. Sandia Resort and Casino, 232 P.3d 901 (N.M. Ct. App. 2010), *cert. denied*, 131 S. Ct. 227 (2010) (allegedly improper nonpayment of jackpot not encompassed within "limited waiver of sovereign immunity [in gaming compact] for the claims of casino patrons that are based on physical injury to their persons or property"); *Holguin v. Tsay Corp.*, 210 P.3d 243, 246 (N.M. Ct. App. 2009) (compact provision waiving sovereign immunity as to bodily injury and property damage claims did not encompass claim for invasion of privacy; "we are dealing solely with an alleged emotional injury resulting from an alleged inchoate, incorporeal invasion of . . . privacy" that "[w]e cannot characterize . . . as one for damages for physical injury to [the plaintiff] or physical damage to property");

Add the following to eleventh-to-last line of the footnote after "*with*":

Guzman v. Laguna Devel. Corp., 219 P.3d 12, 19 (N.M. Ct. App. 2009) (question of fact existed over whether the term "visitor" as used in gaming compact's waiver of immunity for bodily injury or property damage caused by casino operations encompassed employee who became inebriated at the casino and died in automobile accident en route home as to wrongful death claim "to the extent that [the employee] was not within the scope of employment for purposes of the Workers' Compensation Act[,]" but dismissal was proper as to loss of consortium claim not within the "bodily injury" or "property damage"–based waiver);

P.306, n.101.   **Add the following to line 1 of the footnote after "*See*":**

Pales v. Cherokee Nation Enters., 216 P.3d 309, 311 (Okla. Civ. App. 2009) (tribe did not waive immunity from suit under state worker's compensation statute's "estoppel" provision through contract with nontribal insurer where "the policy language in this case also shows expressly and unambiguously that it was not issued to cover Employer under Oklahoma law");

P.308, n.106.　　Add the following to the third-to-last line after *"see also"*:

Tunica-Biloxi Tribe v. Blalock, 23 So. 2d 1041, 1047 (La. Ct. App. 2009) (counter-claim in equitable apportionment suit by intervenor for portion of property acquired by tribe from defendants pursuant to stipulated judgment barred by sovereign immunity where tribe had opposed intervention; "[t]o find that the Tribe waived its sovereign immunity against River View in light of its prayer for damages and a determination as to ownership interest of the property against the Blalocks would require a determination of implied waiver" but "a waiver of sovereign immunity cannot be implied, but must be express");

Add the following to the end of the footnote:

Whether a tribal entity's removal of an action to federal from state court, in the wake of the Eleventh Amendment–based decision in *Lapides v. Board of Regents*, 535 U.S. 613 (2002), remains unresolved. *See Ingrassia v. Chicken Ranch Bingo and Casino*, 676 F. Supp. 2d 953, 961 (E.D. Cal. 2009) (characteriz-ing the decisional law as "not absolutely clear[,]" but declining to find waiver given "a number of cases in which courts have applied tribal sovereign im-munity after removal without addressing the issue" and other cases where "courts have pierced immunity but not based on waiver from removal").

P.308, n. 108.　　Add the following to the end of the footnote:

The district court's permanent injunction was vacated on appeal. *Oglala Sioux Tribe v. C & W Enters., Inc.*, 542 F.3d 224 (8th Cir. 2008). The court of appeals reasoned, with respect to claims arising under a contract that con-tained no immunity waiver, that the tribe had waived any immunity claim by voluntarily participating in the arbitration. *Id.* at 231 ("[w]holly mindful that a waiver of sovereign immunity must be clearly expressed, we hold that, under these conditions, where there are contractual arbitration agreements and a tribe actively participates in that arbitration, and in the course of that arbitra-tion raises its own affirmative claims involving a clearly-related matter, the Tribe voluntarily and explicitly waives any immunity respecting that related matter"). As for the issue of state court jurisdiction, the court relied upon pro-visions in the involved commercial contracts and American Arbitration As-sociation rules, which applied to the arbitration, for the conclusion that "[b]y choosing a hearing forum in South Dakota, the arbitrator ultimately decided which court would have jurisdiction to confirm the award." *Id.* at 232; *see also Oglala Sioux Tribe v. C & W Enters., Inc.*, 607 F. Supp. 2d 1069 (D.S.D. 2009) (de-clining, on the basis of the Anti-Injunction Act, 28 U.S.C. § 2283, and absten-tion principles under *Younger v. Harris*, 401 U.S. 37 (1971), to enjoin C & W Enterprises from pursuing state-court enforcement procedures against tribal assets); *see generally* Christopher McMillin, *Failure to Object: Tribal Waiver of Immunity by Participation in Arbitration*, 2009 J. Disp. Resol. 517, 528–29 (criticizing Eighth Circuit's decision because use of mere participation in the arbitration as basis for waiver "seems like an implied waiver and far from an unequivocal expression" ordinarily necessary and because "[a]n equitable resolution . . . would have been to enforce the arbitration in tribal court" and not "implying that the Tribe submitted to AAA [enforcement] rules").

P.308, n.111.   Add the following to line 5 of the footnote after "E.g.,":

Memphis Biofuels, LLC v. Chickasaw Nation Indus., Inc., 585 F.3d 917, 920, 922 (6th Cir. 2009) (holding that (1) § 17 incorporation does not "automatically divest an entity of its tribal-sovereign immunity given the statute's silence on the immunity issue; (2) sue-and-be-sued clause in corporate charter, standing alone, was "insufficient" to waive immunity since it conditioned waiver on specific authorization by the tribal board of directors; and (3) tribal corporation was not equitably estopped to context immunity waiver in agreement where executing tribal officials lacked authority to effect waiver); *Native Am. Distrib. v. Seneca-Cayuga Tobacco Co.*, 546 F.3d 1288, 1295–96 (10th Cir. 2008) (declining to apply equitable estoppel to alleged misrepresentations by tribal representative; "the plaintiffs point to no prior case, and we have found none, that has taken into account the specific facts before it and extended a waiver of immunity to a suit that was not already within the waiver's scope");

P.311, n.118.   Add the following to line 3 of the footnote after the semi-colon:

Breakthrough Mgmt Group, Inc. v. Chukchansi Gold Casino, 629 F.3d 1173, 1187 (10th Cir. 2010), *petition for cert. filed*, 79 USLW 3662 (U.S. May 9, 2011) (No. 10-1389) (establishing six part test to determine if a tribe's economic entity qualifies as a subordinate economic entity entitled to share in a tribe's immunity); *Native Am. Distrib. v. Seneca-Cayuga Tobacco Co.*, 546 F.3d 1288, 1294 (10th Cir. 2008) (affirming district court determination that the defendant enterprise served as an "arm of the tribe" where, *inter alia*, the resolution authorizing its creation "expressly declares that the tobacco company will function as 'an economic development project to provide employment opportunities and revenue for the Tribe,' and states that the company and its activities are 'essential governmental functions of the . . . Tribe'"); *Cook v. Avi Casino Enters., Inc.*, 548 F.3d 718, 726 (9th Cir. 2008) (corporation operating casino constituted an "arm of the tribe" where "the Tribe created [the corporation] pursuant to a tribal ordinance and intergovernmental agreement, . . . the tribal corporation is wholly owned and managed by the Tribe[,] . . . the economic benefits produced by the casino inure to the Tribe's benefit[,]" and a majority of the corporation's board must be tribal members, with tribe's council serving as the sole shareholder), *cert. denied*, 129 S. Ct. 2159 (2009); *Cash Advance and Preferred Cash Loans v. Colo. ex rel. Suthers*, 242 P.3d 1099, 1103 (Colo. 2010) (establishes a three part test to determine if companies are an arm of the tribe for immunity purposes);

Add the following to line 7 of the footnote after the semi-colon:

Bales v. Chickasaw Nation Indus., 606 F. Supp. 2d 1299, 1306 (D.N.M. 2009) (where corporation chartered by Secretary of the Interior under a provision of the Oklahoma Indian Welfare Act analogous to IRA § 17, "subordinate economic organization"—*i.e.*, arm-of-the-tribe—analysis was unnecessary since the corporation automatically partook of tribe's immunity from suit);

Add the following to line 8 of the footnote after the semi-colon:

Ameriloan v. Superior Ct., 86 Cal. Rptr. 3d 572, 585 (Cal. Ct. App. 2008) (because the arm-of-the-tribe doctrine "does not 'cover tribally chartered corporations that are completely independent of the tribe[,]'" the trial court was instructed to determine on remand "whether the entities are sufficiently related to the tribe to benefit from the application of sovereign immunity"); *State ex rel. Edmondson v. Native Wholesale Supply*, 237 P.3d 199, 210 (Okla. 2010), *cert. denied*, 131 S. Ct. 2150 (2011) ("Tribal freedom from suit is an attribute of Indian sovereignty and may not and should not be extended to cover private entities operating for private gain based solely on the ethnicity of their owners");

Add the following to the end of the footnote before the period:

; Aaron F.W. Meek, *The Conflict Between State Tests of Tribal Entity Immunity and the Congressional Policy of Indian Self-Determination*, 35 Am. Indian L. Rev. 141 (2010/11) (offers several options to address the issue of states adopting varying tests to determine if an economic entity is an arm of the tribe). Issues concerning the extent of discovery allowed against a tribe and tribal economic entities to determine the nature of the relationship and the tribal interests at stake have arisen. *See Breakthrough Mgmt. Group, Inc. v. Chukchansi Gold Casino*, 629 F.3d 1173, 1190, (10th Cir. 2010), *petition for cert. filed*, 79 USLW 3662 (U.S. May 9, 2011) (No. 10-1389) (burden of demonstrating a legal entitlement to jurisdictional discovery and the related prejudice flowing from the discovery's denial rest on the party seeking the discovery); *Cash Advance and Preferred Cash Loans v. Colo. ex rel. Suthers*, 242 P.3d 1099 (Colo. 2010) (tribal entities waived any immunity they might possess with respect only to information directly relevant to their entitlement to immunity by providing state with certain relevant information. On remand, the trial court must determine whether discovery requests are properly tailored to the immunity determination)

P.312, n.119. **Add the following to line 2 of the footnote after the semi-colon:**

Gristede's Foods, Inc. v. Unkechuage Nation, 660 F. Supp. 2d 442, 477–78 (E.D.N.Y. 2009) (applying multi-factor test, and concluding that privately owned, but tribally licensed, smoke shop was not an arm of the tribe);

P.313, n.132.   Add the following to line 1 of the footnote after "E.g.,":

Vann v. Kempthorne, 534 F.3d 741, 750 (D.C. Cir. 2008) (under *Ex parte Young*, "when "[f]aced with allegations of ongoing constitutional and treaty violations, and a prospective request for injunctive relief, officers of the [tribe] cannot seek shelter in the tribe's sovereign immunity");

P.315.   Add the following new footnote 135.1 at the end of the first full sentence:

[135.1] *E.g., Crowe & Dunlevy, P.C. v. Stidham*, 640 F.3d 1140, 1154 (10th Cir. 2011) ("[T]oday we join our sister circuits in expressly recognizing Ex parte Young as an exception not just to state sovereign immunity but also to tribal sovereign immunity"); *Vann v. Kempthorne*, 534 F.3d 741, 750–56 (D.C. Cir. 2008) (applying *Ex parte Young* precedent from non-Indian law contexts to reject tribe's challenge to the doctrine's application).

P.315, n.136.   Add the following to line 1 of the footnote after "see":

Burrell v. Armijo, 603 F.3d 825, 835 (10th Cir. 2010) (pueblo governor possessed immunity from damages verdict with respect to alleged discrimination in leasing relationship where trial evidence established that he "acted within the scope of his authority as a Pueblo official when he issued [the challenged] directive"); *Cook v. Avi Casino Enters., Inc.*, 548 F.3d 718, 727 (9th Cir. 2008) ("[t]he principles that motivate the immunizing of tribal officials from suit—protecting an Indian tribe's treasury and preventing a plaintiff from bypassing tribal immunity merely by naming a tribal official—apply just as much to tribal employees when they are sued in their official capacity"), *cert. denied*, 129 S. Ct. 2159 (2009);

Add the following to line 1 of the footnote after the semi-colon:

Gristede's Foods, Inc. v. Unkechuage Nation, 660 F. Supp. 2d 442, 478 (E.D.N.Y. 2009) (holding that tribal chief sued in official and personal capacities "enjoys tribal immunity from suit only to the extent that his is sued in his official capacity for acts within the scope of his tribal authority" without distinguishing between retroactive and prospective relief);

Add the following to line 4 of the footnote after the semi-colon:

Oberloh v. Johnson, 768 N.W.2d 373, 376 (Minn. Ct. App. 2009) (applying principle that "[t]ribal sovereign immunity extends to individual tribal officials acting in their official capacity and within the scope of their authority[,]" and construing tribal bylaws as not foreclosing treasurer's communications to tribal members alleged to be defamatory);

P.317, n.142.   **Add the following to the end of the footnote:**

This section was amended by the Tribal Law and Order Act of 2010, Pub. L. No. 111-211, 124 Stat. 2258 (2010), to increase the possible term of imprisonment to three years and increase the fine to $15,000 for any one offense and to allow imprisonment for a total of nine years for multiple offenses if the defendant has been previously convicted of the same or comparable offense by any jurisdiction in the United States or is being prosecuted for an offense comparable to an offense that would be punishable by more than one year of imprisonment if prosecuted by the United States or any of the States. If a tribe imposes a sentence of more than one year, the tribe shall: (1) provide the defendant the right to effective assistance of counsel at least equal to that guaranteed by the United States Constitution; (2) at the expense of the tribe, provide indigent defendants with assistance of a defense attorney; (3) require that the judge presiding over the criminal proceeding has sufficient legal training to preside over criminal trials and be licensed to practice law by any jurisdiction in the United States; (4) prior to charging the defendant, make publicly available the criminal laws, rules of evidence and the rules of criminal procedure of the tribal government; and (5) maintain a record of the criminal proceeding, including an audio or other recording of the trial proceeding. If a sentence of more than one year is imposed, the tribal court may require the defendant to serve the sentence: (1) in a tribal correctional center that has been approved by the Bureau of Indian Affairs for long-term incarceration, in accordance with guidelines to be developed by the Bureau, (2) in the nearest appropriate federal facility; (3) in a State or local government approved detention or correctional center pursuant to an agreement between the tribe and the State or local government; or (4) in an alternative rehabilitation center of the tribe. In addition, the tribal court judge may order the defendant to serve an alternative form of punishment pursuant to tribal law. *See also* Quintin Cushner and Jon M. Sands, *Tribal Law and Order Act of 2010: A Primer With Reservations*, 34 Champion 38 (2010).

P.323, n.177.   **Add the following to line 1 of the footnote after the semi-colon:**

but see Miner v. Standing Rock Sioux Tribe, 619 F. Supp. 2d 715, 725 (D.S.D. 2009) (declining to distinguish *Martinez* where the plaintiff was "'not asking the federal court to provide her with relief under ICRA'" but "'merely asking that she be allowed to *enforce her rights under ICRA in Tribal Court*'");

P.324, n.178.   **Add the following to line 1 of the footnote after "*see also*":**

Paul W. Shagen, *Safeguarding the Integrity of Tribal Elections Through Campaign Finance Regulation*, 8 Cardozo Pub. L. Pol'y & Ethics J. 103, 134 (2009) (following *Martinez*, "challenges to tribal action alleged to contravene the ICRA, including campaign finance regulations, must be brought in tribal court, which should have the last word, including in interpreting the breadth of the protections afforded[,]" and, therefore, "each Indian tribe is empowered to interpret the ICRA 'in light of its unique needs, values, customs and traditions'").

P.324, n.181.   Add the following to line 1 of the footnote after "*see*":

Jeffredo v. Macarro, 599 F.3d 913, 919 (9th Cir. 2010) (agreeing with *Poodry* for the principle that "§ 1303 does require 'a severe actual or potential restraint on liberty[,]'" and declining to find such restraint in the denial of access to certain facilities, a continuing threat of banishment/exclusion, and disenrollment from tribal citizenship);

P.325.   Add the following to the text at the end of the carry-over paragraph:

Even where the requisite detention or comparable restraint exists, exhaustion of available tribal remedies is generally necessary as a predicate to *habeas corpus* relief.[185.1]

[185.1]   *E.g.*, *Jeffredo v. Macarro*, 599 F.3d 913, 921 (9th Cir. 2010) (*habeas* jurisdiction absent over one type of claimed restraint given failure to exhaust tribal remedies); *Acosta-Vigil v. Delorme-Gaines*, 672 F. Supp. 2d 1194, 1196–97 (D.N.M. 2009) (applying "generally recognized" rule that a habeas petitioner "must fully exhaust tribal-court remedies before a federal court can review challenges to his detention[,]" and declining to find futility exception "at this stage" predicated on claim that petitioner would not be permitted appellate counsel since it was not clear that such denial would occur).

P.327, n.193.   Add the following to line 1 of the footnote after "*Compare*":

Davison v. Mohegan Tribe Elec. Cmte., 36 Indian L. Rep. 6056 (Mohegan Tr. Ct. May 18, 2009) (applying federal case law, but rejecting free speech and equal protection-based challenges to tribal election code);

Add the following to the twenty-seventh-to-last line of the footnote after "*see generally*":

Ann E. Tweedy, *Sex Discrimination Under Tribal Law*, 36 Wm. Mitchell L. Rev. 392, 408–40 (2010) (examining three tribal court decisions that address sex discrimination, and various tribal constitution or ordinance provisions concerned with sex discrimination); Paul W. Shagen, *Safeguarding the Integrity of Tribal Elections Through Campaign Finance Regulation*, 8 Cardozo Pub. L. Pol'y & Ethics J. 103, 138–40, 174–75 (2009) (discussing tribal court decisions that resolve First Amendment issues in the tribal election context; suggesting, *inter alia*, as compliant with ICRA an approach under which "tribes that wish to impose strict contribution or expenditure limits should assess whether tribal traditions and customs support treating the 'potential for distortion' or 'equalization' (the restriction of speech to 'enhance the relative voice of others') as a significantly 'compelling' interest"—*i.e.*, that "a tribal court may be more likely to uphold contribution, expenditure, and disclosure requirements, particularly against a tribal member challenge, if developed in light of the *Buckley* [*v. Valeo*, 424 U.S. 1 (1976)] framework, as specifically modified by tribal mores");

P.329, n.195.   **Add the following to line 1 of the footnote after "*See*":**

Laverdure v. Turtle Mountain Hous. Auth., 35 Indian L. Rep. 6131 (Turtle Mtn. Ct. App. Feb. 14, 2008) ("[o]fficials may be sued for injunctive relief when they act outside the scope of their authority");

Add the following to the tenth-to-last line of the footnote after "*see generally*":

Ann E. Tweedy, *Sex Discrimination Under Tribal Law*, 36 Wm. Mitchell L. Rev. 392, 443–44 (2010) ("most tribes will permit ICRA suits in which only equitable relief is sought to be brought against them in tribal court[,]" while "[o]ther civil rights claims based on the tribal constitution or a statutory bill of rights also appear to be permitted fairly commonly when only equitable relief is sought").

P.330, n.196.   **Add the following to the beginning of the footnote:**

Miss. Band of Choctaw Indians v. Peeples, 37 Indian L. Rep. 6004 (Miss. Band Choct. S. Ct. Oct. 14, 2009) (no sovereign immunity waiver with respect to employment discharge and due process claims); *Lower Sioux Indian Cmty. v. Prescott*, 35 Indian L. Rep. 6050 (L. Sx. Cmty. Ct. App. May 1, 2008) (lease provision subjecting disputes to binding arbitration under American Arbitration Association rules and making any award enforceable in tribal court or any other court with jurisdiction did not contain the express sovereign immunity waiver required by the applicable judicial ordinance);

Chapter 8
Indian Reserved Water Rights

P.331, n.6.   **Add the following to the end of the footnote:**

See also Jeff Candrian, Note & Comment: *Building With Blinders On: How Policymakers Ignored Indian Water Rights to the Colorado, Setting the Stage for the Navajo Claim*, 22 Colo. J. Int'l Envtl. L. & Pol'y 159 (2011) (discussing how the lower basin states of the Colorado River failed to take into account the potential tribal claims to water and how those claims may upend the current water allocation system).

P.332, n.7.   **Add the following to the end of the footnote before the period:**

; Robert T. Anderson, *Indian Water Rights, Practical Reasoning, and Negotiated Settlements*, 98 Cal. L. Rev. 1133 (2010)

P.332, n.9.   **Add the following to the end of the footnote before the period:**

; *see generally* Charles Carvell, *Indian Reserved Water Rights: Impending Conflict or Coming Rapprochement Between the State of North Dakota and North Dakota Indian Tribes*, 85 N.D. L. Rev. 1 (2009) (discussing the foundation of North Dakota water law, the modern-day presence of non-Indians residing on Indian reservations and the doctrine of Indian reserved water rights).

P.344, n.91.   **Add the following to the fifth-to-last line of the footnote after "*see generally*":**

Sidney P. Ottem, *The General Adjudication of the Yakima River: Tributaries for the Twenty-First Century and a Changing Climate*, 23 J. Envtl. L. & Litig. 275, 298–310 (2008) (reviewing the Yakima River Basin general adjudication's rulings related to the Yakama Nation's reserved rights);

P.346, n.105.   **Add the following to the end of the footnote before the period:**

; *see also San Carlos Apache Tribe v. United States*, 639 F.3d 1346 (Fed. Cir. 2011) (holding that six year statute of limitations under 28 U.S.C. § 2501 precludes tribe from bringing claim against the United States for monetary damages for breach of fiduciary duty related to establishing reserved water rights in the Gila River)

P.349, n.123. Add the following to the end of the footnote before the period:

; Michelle Uberuaga Zanoni, *Evaluating the Consequences of Climate Change on Indian Reserved Water Rights and the PIA: The Impracticable Irrigable Acreage Standard*, 31 Pub. Land & Resources L. Rev. 125 (2010) (discussing the alternative homeland standard to determine Indian reserved water rights as climate change makes irrigation less practicable).

P.355, n.176. Add the following to the end of the footnote before the period:

; *cf. United States v. Orr Water Ditch Co.*, 600 F.3d 1152, 1158 (9th Cir. 2010) (State Engineer may not issue groundwater permits to non-Indians if groundwater use would diminish tribal decreed surface water rights since "[s]urface water contributes to groundwater and groundwater contributes to surface water"); *see generally* Liana Gregory, Note, *"Technically Open": The Debate Over Native American Reserved Groundwater Rights*, 28 J. Land Resources & Envtl. L. 361, 365–67 (2008) (discussing the Wyoming and Arizona decisions, and concluding that "there is no clear common law path for the debate to follow" since "[i]t is evident from the behavior on the state level that the holding in *Cappaert* did not settle the issue of groundwater reservation"); Aubri Goldsby, Note, *The McCarran Amendment and Groundwater: Why Washington State Should Require Inclusion of Groundwater in General Stream Adjudications Involving Federal Reserved Water Rights*, 86 Wash. L. Rev. 185 (2011) (discussing hydrologic comprehensiveness and the relationship between surface and groundwater)

P.356, n.178. Add the following to the end of the footnote before the period:

; *see generally* John B. Carter, *Montana Groundwater Law in the Twenty-First Century*, 70 Mont. L. Rev. 221 (2009) (discussing the development of Montana groundwater law and Indian reserved water rights as they relate to groundwater)

P.357, n.188. Add the following to the end of the footnote before the period:

; *see generally* Nicole C. Salamander, *A Half Full Circle: The Reserved Rights Doctrine and Tribal Reacquired Lands*, 12 U. Denv. Water L. Rev. 333, 347–51 (2009) (discussing reserved water rights for allotted lands reacquired by the original Native American owners)

**P.371, n.271.   Add the following to the end of the footnote before
the period:**

; *see also In re Gen. Adjudication of All Rights to Use Water in the Gila River Sys.
and Source*, 224 P.3d 178 (Ariz. 2010) (approving reserved water rights settlement for the Gila River Indian Community over objections of other tribes
and non-Indians)

P.371, n.272.   ERRATA: Replace *"Id."* with the following:

United States v. Oregon, 44 F.3d 758, 765–67 (9th Cir. 1994).

**P.373, n.282.   Add the following to line 1 of the footnote before
the period:**

; *see generally* Alexander Wood, Note & Comment, *Watering Down Federal
Court Jurisdiction: What Role Do Federal Courts Play in Deciding Water Rights?*,
23 J. Envtl. L. & Litig. 241, 252–61 (2008) (discussing *Colorado River* and its
subsequent application by the Supreme Court and lower federal courts)

Chapter 9
Fish and Wildlife Regulation

P.385, n.13.   **Add the following to line 1 of the footnote after "*see*":**

San Luis & Delta-Mendota Water Auth. v. Salazar, 638 F.3d 1163 (9th Cir. 2011), *petition for cert. filed*, 80 USLW 3004 (U.S. June 22, 2011) (No.10-1551); *Alabama-Tombigbee Rivers Coalition v. Kempthorne*, 477 F.3d 1250 (11th Cir. 2007);

P.386, n.21.   **Add the following to the end of the footnote before the period:**

; *but see State v. Guidry*, 223 P.3d 533 (Wash. Ct. App. 2009) (state law could not be enforced against non-Indian who was "assisting" member spouse in the exercise of treaty fishing in a manner approved by law of spouse's tribe)

P.387, n.24.   **Add the following to the end of the footnote before the period:**

; Marc Slonim, *Indian Country, Indian Reservations, and the Importance of History in Indian Law*, 45 Gonz. L. Rev. 517 (2010)

P.387, n.29.   **Delete the text of the footnote and replace it with the following:**

25 U.S.C. § 1302(7). The Tribal Law and Order Act of 2010 amended the Indian Civil Rights Act to authorize harsher penalties under some circumstances. Pub. L. No. 111-211, 124 Stat. 2258 (2010).

P.389, n.41.   **Replace "543 N.W.2d 246" with "543 N.W.2d 426".**

P.389, n.42.   **Delete the text of the footnote after the semi-colon in line 2 and add the following:**

cf. State v. Cayenne, 195 P.3d 521 (Wash. 2008) (when sentencing a tribal member for an off-reservation crime, the trial court may impose crime-related conditions that apply on-reservation as well as off-reservation, and which limit the means by which that member can exercise fishing rights secured to the member's tribe).

P.389, n.43. **Delete "128 S. Ct. 2709, 2719–20" in the first line of the footnote and replace it with the following:**

554 U.S. 316, 328–30

Add the following to the end of the footnote:

But see Water Wheel Camp Recreational Area, Inc. v. LaRance, 642 F.3d 802, 808 (9th Cir. 2011) ("Indian tribes possess inherent sovereign powers, including the authority to exclude, . . . unless Congress clearly and unambiguously says otherwise").

P.389, n.44. **Delete "128 S. Ct. at 2719–20" in the third line of the footnote and replace it with the following:**

554 U.S. at 328–30

P.389, n.45. **Add the following to the end of the footnote:**

See Pub. L. No. 111-211, § 206, 124 Stat. 2258, 2264 (to be codified as a note to 25 U.S.C. § 2801) ("Nothing in this [Tribal Law and Order] Act [of 2010] confers on an Indian tribe criminal jurisdiction over non-Indians.")

P.390, n.48. **Delete "128 S. Ct. 2709, 2720" in the second line of the footnote and replace it with the following:**

554 U.S. 316, 330–31

P.390, n.50. **Add the following to line 1 of the footnote before the semi-colon:**

; *Water Wheel Camp Recreational Area, Inc. v. LaRance*, 642 F.3d 802, 812 (9th Cir. 2011) (tribe's "right to exclude non-Indians from tribal land includes the power to regulate them unless Congress has said otherwise, or unless the Supreme Court has recognized that such power conflicts with federal interests promoting tribal self-government") (footnote omitted)

P.392, n.68. **Add the following to the end of the footnote:**

The Oregon Court of Appeals has held that the Oregon Fish and Wildlife Commission may authorize ceremonial hunting permits for the Grand Ronde Tribes to engage in off-reservation hunting not specifically described in the congressionally-authorized agreement. *Confederated Tribes of Siletz Indians v. Fish & Wildlife Comm'n*, ___ P.3d ___ , 2011 WL 3117880 (Or. Ct. App. 2011).

P.394, n.82. **Add the following to the end of the footnote before the period:**

; *see generally* Michelle Smith & Janet C. Neuman, *Keeping Indian Claims Commission Decisions in Their Place: Assessing the Preclusive Effect of ICC Decisions in Litigation Over Off-Reservation Treaty Fishing Rights*, 31 U. Haw. L. Rev.

475, 505 (2009) (criticizing *Molini* as an improper application of claim preclusion principles because (1) "a claim will not be precluded if a party could not have relied on a particular theory of the case or pursued a certain remedy or form of relief . . . [and] tribes were unable to request the equitable relief necessary to recognize usual and accustomed fishing locations" by virtue of limitations on ICC remedial authority, and (2) "issue preclusion should not normally be available when the prior litigation ended in settlement unless the same issue was actually litigated in the liability phase of an ICC case . . . [and] ICC was usually concerned with the determination of a tribe's aboriginal territory"—not with non-treaty aboriginal usufructuary rights claimed to exist outside areas where a tribe possessed exclusive occupancy rights)

P.394, n.83.   **Add the following to line 4 of the footnote before the semi-colon:**

, *aff'd on other grounds*, 577 F.3d 634 (6th Cir. 2009)

P.395, n.85.   **Add the following to the end of the footnote before the period:**

, *aff'd on other grounds*, 577 F.3d 634 (6th Cir. 2009)

P.395, n.87.   **Delete the text after *"but see"* from line 2 of the footnote to the end and add the following:**

United States v. Confederated Tribes of the Colville Indian Reservation, 606 F.3d 698, 715 (9th Cir. 2010) (holding that a post-statehood congressionally ratified agreement between a tribe and the United States granted "new fishing rights" to a nonparty Indian band).

P.395, n.91.   **In the second line of the footnote, replace "485 N.W.2d 24" with "485 N.W.2d 724".**

P.396, n.93.   **Delete the text of line 1 in the footnote through the first semi-colon.**

P.396.   **Add the following to the text at the end of the first full paragraph:**

Though the facts a group must establish to gain federal acknowledgement as an Indian tribe are similar to those it must establish to show that it is entitled to exercise treaty rights, the two inquiries address legally distinct issues. Federal acknowledgement establishes no presumption that a tribe is entitled to exercise treaty rights, while a determination that a group is not entitled to exercise treaty rights does not preclude it from gaining federal acknowledgement.[94.1]

[94.1] *Evans v. USDOI*, 604 F.3d 1120, 1123 (9th Cir. 2010); *United States v. Washington*, 593 F.3d 790, 800–01 (9th Cir. 2010) (*en banc*).

P.396, n.99.   **Add the following to the end of the footnote before the period:**

; *see State v. Guidry*, 223 P.3d 533, 536–37 (Wash. Ct. App. 2009) (where tribal code permitted nonmember spouse to assist member by fishing in her absence, state could not impose different conditions on nonmember without showing that they were reasonable and necessary for conservation)

P.397, n.101.   **Insert the following at the end of the second line of the footnote before the period:**

; *Confederated Tribes of the Colville Reservation v. Anderson*, 761 F. Supp. 2d 1101, 1112 (E.D. Wash. 2011) (rejecting tribal theory that, inter alia, tribal self-regulation must be shown to be "ineffective" before state can enforce public safety laws against tribal members exercising federally-secured nonexclusive hunting rights on lands formerly within tribe's reservation)

P.397, n.103.   **Add the following to the end of the footnote:**

Because primary rights preserve intertribal relationships as they existed at treaty time, they arise only when tribes claim the same usual and accustomed fishing places under a treaty or treaties executed at approximately the same time. *United States v. Confederated Tribes of the Colville Indian Reservation*, 606 F.3d 698, 714 (9th Cir. 2010).

P.400.   **In the second and third line of the Suquamish paragraph, delete "*United States v. Washington*, 2007 WL 30869 (W.D. Wash. 2007)" and add the following:**

Upper Skagit Indian Tribe v. Washington, 590 F.3d 1020 (9th Cir.), *cert. denied*, 131 S. Ct. 414 (2010)

P.401, n.125.   **Add the following to the end of the footnote:**

In *United States v. Confederated Tribes of the Colville Indian Reservation*, 606 F.3d 698, 711–12 (9th Cir. 2010), the court determined that the Wenatshapam Fishery on Icicle Creek, a tributary to the Wenatchee River in central Washington State, is a usual and accustomed place of the Yakama Nation. *See generally* Angelique EagleWoman, *Tribal Hunting and Fishing Lifeways & Tribal-State Relations in Idaho*, 46 Idaho L. Rev. 81, 110–115 (2009) (discussing usual and accustomed fishing places on Rapid River, which is within the Columbia River Basin, reserved to Nez Perce Tribe under 1855 Stevens treaty).

P.403, n.144.   **Delete the second line of the footnote and replace it with the following:**

http://wdfw.wa.gov/fishing/salmon/who_in_charge_fishing.pdf (last visited July 28, 2011).

P.405, n.162.   Add the following to line 6 of the footnote after "*see*":

United States v. Fox, 573 F.3d 1050 (10th Cir.) (treaty hunting right did not insulate tribal member from prosecution under federal statute prohibiting felon from possessing firearm), *cert. denied*, 130 S. Ct. 813 (2009);

Add the following to line 8 of the footnote before the semi-colon:

; *State v. Roy*, 761 N.W.2d 883 (Minn. Ct. App.) (state law prohibiting felon from possessing firearms was a generally applicable criminal statute, not a hunting regulation, and could be enforced against member of tribe with hunting rights under Public Law 280–conferred authority), *cert. denied*, 130 S. Ct. 1022 (2009); *State v. Jacobs*, 735 N.W.2d 535 (Wis. Ct. App. 2007) (same)

Add the following to line 9 of the footnote before the semi-colon:

; *see also Confederated Tribes of the Colville Reservation v. Anderson*, 761 F. Supp. 2d 1101, 1112 (E.D. Wash. 2011) (discussing the applicability of health- and safety-related state laws to tribal members exercising federally-secured non-exclusive hunting rights)

P.405.   Add the following to the text at the end of the second full paragraph:

In *Confederated Tribes of the Colville Reservation v. Anderson*, 761 F. Supp. 2d 1101 (E.D. Wash. 2011), the court articulated a standard for determining whether state public-safety laws can be enforced against tribal members exercising hunting rights under a congressionally-ratified agreement that secures to the tribe "the right to hunt and fish in common with all other persons" on former reservation lands ceded to the United States. The court held that the state may enforce a law that "1) reasonably prevents a public-safety threat; 2) is necessary to prevent the identified public-safety threat; 3) does not discriminate against Indians; and 4) application to the Tribe is necessary in the interest of public safety."[162.1]

[162.1] *Confederated Tribes of the Colville Reservation v. Anderson*, 761 F. Supp. 2d 1101, 1112 (E.D. Wash. 2011) (citations omitted).

P.409, n.192.   Add the following to the end of the footnote before the period:

, *aff'd on other grounds*, 573 F.3d 701 (9th Cir. 2009)

P.409.   Add the following to the text at the end of the first full paragraph:

The Ninth Circuit subsequently affirmed the district court but on somewhat different grounds, holding that intertribal claims for equitable allocation of fish are analogous to interstate claims for equitable apportionment of fish under the doctrine described in *Idaho ex rel. Evans v. Oregon*[192.1] and that a tribe seeking an equitable apportionment against another tribe thus must plead and prove by clear and convincing evidence some real and substantial injury or damage.[192.2]

[191.1]   462 U.S. 1017 (1983).

[191.2]   *United States v. Washington*, 573 F.3d 701, 707–08 (9th Cir. 2009).

P.411, n.208.   Add the following to the beginning of the footnote:

Ruth Langridge, *The Right to Habitat Protection*, 29 Pub. Land & Resources L. Rev. 41 (2008);

P.414, n.221.   Add the following to line 1 of the footnote after "*See*":

Michael C. Blumm & Jane G. Steadman, *Indian Treaty Fishing Rights and Habitat Protection: The Martinez Decision Supplies a Resounding Judicial Reaffirmation*, 49 Nat. Resources J. 653 (2009); Mason D. Morisset & Carly A. Summers, *Clear Passage: The Culvert Case Decision as a Foundation for Habitat Protection and Preservation*, 1 Bellwether: The Seattle J. Envtl. L. & Pol'y 29 (2009), available at http://www.sjel.org/images/pdf/2009/Bellwether2009-3-MorissetSummers.pdf (last visited July 28, 2011); William Fisher, Note, *The Culverts Opinion and the Need for a Broader Property-Based Construct*, 23 J. Envtl. L. & Litig. 491 (2008);

P.414.   Add the following to the text after footnote 221:

Settlement negotiations failed, and the remedy phase of the culvert litigation went to trial in October 2009. As of mid-2011, the parties are awaiting a decision.

P.416, n.235.   Add the following to the end of the footnote before the period:

; *see generally* Sidney P. Ottem, *The General Adjudication of the Yakima River: Tributaries for the Twenty-First Century and a Changing Climate*, 23 J. Envtl. L. & Litig. 275 (2008)

P.416, n.236.   Add the following to line 2 of the footnote before the semi-colon:

; *United States v. Stone*, 112 F.3d 971, 973–74 (8th Cir. 1997) (member of tribe with treaty hunting rights could be prosecuted under Airborne Hunting Act)

P.421, n.280.   Add the following to the end of the footnote:

See generally Carol B. Koppelman, *Anderson v. Evans: The Ninth Circuit Harmonizes Treaty Rights and the Marine Mammal Protection Act*, 16 Hastings W.-Nw. J. Envtl. L. & Pol'y 353 (2010).

P.422, n.289. **Add the following to the end of the footnote before the period:**

; *see generally* Emily Brand, *The Struggle to Exercise a Treaty Right: An Analysis of the Makah Tribe's Path to Whale*, 32 Environs Envtl. L. & Pol'y J. 287 (Spring 2009)

P.422, n.293. **Add the following to line 5 of the footnote after "*see generally*":**

Michael Davidson, Comment, *United States v. Friday and the Future of Native American Religious Challenges to the Bald and Golden Eagle Protection Act*, 86 Denv. U. L. Rev. 1133 (2009);

P.423, n.298. **Add the following to the end of the footnote:**

When the case returned to the Tenth Circuit after a remand, the court determined that the government had made the required showing. The Tenth Circuit has now aligned with the Ninth and Eleventh Circuits. *United States v. Wilgus*, 638 F.3d 1274 (10th Cir. 2011), *rev'g* 606 F. Supp. 2d 1308 (D. Utah 2009).

P.423, n.299. **Add the following to the beginning of the footnote:**

Jessica L. Fjerstad, *The First Amendment and Eagle Feathers: An Analysis of RFRA, BGEPA, and the Regulation of Indian Religious Practices*, 55 S.D. L. Rev. 528 (2010); Kyle Persaud, *A Permit to Practice Religion for Some but Not for Others: How the Federal Government Violates Religious Freedom When It Grants Eagle Feathers Only to Indian Tribe Members*, 36 Ohio N. U. L. Rev. 115 (2010); Alex Tallchief Skibine, *Culture Talk or Culture War in Federal Indian Law?*, 45 Tulsa L. Rev. 89 (2009); Stephen Rosecan, Note, *A Meaningful Presentation: Proposing a Less Restrictive Way to Distribute Eagle Feathers*, 42 New Eng. L. Rev. 891 (2008);

P.423, n.302. **Add the following to the end of the footnote before the period:**

; 76 Fed. Reg. 17,353 (March 29, 2011)

P.424, n.303. **Add the following to line 1 of the footnote after "*see, e.g.,*":**

75 Fed. Reg. 53,774 (Sept. 1, 2010) (2010–11 regulations for hunting by certain tribes);

P.426, n.322. **Add the following to the end of the footnote:**

See generally Jack B. McGee, *Subsistence Hunting and Fishing in Alaska: Does ANILCA's Rural Subsistence Priority Really Conflict With the Alaska Constitution?*, 27 Alaska L. Rev. 221 (2010).

P.426, n.325.   **Add the following to line 1 of the footnote after "*See*":**

76 Fed. Reg. 12,564 (March 8, 2011);

Add the following to the end of the footnote before the period:

; *see also Alaska v. Fed. Subsistence Bd.*, 544 F.3d 1089 (9th Cir. 2008) (upholding determination issued under ANILCA regulations regarding customary and traditional use of moose). During 2009 and 2010, the Department of the Interior conducted a review of the Federal Subsistence Management Program in Alaska. In September 2010, the Department released a report describing changes that would be made to the program with the assumption that federal subsistence management would continue for the foreseeable future. *See* 76 Fed. Reg. 7,758 (Feb. 11, 2011) (proposed rule that would change structure of Federal Subsistence Board)

Chapter 10
Environmental Regulation in Indian Country

P.428, n.10.   Add the following to the end of the footnote:

Although this chapter focuses principally on regulatory schemes administered by EPA, other federal statutes designed in whole or part to address environmental concerns play an important role both as to Indian country and lands outside Indian country where a tribe claims some interest. As to the latter laws, tribes have access to, and often use, the judicial remedies available to other entities or individuals. *E.g., Te-Moak Tribe v. USDOI*, 608 F.3d 592, 599–601 (9th Cir. 2010) (challenge to amendment of gold mine's operation plan under National Environmental Policy Act claiming, *inter alia*, that federal agency had failed, to take "hard look" at the amendment's effect on tribal cultural resources); *S. Fork Council of W. Shoshone v. USDOI*, 586 F.3d 718, 723–25 (9th Cir. 2009) (rejecting claim by tribe under Federal Land Policy and Management Act over agency's alleged failure to accommodate tribal access and ceremonial use of sacred sites as required under Executive Order No. 13007). Tribes additionally may possess state law-created rights to avoid or seek damages for environmental harm. *E.g., Quapaw Tribe v. Blue Tee Corp.*, 653 F. Supp. 2d 1166, 1192 (N.D. Okla. 2009) (tribe had *parens patriae* standing to maintain natural resource damages action predicated, in part, on common law public trust and public nuisance theories although "Defendants have shown that Oklahoma law may limit the remedies available to a plaintiff for a nuisance claim, whether it is a public or private nuisance claim").

P.433, n.54.   Add the following to the end of the footnote before the period:

; *cf. Elliot v. White Mountain Apache Tribal Court*, 566 F.3d 842, 850 (9th Cir. 2009) (exhaustion of tribal court remedies required with respect to suit by tribe against nonmember for violation of tribal regulations and damages caused by forest fire given plausible presence of inherent adjudicatory authority; reasoning in part that "the tribe makes a compelling argument that the regulations at issue are intended to secure the tribe's political and economic well-being, particularly in light of the result of the alleged violations of those regulations in this very case: the destruction of millions of dollars of the tribe's natural resources"), *cert. denied*, 130 S. Ct. 624 (2009)

P.435, n.67.   ERRATA: The reporter volume number should read "752".

p.435, n.68.   Add the following to the end of the footnote before the period.

; Cassandra Barnum, Note: *A Single Penny, an Inch of Land, or an Ounce of Sovereignty: The Problem of Tribal Sovereignty and Water Quality Regulation under the Maine Indian Claims Settlement Act,* 37 Ecology L. Q. 1159 (2010) (commenting on solutions to tribal water quality concerns in response to the *Maine v. Johnson* decision)

P.436, n.76.   ERRATA: The specific page reference should read: "257–58".

P.437, n.82.   In the fourth line from the top, delete "Aug. 2, 2008" and insert "June 23, 2011".

In the eighth line from the top, delete "Jul. 31, 2008" and insert "June 29, 2011".

P.437, n.84.   Delete lines two and three and insert the following:

The EPA also discontinued the use of the term "treated as a state," substituting in its place, except where the relevant statute provided otherwise, the term treatment "in a manner to that in which it treats a state." *Id.* at 64,343.

P.439, n.97.   The statutory citation in line one should read as follows:

"33 U.S.C. § 1369(b)(1)"

The statutory citation in line two should read as follows:

"42 U.S.C. § 300j–7(a)"

P.439, n.101.   In the third line from the top, delete "Aug. 3, 2008" and insert "June 23, 2011".

Add the following to the end of the footnote:

Most recently, the EPA has issued a memorandum, *Strategy for Reviewing Tribal Eligibility Applications to Administer EPA Regulatory Programs* (Jan. 23, 2008), *available at* http://www.epa.gov/tribal/pdf/strategy-for-reviewing-applications-for-tas-01-23-08.pdf (last visited Jul. 28, 2009), aimed at improving the process for TAS application review under the CWA, CAA and SDWA. *See generally* James M. Grijalva, *EPA's Indian Policy at Twenty-Five,* 25-SUM Nat. Resources & Env't 12 (2010) (discussing development and implementation of EPA's Indian policy, together with related litigation, since its initial 1984 promulgation by then-Administrator William Ruckelshaus); David F. Coursen, *EPA's New Tribal Strategy*, 38 Envtl. L. Rep. News & Analysis 10643 (2008) (discussing the background and development of the TAS process generally under the three statutes and the new strategy's components).

P.439, n.103.   **In the third line from the top, delete "Aug. 4, 2008" and insert "June 23, 2011".**

P.443, n.127.   **Add the following to line 1 of the footnote after "See generally":**

Taylor Reinhard, Comment, *Advancing Tribal Law Through "Treatment as a State" Under the Obama Administration: American Indians May Also Find Help from Their Legal Relative, Louisiana—No Blood Quantum Necessary*, 23 Tul. Envtl. L.J. 537 (2010);

Add the following to the end of the footnote:

One commentator examining "the requirements that tribes must satisfy in order to exercise their sovereign right to environmental regulation within the reservation" under EPA regulations and particularly stressed the need for them to develop "institutional capacity" to develop and implement WQSs. Marren Sanders, *Clean Water in Indian Country: The Risks (and Rewards) of Being Treated in the Same Manner as a State*, 36 Wm. Mitchell L. Rev. 533, 534, 553–63 (2010). In the latter regard, the author relies extensively on the analysis in a 1998 joint project between the Harvard Project on American Indian Economic Development at Harvard University and the Native Nations Institute for Leadership, Management, and Policy at the University of Arizona. *Id.* at 558–63 (citing Stephen Cornell & Joseph P. Kalt, *Sovereignty and Nation-Building: The Development Challenge in Indian Country Today*, 22 Am. Indian Culture & Res. J. 187 (1998)).

P.443, n.130.   **Add the following to the end of the footnote before the period:**

(1)

P.447, n.162.   **ERRATA: In the first statutory citation, delete "(I)" and insert "(i)".**

P.448, n.169.   **Add the following before the period in the first line.**

(B) and (C)

P.449, n.178.   **Add the following to the end of the footnote:**

The Tenth Circuit subsequently upheld the EPA's determination that the involved land constituted a "dependent Indian community," as such term is used in 18 U.S.C. § 1151(b), for "Indian country" purposes. *Hydro Res., Inc. v. USEPA*, 562 F.3d 1249, 1262–67 (10th Cir. 2009). However, the panel opinion was overruled by the full Circuit sitting *en banc* in *Hydro-Resources, Inc. v. USEPA*, 608 F.3d 1131 (10th Cir. 2010) (*en banc*). The *en banc* six-judge majority found that use of the "community of reference" test would be inconsistent with *Alaska v. Native Village of Venetie*, 522 U.S. 520 (1997), which "rejected the idea that the boundaries of a federally dependent Indian community should be determined by a sort of judicially administered census study of the nature of 'the Indian tribe inhabiting' the area" and instead identified as "[t]he right question . . . whether Congress has taken some action to designate and maintain the land in question for Indian use." 608 F.3d at 1150. The principal five-judge dissent deemed *Venetie* not dispositive because, in its view, "the Supreme Court did not address a separate, antecedent question: to what area of land should this two-part test be applied" and argued that "[o]ver the last twenty years in this circuit, we have held that a 'community-of-reference' test must be employed to determine the appropriate community, before determining whether that community is both 'dependent' and 'Indian.'" *Id.* at 1168 (Ebel, J., dissenting). The dissent further suggested that United States Supreme Court review may be required to address what it deemed the "confusion and the serious consequences generated by today's [majority] opinion." *Id.* at 1182 (Ebel, J., dissenting); *accord id.* at 1185 (Henry, J., dissenting).

P. 450, n. 191.   **Add the following to the end of the footnote:**

Where a tribe has not submitted a plan, the EPA construes its regulations to permit it to adopt a federal plan that incorporates "a previously-approved state plan" and "to take limited action to fill a regulatory gap without having to conduct extensive, area-wide modeling and analysis." *Ariz. Pub. Serv. Co. v. USEPA*, 562 F.3d 1116, 1124 (10th Cir. 2009). The Tenth Circuit extended deference to this construction, at least when "[t]he federal plan codifies in part [a state's] plan—previously studied, analyzed, approved, and in place—and relies on current data demonstrating that the air quality in the area of the [involved facility] is better than the national air standards for criteria pollutants." *Id.* at 1126.

P. 451, n. 197.   **Add the following to the end of the footnote before the period:**

; *see Michigan v. USEPA*, 581 F.3d 524, 527–28 (6th Cir. 2009) (state lacked standing to challenge EPA redesignation of tribal lands to class I status under its federal implementation program pursuant to tribe's request)

P. 456, n. 249.   **ERRATA: Delete "§ 9607(f)(1)" in the first line.**

P. 458, n. 263.   **Add the following to the end of the footnote:**

Where tribes support activities believed to be in violation of federal environmental law, the issue of sovereign immunity because suit under the Administrative Procedure Act against responsible federal officials will be available if the challenged activity has been authorized through agency action. *See generally* Ezra Rosser, *Ahistorical Indians and Reservation Resources*, 40 Envtl. L.

437, 507 (2010) ("[F]ederal administrative primacy largely defines the current environmental regulation of reservations. This is not to say that tribes and states play no role, but the regulatory framework is decidedly federal").

P.459   **In the tenth line of the first paragraph of the text, delete the word "purposes" and insert the words "a purpose".**

P.461, n.296.   **Delete the text of the footnote between "30 U.S.C. § 1292(b)" in the third-to-last line and the period at the footnote's conclusion.**

P.462.   **Delete from the last sentence of the first paragraph "may be expended in any state at the Secretary's discretion", and replace the deletion with "are subject to distribution to otherwise eligible tribes in the form of 'tribal share funds' under a formula prescribed by regulation".**

P.462, n.299.   **Delete the text of the current footnote before the period, and substitute the following:**

73 Fed. Reg. 67,576, 67,635 (Nov. 14, 2008) (codified at 30 C.F.R. § 872.18)

Chapter 11
Taxation in Indian Country

P.465, n.7.   **Add the following to the end of the footnote before the period:**

; *see generally* Alex Tallchief Skibine, *Tribal Sovereign Interests Beyond the Reservation Borders*, 12 Lewis & Clark L. Rev. 1003, 1006, 1042 (2008) (reasons that "because the concept of territorial sovereignty, both in the United States and abroad, has been significantly eroded or modified, there are no valid reasons why tribal sovereign interests should be strictly limited to the reservation setting[;]" identifies tribal taxation of income earned by members residing off reservation as a possible application of this concept, with "the tribal income tax . . . treated the same as state income taxes relative to the federal income tax and . . . deducted from the amount of tax owed to the federal government")

P.469, n.38.   **Add the following to the end of the footnote before the period:**

; *see generally* Scott A. Taylor, *Taxation in Indian Country After Carcieri v. Salazar*, 36 Wm. Mitchell L. Rev. 590 (2010) (discussing importance of Indian country status for purposes of determining permissible scope of federal, state and tribal taxation; and identifying possible ramifications on the several sovereigns' taxing authority from *Carcieri v. Salazar*, 129 S. Ct. 1058 (2009), where the Supreme Court construed the definition of "Indian" in 25 U.S.C. § 469 to exclude members of Indian tribes not federally recognized as of June 18, 1934 and, therefore, removed them from "Indian" status under 25 U.S.C. § 465 for land-into-trust purposes)

P.470, n.44.   **Add the following to the end of the footnote before the period:**

; *cf. Big Lagoon Rancheria v. California*, 759 F. Supp. 2d 1149 (N.D. Cal. 2011) (holding that, despite IGRA's allowance of revenue sharing under conditions specified in *Rincon Band of Luiseno Mission Indians v. Schwarzenegger*, 602 F.3d 1019, 1033 (9th Cir. 2010), *cert. denied*, ___ S. Ct. ___ (2011), California's insistence on a 15% revenue share in exchange for geographic exclusivity, amounted to a demand for impermissible direct taxation of the tribe and constituted bad faith negotiations)

P.470, n.45.   **Add the following to the end of the footnote before the period:**

; *see generally* Scott A. Taylor, *The Unending Onslaught of Tribal Sovereignty: State Taxation of Non-Member Indians*, 91 Marq. L. Rev. 917, 976 (2008) (analyzing decisional authority relevant to the principle that nonmember Indians and non-Indians are similarly situated for civil regulatory purposes and that the rule "ignores [nonmember Indians'] important place in the history of Indian Country and . . . their current roles as mothers and fathers, husbands and wives, members of extended families, federal employees, tribal employees, teachers, lawyers, doctors, accountants, and entrepreneurs[;]" instead, nonmember Indians "were and are a critical part of the social, cultural, and political fabric of those communities that we call reservation Indians")

P.472, n.56.   **Add the following to line 8 of the footnote after *"see generally"*:**

Scott A. Taylor, *Taxation in Indian Country After Carcieri v. Salazar*, 36 Wm. Mitchell L. Rev. 590, 602 (2010) ("the 'where' question is often critical when deciding whether a state or tribal tax is valid[,]" but, as a result of *Carcieri v. Salazar*, 129 S. Ct. 1058 (2009), "many tens of thousands of acres of land are not so clearly Indian Country anymore. . . [which] means that state taxation is less restricted and that tribal taxation is barred on these '*Carcieri*' lands");

P.472.   **Delete "415" in the sixth-to-last line in the text, and replace the deletion with "465".**

P.474, n.73.   **Add the following to the end of the footnote before the period:**

; *but see generally* Scott A. Taylor, *The Importance of Being Interest: Why a State Cannot Impose Its Income Tax on Tribal Bonds*, 25 Akron Tax J. 123, 167 (2010) (arguing that the "infringement" prong of preemption has relevance in the context of states' taxing tribal bond proceeds received by nonmember bond holders: "Given the federal and state context in which governmental borrowing is a core function and the federal law restricting spending of tribal bond proceeds to essential governmental functions, it becomes clear that state income taxation of tribal bond interest infringes a tribe's right to self-government[,]" and, therefore, "direct state taxation of a tribe, which the Supreme Court has found to be categorically improper, is really no different, as a matter of substance, from direct state taxation of tribal borrowing")

P.477, n.89.   **Add the following to the end of the footnote before the period:**

; *see Attea v. Tax Appeals Tribunal*, 883 N.Y.S.2d 610, 612 (A.D. 2009) (tobacco wholesale distributor subject to state law recordkeeping requirements with respect to on-reservation sales: "it is now well established that 'Indian traders are not wholly immune from state regulation that is reasonably necessary to the assessment or collection of lawful state taxes'")

P.478, n.90.   **Add the following to line 2 of the footnote after "*see generally*":**

Angelique A. EagleWoman, *Tribal Values of Taxation Within Tribalist Economic Theory*, 18-FALL Kan. J.L. & Pub. Pol'y 1, 14, 17 (2008) (summarizing Supreme Court decisions that sanction "state and federal taxing encroachment into the tribal territory[;]" positing that tribal governments embody a unique model—neither "communistic socialists [n]or early capitalists"—and that "the most appropriate label for tribal commercial activity should be summed up in the term 'tribalist'" meaning "an integration of both the contemporary revenue generating activities of Tribal Nations through economic development and the values traditional to tribal peoples of generosity, service, stewardship, conservationism, humility, connectedness, and responsibility");

P.480, n.109.   **Add the following to the end of the footnote before the period:**

; *see generally* David D. Haddock, *To Tax Tribes or Not to Tax Tribes? That Is the Question*, 12 Lewis & Clark L. Rev. 971, 983–86 (2009) (arguing that, from an economic perspective, *Blackfeet* and *Cotton Petroleum* reflect "incoherence" because revenue from a state tax would likely be the same whether the tax was imposed on the nontribal entity or the tribe)

P.482, n.131.   **Add the following to the end of the footnote before the period:**

; *but see Confederated Tribes of the Chehalis Reservation v. Thurston County Bd. of Equalization*, No. CO8-5562 BHS, 2010 WL 1406524 (W.D. Wash. April 2, 2010) (state was permitted to collect personal property tax from corporation that was 51% tribally owned and that operated a recreational facility on trust land within the boundaries of the reservation, because tribal and federal interests were weak and state interests strong)

P.486, n.154.   **In line 6 of the footnote, replace "*Quinnault*" with "*Quinault*".**

     Add the following to line 11 of the footnote after the semi-colon:

White Earth Band of Chippewa Indians v. County of Mahnomen, 605 F. Supp. 2d 1034, 1047 (D. Minn. 2009) (where reserved status of lands acquired with settlement funds was made retroactive under the involved legislation to the date on which the tribe's reservation had been established, Congress "clearly manifested its intent to preclude *ad valorem* taxation on [such] lands");

Add the following to line 31 of the footnote before the semi-colon:

, *aff'd*, 605 F.3d 149 (2d Cir. 2010), *vacated*, 131 S. Ct. 704 (2011)

Add the following to line 32 of the footnote before the semi-colon:

, *aff'd*, 605 F.3d 149 (2d Cir. 2010), *vacated*, 131 S. Ct. 704 (2011)

Add the following to the end of the footnote:

Oneida Indian Nation v. Madison County, 401 F. Supp. 2d 219 (N.D.N.Y. 2005), was subsequently affirmed by *Oneida Indian Nation of New York v. Madison County*, 605 F.3d 149 (2d Cir. 2010). Certiorari was granted on the questions of whether tribal sovereign immunity bars taxing authorities from foreclosing to collect lawfully imposed property taxes and whether the ancient Oneida reservation was disestablished. *Madison County v. Oneida Indian Nation*, 131 S. Ct. 459 (2010). While review was pending, Counsel for the Oneida Nation advised the Court that the Nation had passed a declaration and ordinance waiving "its sovereign immunity to enforcement of real property taxation through foreclosure by state, county and local governments within and throughout the United States." As a consequence, the Court vacated the judgment on review and remanded to the Second Circuit. *Madison County v. Oneida Indian Nation*, 131 S. Ct. 704 (2011)).

P.494, n.219. **Add the following to line 5 of the footnote before the first semi-colon:**

, *on appeal after remand completion*, 778 N.W.2d 602, 606 (S.D. 2010) (applicable state law did not authorize plaintiff taxpayer to bring class action suit on behalf of taxpayers who had failed to exhaust statutory prerequisites to such relief; noting that "[o]ther jurisdictions have found that class action suits to recover illegal taxes are not allowed in the absence of a specific statute authorizing recovery")

P.501, n.270. **Add the following to the end of the footnote:**

The Ninth Circuit recently held that Washington tobacco tax contract legislation, under which the Governor may enter into cigarette tax compacts with Washington tribes, provides no private right of action which would permit a tribe to bring suit to enforce the contracting laws, in the context of one tribe's challenge to another tribe's compact. *Nisqually Indian Tribe v. Gregoire*, 623 F.3d 923 (9th Cir. 2010).

P.502, n.276. **Add the following to the end of the footnote:**

The New York Court of Appeals finally addressed the operation of the 2005 amendments in *Cayuga Indian Nation v. Gould*, 930 N.E.2d 233 (N.Y. 2010), *cert. denied*, 131 S. Ct. 353 (2010), where a four-member majority concluded that the new provision, N.Y. Tax Law § 471-e, could not be given effect with respect to the collection and remittance of cigarette taxes by tribal retailers doing business on a "qualified reservation" in the absence of implementing regulations. The court nevertheless made clear that non-Indian consumers—who bear the cigarette tax's legal incidence under N.Y. Tax Law § 471—continue to have the obligation to pay the tax but that the retailers could not "be criminally prosecuted for failing to collect the sales taxes from consumers and forward them to the Department" without "a methodology developed by the State that respects the federally protected right to sell untaxed cigarettes to members of the [Cayuga] Nation while at the same time providing for the calculation and collection of the tax relating to retail sales to non-Indian consumers, we answer this question in the negative." The *Cayuga* decision also answers, as a practical matter, certified questions posed by the Second Circuit Court of Appeals two months earlier in other cigarette tax litigation. *City of New York v. Golden Feather Smoke Shop, Inc.*, 597 F.3d 115, 127–28 (2d Cir. 2010) (asking "[d]oes N.Y. Tax Law § 471-e, either by itself or in combination with the provisions of § 471, impose a tax on cigarettes sold on Native American reservations when some or all of those cigarettes may be sold to persons other than members of the reservation's nation or tribe[,]" and, if it does not, "does N.Y. Tax Law § 471 alone impose a tax on cigarettes sold on Native American reservations when some or all of those cigarettes may be sold to persons other than members of the reservation's nation or tribe?"); *see also United States v. Morrison*, 596 F. Supp. 2d 661 (E.D.N.Y. 2009), *recons. granted*, 706 F. Supp. 2d 304, 312 (E.D.N.Y. 2010) (granting motion to dismiss on vagueness grounds Racketeer Influenced and Corrupt Organizations Act conviction based on Contraband Cigarette Trafficking Act; "the detailed analysis provided by the Circuit in *Golden Feather* is at odds with my conclusion that a fair reading of § 471, unencumbered by the confusion arguably interjected into the analysis via the enactment of § 471-e, provided more than adequate notice that on-reservation sales of unstamped cigarettes to non–Native Americans is illegal"). In the latest opinion to address New York's efforts to tax on-reservation cigarette sales to non-members, the Second Circuit denied injunctive relief to three plaintiff tribes (Seneca, Oneida and Unkechauge). After a tumultuous history of legislative efforts to impose the taxes, and regulatory forbearance from their enforcement, in June of 2010, the New York Legislature amended New York tax laws in order to implement a tax on reservation sales of cigarettes. In separate actions, consolidated on appeal, three tribes sought to enjoin enforcement of the new laws. In denying injunctive relief, the Second Circuit held that the plaintiff tribes had failed to demonstrate a likelihood of success on the merits of their claims that (1) the precollection scheme instituted by the new law, was (a) an impermissible direct tax on tribal retailers, or (b) imposed undue and unnecessary economic burdens on tribal retailers, and (2) that the coupon and prior approval systems employed by the new law in order to apportion taxable from non-taxable cigarettes, impermissibly interfered with tribal rights of self-government and rights to be free of state taxation. *Oneida Nation of N.Y. v. Cuomo*, 645 F.3d 154 (2d Cir. 2011). The cases were remanded for trial. *See also* Amanda M. Murphy, Note, *A Tale of Three Sovereigns: The Nebulous Boundaries of the Federal*

Government, New York State, and the Seneca Nation of Indians Concerning State Taxation of Indian Reservation Cigarette Sales to Non-Indians, 79 Fordham L. Rev. 2301, 2338–40 (2011).

P.502, n.277.   Add the following to the end of the footnote before the period:

, aff'd in part, vacated in part and remanded, 569 F.3d 589, 592–93 (6th Cir. 2009) (declining to address challenge to state sales use taxes and post-payment refund process in the absence of a concrete dispute over a refund denial; "[i]f the Community files, and the State denies, a request for an exemption or refund based on a transaction occurring within Indian country and involving a member of the Community, the courthouse doors will be open to an appropriate challenge"). *See also Muscogee (Creek) Nation v. Okla. Tax Comm'n,* 611 F.3d 1222, 1236–37 (10th Cir. 2010) (Indian Commerce Clause did not bar state from seizing unstamped cigarettes in transit between parcels of Indian country); *Muscogee (Creek) Nation v. Henry,* No. CIV 10-619-JHP, 2010 WL 1078438 (E.D. Okla. Mar. 18, 2010) (rejecting claim that "Nation to Nation" cigarette purchases from "Native Manufacturers" were exempt from state regulation and taxation, even where cigarettes were transported outside reservation boundaries and sales were made to non-members; "[t]he Supreme Court has repeatedly held that Native American immunities from state taxation and regulation only extend to commerce *within* a particular tribe, not to commerce *among* different tribes or their members"); *accord State ex rel. Edmondson v. Native Wholesale Supply,* 237 P.3d 199, 215 (Okla. 2010), *cert. denied,* 131 S. Ct. 2150 (2011) (Indian Commerce Clause did not deprive state court of subject matter jurisdiction in state enforcement action involving tribe-to-tribe cigarette shipments)

P.503, n.278.   Add the following to line 8 of the footnote after *"see generally"*:

Benjamin Fenner, *Indian Country in Cyber Space: Tribal Tax and Regulatory Jurisdiction and Online Business,* 12 No. 5 J. Internet L. 3, 7 (2008) (discussing Indian law and Commerce Clause decisional authority, and arguing that dormant Commerce Clause principles should apply—given "that the Indian Commerce Clause is broader (giving Congress power to regulate commerce with the Indian tribes as a whole regardless of their geographical scope) and as comprehensive as (with the common purpose of ensuring federal oversight of 'inter-sovereign' commerce)"—and that, therefore, "a state that receives goods or services from Indian country via the mail or common carrier is without jurisdiction to tax that reservation retailer" unless the reservation retailer has "establish[ed] some physical presence in the state");

P.506, n.304.   Delete *"but see"* in line 1 of the footnote, and replace the deletion with the following:

compare Osage Nation v. Oklahoma ex rel. Oklahoma Tax Comm'n, 597 F. Supp. 2d 1250, 1262–63 (N.D. Okla. 2009), *aff'd,* 597 F.3d 1117 (10th Cir.

2010), *cert. denied*, ___ S. Ct. ___ (2011) (declining to find state income tax inapplicable to compensation earned by tribal members who reside and work on fee land within boundaries of disestablished reservation; observing further that "income of a tribal member resident on fee lands earned from sources in which the Nation does not have a significant interest, i.e., from employment with the State or a non-member enterprise or entity, even in Osage County (assuming it were a reservation), would be subject to state income tax") *with*

P.507, n.306.   Add the following to the seventh-to-last line of the footnote after *"compare"*:

Mike v. Franchise Tax Bd., 106 Cal. Rptr. 3d 139, 148 (Ct. App. 2010) (state taxation of income earned from activity on tribal member taxpayer's reservation not preempted where taxpayer resided on another tribe's reservation; citing *McClanahan* for principle that "an Indian may not move away from the lands reserved for the exclusive use of the tribe in which he or she is enrolled and into the general population while nevertheless retaining the tax exemption for income afforded to that Indian"—a principle that after *Colville* and *Duro v. Reina*, 495 U.S. 676 (1990), "courts appear unanimous in their conclusion that the same rule applies when an Indian moves away from the lands reserved for the exclusive use of the tribe in which he or she is enrolled even though the new residence might qualify as 'Indian lands' for other purposes or other persons");

Add the following to the end of the footnote before the period:

; *see generally* Drew K. Barber, Note, *The Power of Indian Tribes to Tax the Income of Professional Athletes and Entertainers Who Perform in Indian Country*, 41 Conn. L. Rev. 1785, 1813 (2009) (arguing that concurrent tribal and state taxation authority—as found, *inter alia*, in *Colville*—should be answered "by asking 'what is fair?'" and proposed, as an answer in the context of taxing professional athletes and entertainers for their work at the Mohegan Sun Casino on the Mashantucket Reservation, "a tax framework under which the Mohegan Tribe will benefit as the primary taxing entity of the athletes' and entertainers' incomes while Connecticut will continue to receive a fair proportion of the income tax revenue" through "a tribal flat income tax with a corresponding state tax credit")

P.507, n.307.   Add the following to the end of the footnote before the period:

; *Miccosukee Tribe of Indians v. United States*, 730 F. Supp. 2d 1344 (S.D. Fla. 2010) (tribal council member not exempted from the payment of federal income taxes merely as a consequence of council membership)

P.507, n.309. **Add the following to line 1 of the footnote after "*see also*":**

Barrett v. United States, 561 F.3d 1140, 1146 (10th Cir. 2009), *cert. denied*, 130 S. Ct. 396 (2009) (compensation received by tribal chairman was subject to federal income tax under *Capoeman*'s "clearly expressed" standard notwithstanding claim that it was exempt under a 1983 tribal plan adopted pursuant to the Indian Tribal Judgment Funds Use or Distribution Act as monies used for "development"—*i.e.*, for "'those activities and/or actions undertaken by the Tribe to in some way cause growth, building up, expansion, strengthening, increased effectiveness or other evolutionary process toward the progress of the Tribe economically and/or socially, and/or governmentally'");

Chapter 12
Indian Lands Gaming

P.510, n.3.   **Add the following to the end of the footnote:**

See generally Allison Sirica, *A Great Gamble: Why Compromise is the Best Bet to Resolve Florida's Indian Gaming Crisis*, 61 Fla. L. Rev. 1201, 1201–31 (2009) (examining in detail the two-decade clash between the Seminole Tribe and Florida over the operation of class III gaming in the state); Matthew G. Struble, *Seminole Gaming Compact Part II: Whether Senate Bill 788 Satisfies the Compact Process Requirements as Written*, 34 Nova L. Rev. 296, 315–20 (2009) (reviewing history of the dispute between the tribe and state and examining whether new compact framework drafted by Florida legislature will meet IGRA requirements and resolve conflict).

P.511, n.5.   **Add the following to the end of the footnote:**

In 2008, more than 240 of 562 federally recognized tribes engaged in gaming. Press Release, Nat'l Indian Gaming Comm'n, NIGC Announces 2008 Revenues (Jun. 3, 2009), available at http://www.nigc.gov/ReadingRoom/PressReleases/PressReleasesMain/PR113062009/tabid/918/Default.aspx (last visited Jul. 1, 2009). Current statistics on the number of gaming tribes and gaming revenues can be found through the website of the National Indian Gaming Commission at www.nigc.gov.

P.511, n.6.   **Add the following to line 3 of the footnote after the period:**

Tribal gaming revenue for 2008 totaled $26.7 billion, a 2.3 percent increase over the prior year. Press Release, Nat'l Indian Gaming Comm'n, NIGC Announces 2008 Revenues (Jun. 3, 2009). The total gross gaming revenue for tribal gaming remained stable in 2009 at $26.5 billion. Press Release, Nat'l Indian Gaming Comm'n, 2009 Indian Gaming Revenues Remain Stable (Jun. 11, 2010). The above press releases are available at the website of the National Indian Gaming Commission, www.nigc.gov. *See also* Aaron Drue Johnson, *Comment: Just Say No (To American Capitalism): Why American Indians Should Reject the Model Tribal Secured Transactions Act and Other Attempts to Promote Economic Assimilation*, 35 Am. Indian L. Rev. 107 (2010/2011) (review of tribal economic development options, noting in 2005 that only 254 of 560 tribes had gaming operations and arguing gaming cannot be relied upon to lift all tribes out of poverty).

Add the following to line 7 of the footnote after "*See*":

Marcia A. Zug, *Dangerous Gamble: Child Support, Casino Dividends, and the Fate of the Indian Family*, 36 Wm. Mitchell L. Rev. 738 (2010) (examining the "consequences of permitting casino dividends to eliminate an Indian parent's child support obligation" in light of the increased wealth of certain gaming tribes); Suzianne D. Painter-Thorne, *If You Build It, They Will Come: Preserving Tribal Sovereignty in the Face of Indian Casinos and the New Premium on Tribal Membership*, 14 Lewis & Clark L. Rev. 311 (Spring 2010) (discussing the growth of tribal gaming operations and the resulting growth in tribal membership disputes, acknowledging lack of recourse for excluded members and proposing intertribal appellate court to provide independent review of tribal membership decisions); Audrey Bryant Braccio, *Special Feature: How the Anti-Gaming Backlash is Redefining Tribal Government Functions*, 34 Am. Indian L. Rev. 171 (2009/2010) (review of caselaw interpreting tribal government functions during post-IGRA period of expanded tribal gaming, concluding that increased anti-gaming sentiment coincides with "gradual infringement on the tribal governmental sphere through a redefinition of what constitutes tribal government functions"); Ezekiel J.N. Fletcher, *Negotiating Meaningful Concessions from States in Gaming Compacts to Further Tribal Economic Development: Satisfying the "Economic Benefits" Test*, 54 S.D. L. Rev. 419, 421 (2009) (noting that the majority of tribal gaming revenue is generated by only one-third of the tribes); Alan P. Meister, Kathryn R.L. Rand & Steven Andrew Light, *Indian Gaming and Beyond: Tribal Economic Development and Diversification*, 54 S.D. L. Rev. 375, 380–96 (2009) (discussing the growth of Indian gaming since IGRA's enactment in 1988, the related economic and fiscal impacts and current economic trends, and recommending tribal economic diversification in the face of an uncertain future for Indian gaming);

P.511, n.7.   Add the following to line 1 of the footnote after "*see generally*":

Guadalupe Gutierrez, Note, *Jurisdictional Ambiguities Among Sovereigns: The Impact of the Indian Gaming Regulatory Act on Criminal Jurisdiction on Tribal Lands*, 26 Ariz. J. Int'l & Comp. L. 229, 250–58 (2009) (reviewing economic and social effects of gaming on tribal life, and criminal incidence related to tribal gaming); Matthew L.M. Fletcher, *Indian Tribal Businesses and the Off-Reservation Market*, 12 Lewis & Clark L. Rev. 1047, 1058–64 (2008) (acknowledging that "Indian gaming creates some new wealth" but to "generate significant and sustainable economic development," it must expand beyond the closed circle of reservation economies and into the off-reservation market);

Add the following to line 13 of the footnote after the semicolon:

The Harvard Project on Am. Indian Econ. Dev., Cabazon, the Indian Gaming Regulatory Act, and the Socioeconomic Consequences of American Indian Governmental Gaming, http://www.ksg.harvard.edu/hpaied/pubs/cabazon.htm (reviewing tribal gaming's social and economic impacts between the 1990 and 2000 censuses, and listing related case studies);

P.518, n.50.　　Add the following to end of the footnote:

See generally Robert N. Clinton, *Enactment of the Indian Gaming Regulatory Act of 1988: The Return of the Buffalo to Indian Country or Another Federal Usurpation of Tribal Sovereignty?*, 42 Ariz. St. L.J. 17, 42 (2010) (asserting that *Cabazon* was not the catalyst, but rather the culmination of a long train of federal analysis of Indian gaming starting which began in 1949).

P.518, n.51.　　Add the following to line 6 of the footnote before the period:

; Virginia W. Boylan, *Reflections on IGRA 20 Years After Enactment*, 42 Ariz. St. L.J. 1, 1–14 (2010) (personal account of staff attorney on Senate Committee on Indian Affairs responsible for the IGRA legislation of IGRA's enactment); Robert N. Clinton, *Enactment of the Indian Gaming Regulatory Act of 1988: The Return of the Buffalo to Indian Country or Another Federal Usurpation of Tribal Sovereignty?*, 42 Ariz. St. L.J. 17, 53–97 (2010) (exploring events leading up to IGRA and the tribal responses to IGRA at the time of its enactment); Franklin Ducheneaux, *The Indian Gaming Regulatory Act: Background and Legislative History*, 42 Ariz. St. L.J. 99, 100–82 (2010) (exhaustive review of IGRA background and legislative history, including section by section analysis of IGRA's provisions); G. William Rice, *Some Thoughts on the Future of Indian Gaming*, 42 Ariz. St. L.J. 219, 220–52 (2010) (overview of IGRA's history and developments as well as predictions for future developments); Alex Tallchief Skibine, *Indian Gaming and Cooperative Federalism*, 42 Ariz. St. L.J. 253, 288–298 (2010) (evaluating the structure and implementation of IGRA and suggesting possible amendments to IGRA to conform to proper place for tribes in the federal system)

P.518, n.53.　　Add the following to the end of the footnote:

See generally Kevin K. Washburn, *Agency Conflict and Culture: Federal Implementation of the Indian Gaming Regulatory Act by the National Indian Gaming Commission, the Bureau of Indian Affairs, and the Department of Justice*, 42 Ariz. St. L.J. 303, 306–34 (2010) (examining the history of "cooperation and conflict" between the three federal actors involved in the oversight and regulation of Indian gaming-NIGC, Department of the Interior, including the BIA, and Department of Justice).

P.521, n.64.   Add the following to line 5 of the footnote after *"see"*:

Sault Ste. Marie Tribe v. United States, 576 F. Supp. 2d 838, 848–51 (W.D. Mich. 2008) (applying Indian canon of construction to interpret provision of IGRA where it conflicted with *Chevron* deference, and finding Commission's definition of the term "reservation" not entitled to deference);

Add the following to the end of the footnote:

In 2008, the previously cooperative relationship between the NIGC and the Department of the Interior disintegrated. Interior's Solicitor directed the NIGC chairman to stand down from his decision that an Alabama Indian tribe has the right to conduct gaming on newly acquired land. Letter from David L. Berhnardt, Solicitor, Dep't of the Interior, to Philip N. Hogen, Chairman, Nat'l Indian Gaming Comm'n (Jun. 13, 2008), *reprinted in* 12 Gaming L. Rev. & Econ. 430 (2008). Because the DOI believed the land did not qualify for gaming and the NIGC lacked statutory authority to issue Indian lands opinions independently, the Secretary invoked his general authority in 43 C.F.R. § 4.5 to review the chairman's decision. *Id.* The Solicitor asserted that the Secretary alone has authority to decide issues concerning Indian lands and tribal jurisdiction, and resolution of such issues requires the Solicitor's particular expertise regarding overall Indian issues and not just Indian gaming concerns. *Id.* at 433–34. In an effort toward clarity, the DOI corrected the final rule regarding gaming on newly acquired land to specify that "[r]egardless of where the tribe sends its request for an Indian lands opinion, the Department will coordinate the completion of the request by the appropriate offices." 73 Fed. Reg. 35,579 (Jun. 24, 2008). The NIGC's Acting General Counsel responded that the Secretary's authority under IGRA is limited, Congress specifically delegated NIGC the authority to make Indian lands determinations, the NIGC is an independent agency beyond the Secretary's control, and the Secretary proposes to grant himself more power than did Congress. Letter from Penny J. Coleman, Acting General Counsel, Nat'l Indian Gaming Comm'n, to David L. Bernhardt, Solicitor, Dep't of the Interior (Jul. 30, 2008), *reprinted in* 12 Gaming L. Rev. & Econ. 413, 415–29 (2008). It remains to be seen whether this conflict will require judicial resolution. *See generally* Dennis J. Whittlesey, *Washington's Newest Battle: Indian Gaming v. Indian Gaming*, 12 Gaming L. Rev. & Econ. 408 (2008) (discussing the conflicting opinions of the Solicitor and NIGC's Acting General Counsel). *See also Neb. ex rel. Bruning v. U.S. Dept. of Interior*, 625 F.3d 501, 511 (8th Cir. 2010) ("we need not divine whether the DOI or NIGC possess the authority to make such a determination . . . the NIGC and DOI aver that, upon remand, the NIGC would not issue a 'restored lands' opinion without obtaining the concurrence of the DOI").

P.521, n.65.   Add the following to line 1 of the footnote after *"E.g.,"*:

Sault Ste. Marie Tribe v. United States, 576 F. Supp. 2d 838, 861 (W.D. Mich. 2008) ("[g]oing forward, it appears that the definition of reservation pursuant to IGRA will less ambiguous with the enactment of 25 C.F.R. § 292.2");

P.524, n.86.   **Add the following to the end of the footnote before the period:**

; *see supra* note 64

P.524, n.87.   **ERRATA: The pincite to page "1272" should read "1204–19".**

P.524, n.89.   **Add the following to the end of the footnote before the period:**

; *see generally* Matthew Murphy, *Betting the Rancheria: Environmental Protections as Bargaining Chips under the Indian Gaming Regulatory Act*, 36 B.C. Envtl. Aff. L. Rev. 171, 196–200, 204 (2009) (pointing to agreement between California and the Big Lagoon Rancheria to build a casino on land other than the Tribe's environmentally sensitive lands as a creative new way to approach the compact process that addresses federal, state, tribal, and local concerns, suggesting Secretary should abandon guidance memorandum and develop new rules to allow similar creative compact provisions); Matthew L.M. Fletcher, *Indian Tribal Businesses and the Off-Reservation Market*, 12 Lewis & Clark L. Rev. 1047, 1058–59, 1062–64 (2008) (arguing that the new regulations: restrict off-reservation gaming opportunities, reflect a "tortured reading of the IGRA and its legislative history," and constitute "a patent restoration of measured separatism at a time when tribal economies are expanding into the off-reservation market")

P.524, n.91.   **Add the following to line 13 of the footnote after "*with*":**

Butte County v. Hogen, 609 F. Supp. 2d 20, 25–27 (D.D.C. 2009) (finding county had standing to challenge Commission's approval of tribal gaming ordinance and Secretary's decision to acquire trust land), *remanded*, 613 F.3d 190 (D.C. Cir. 2010) (agency's response provided no basis for concluding that it resulted from "'reasoned decisionmaking'" and "sp[oke] as if the Secretary had already decided the issues"); *Amador County, Cal.*, 592 F. Supp. 2d at 104–05 (finding county had standing to challenge Secretary's decision not to affirmatively disapprove amended compact), *aff'd in part and rev'd on other grounds*, 640 F.3d 373 (D.C. Cir. 2011);

Add the following to the end of the footnote on P.525 before the period:

; *Patchak v. Salazar*, 632 F.3d 702, 704 (D.C. Cir. 2011) (finding all Article III standing requirements met in challenge by a neighboring landowner to the Secretary's decision to take tribal land into trust, thereby allowing the tribe to proceed with plans to construct a gambling facility); *See also* Brian L. Lewis, *A Day Late and a Dollar Short: Section 2719 of the Indian Gaming Regulatory Act, the Interpretation of its Exceptions and the Part 292 Regulations*, 12 T.M. Cooley J. Prac. & Clinical L. 147 (2010) (arguing that the Part 292 Regulations contain inconsistencies with the caselaw interpreting Section 2719 which effectively narrow the four exceptions to gaming on after-acquired land, making it more burdensome for tribes to meet the exceptions)

P.525, n.94.   Add the following to line 1 of the footnote after "*See*":

Sault Ste. Marie Tribe v. United States, 576 F. Supp. 2d 838, 848–51 (W.D. Mich. 2008) (finding newly acquired trust parcel contiguous to another parcel taken in trust for the tribe in 1983 that had never been declared a reservation, despite tribal requests to do so in 1986 and 1988, fit "contiguous to the boundaries of the reservation" exception);

Add the following to the end of the footnote before the period:

, *rev'd on other grounds*, 555 U.S. 379 (2009)

P.527, n.105.   Add the following to the end of the footnote:

Before the Department of the Interior promulgated the new regulations, it issued guidance for evaluating off-reservation land acquisitions for gaming purposes. Mem. from Carl J. Artman, Asst. Secretary-Indian Affairs, Dep't of the Interior, to Bureau of Indian Affairs Regional Directors & Office of Indian Gaming, Guidance on Taking Off-reservation Land in Trust for Gaming Purposes (Jan. 3, 2008). The so-called "guidance memorandum" has been widely criticized as constituting a significant change in the Department's position on off-reservation gaming, and unnecessarily, if not unlawfully, restricting off-reservation gaming opportunities. *See, e.g., Oversight Hearing on Dep't of Interior's Recently Released Guidance on Taking Land into Trust for Indian Tribes and its Ramifications Before the H. Comm. on Natural Resources*, 110th Cong. 1 (Feb. 27, 2008) (statement of Rep. Rahall, Chairman, House Comm. on Natural Resources); *see generally* Kathryn R.L. Rand, Alan P. Meister & Steven Andrew Light, *Questionable Federal "Guidance" on Off-reservation Indian Gaming: Legal and Economic Issues*, 12 Gaming L. Rev. & Econ. 194, 200–06 (2008) (discussing whether the "guidance memorandum" violates the Administrative Procedure Act, is arbitrary and capricious, or undermines congressional intent, and evaluating the memorandum's various economic components). The "guidance memorandum" was withdrawn on June 14, 2011, by Assistant Secretary for Indian Affairs Larry EchoHawk.

P.530, n.115.   Add the following to line 12 of the footnote before "*with*":

rev'd on other grounds, 555 U.S. 379, 129 S. Ct. 1058, 1064–68 (2009) (holding that, for purposes of 25 U.S.C. § 479, the phrase "now under Federal jurisdiction" refers to the time of the statute's enactment, and limits the Secretary's authority to acquire trust land for members of recognized tribes that were "under Federal jurisdiction" when the Indian Reorganization Act was enacted in June 1934),

P.531, n.121.   Add the following to line 1 of the footnote after "*See*":

Butte County v. Hogen, 609 F. Supp. 2d 20, 27–29 (D.D.C. 2009) (following *Grand Traverse Band* factors and finding tribe's former rancheria no longer available for restoration, and parcel located "as near as possible" to former rancheria and within original ancestral homeland constitutes tribe's restored lands), *remanded*, 613 F. 3d 190 (D.C. Cir. 2010) (agency determination invalid for failure to explain rationale adequately);

P. 533, n. 130.   Add the following to the end of the footnote:

See generally Antonia Cowan, *You Can't Get There from Here: IGRA Needs Reinvention into a Relevant Statute for a Mature Industry,* 17 Vill. Sports & Ent. L.J. 309 (2010) (arguing that technology has made the distinctions between Class II bingo machines and Class III slot machines an anachronism, proposing to amend IGRA to base the Class II and III categories on the size of the gaming operation rather than the type of games offered).

P.536, n.143.   Add the following to the end of the footnote:

The Commission subsequently withdrew the proposed amendments concerning classification standards appearing in 25 C.F.R. §§ 502 and 546, and the definition for electronic or electromechanical facsimile in 25 C.F.R. § 502, 73 Fed. Reg. 60,490 (Oct. 10, 2008), and made final a new rule for technical standards for electronic class II gaming in 25 C.F.R. § 547, that pertains only to equipment and system certification, 73 Fed. Reg. 60,508 (Oct. 10, 2008).

P.542, n.171.   Add the following to the end of the footnote before the period:

, *cert. denied*, 129 S. Ct. 1038 (2009); *but see Catskill Dev., L.L.C. v. Park Place Entm't Corp.*, 547 F.3d 115, 126 & n.16 (2d Cir. 2008) (distinguishing *Guidiville Band* insofar as it interpreted 25 U.S.C. § 81 and involved land neither acquired nor identified for gaming purposes, and following *Guidiville Band* dissent for separate reasons), *cert. denied*, 129 S. Ct. 1908 (2009); *cf. N. County Cmty. Alliance, Inc. v. Salazar*, 573 F.3d 738, 747 (9th Cir. 2009) (holding that IGRA does not require tribe to submit a site-specific proposed gaming ordinance as a condition of approval by the NIGC under § 2710(b), nor is the NIGC required to make an Indian lands determination before approving a non-site specific gaming ordinance), *cert. denied*, 130 S. Ct. 2095 (2010)

P.543, n.174.   Add the following to the end of the footnote before the period:

, *rev'd on other grounds*, 396 B.R. 222, 225 (W.D. Wis. 2008) ("[t]he right of the [tribe] to distribute its own assets as it sees fit is central to self-governance")

P.544, n.177.   Add the following to line 7 of the footnote after "*cf.*":

Catskill Dev., L.L.C. v. Park Place Entm't Corp., 547 F.3d 115 (2d Cir. 2008), *cert. denied* 129 S. Ct. 1908 (2009) (following dissent in *Guidiville Band of Pomo Indians v. NGV Gaming, Ltd.*, 531 F.3d 767 (9th Cir. 2008), *cert. denied*, 129 S. Ct. 1038 (2009), to hold that IGRA's "Indian lands" definition encompasses not only land presently held in trust but also land "that *will* be held in trust," and giving opinion by Commission's deputy general counsel limited *Skidmore* deference but ultimately finding it unpersuasive); *see also N. County Cmty. Alliance, Inc. v. Salazar*, 573 F.3d 738, 747 (9th Cir. 2009) (NIGC was under no "judicially enforceable obligation" to make an Indian lands determination when it licensed the tribe's casino), *cert. denied*, 130 S. Ct. 2095 (2010);

Add the following to the end of the footnote:

The Commission subsequently adopted the proposed rule without significant substantive change. 73 Fed. Reg. 6019 (Feb. 1, 2008).

P.545, n.182.   Add the following to the end of the footnote:

In October 2008, the Commission made final the new Minimum Internal Control Standards for class II gaming, codified at 25 C.F.R. § 543. 73 Fed. Reg. 60,492 (Oct. 10, 2008).

P.545, n.183.   Add the following to line 4 of the footnote after "*generally*":

Panel discussion, *Paternalism or Protection? Federal Review of Tribal Economic Decisions in Indian Gaming*, 12 Gaming L. Rev. & Econ. 435 (2008) (discussing the need for continued federal oversight of management and gaming-related contracts where tribes employ skilled legal and financial analysts to inform gaming development and operation decisions);

P.545, n.184.   Add the following to line 1 of the footnote after "*see*":

Catskill Dev., L.L.C. v. Park Place Entm't Corp., 547 F.3d 115, 126 & n.16 (2d Cir. 2008) (casino management agreement was unquestionably a management contract; land purchase agreement and development and construction agreement were collateral agreements incorporated into the management agreement as defined in 25 C.F.R. § 502.5; and, under 25 C.F.R. § 533.7, all three agreements held invalid failing approval by Secretary or Commission chairman), *cert. denied*, 129 S. Ct. 1908 (2009); *Wells Fargo Bank v. Lake of the Torches Econ. Dev. Corp.*, 677 F. Supp. 2d 1056, 1059–61 (W.D. Wis. 2010) (bond contract between bank and tribe held to be an unapproved management contract and therefore void *ab intitio*);

Add the following to line 15 of the footnote after "*generally*":

Heidi McNeil Staudenmaier & Anne W. Bishop, *The Three-Billion Dollar Question*, 57 Drake L. Rev. 323 (2009) (providing extensive discussion of *Catskill Development* and possible federal district court enforcement of tribal court's three billion dollar judgment against casino developer);

P.547, n.190   Add the following to line 10 after "*and*":

Wells Fargo Bank v. Lake of the Torches Econ. Dev. Corp., 677 F. Supp. 2d 1056, 1061 (W.D. Wis. 2010) (unapproved bond contract held to be void *ab initio*, invalidating tribe's express waiver of sovereign immunity and destroying court's jurisdiction over tribe);

P.551, n.207.   Add the following to the end of the footnote:

The court in *McCracken & Amick, Inc. v. Purdue*, 687 S.E. 2d 690 (N.C. Ct. App. 2009), also addressed the issue of whether a state can allow tribes to conduct class III games that are otherwise banned by statute. North Carolina passed a statute that banned video poker machines except when operated by a tribe pursuant to a class III gaming compact. A party that sold, serviced, and operated video poker machines challenged the statute, claiming that it violated IGRA because the gaming activity was not located in a state that permits such gaming by any person, organization, or entity as required by 25 U.S.C. § 2710(d)(1)(B). The court accepted North Carolina's position that IGRA permits states to grant tribes preferential gaming rights. *Id.* at 695. The court examined the meaning of the phrase "any person, organization, or entity" and deemed the word "any" to be ambiguous and therefore resorted to principles of statutory construction. *Id.* at 696–97. Applying the Blackfeet presumption, the court adopted North Carolina's interpretation of the ambiguous phrase and concluded that the statute satisfied IGRA's requirement that North Carolina is a state that "permits such gaming for any purpose by any person, organization or entity." *Id.* at 698; *see also Knox v. Idaho*, 223 P.3d 266 (Idaho 2010) (suit challenging constitutionality of Idaho statute that authorized Indian tribes to operate video gaming machines dismissed on standing grounds).

P.553, n.220.   Add the following to line 4 of the footnote after "*see generally*":

Kevin Gover & Tom Gede, *The States as Trespassers in a Federal-Tribal Relationship: A Historical Critique of Tribal-State Compacting Under IGRA*, 42 Ariz. St. L.J. 185, 193–201, 206–16 (2010) (arguing that IGRA's requirement that tribes and states negotiate a compact serves as the "flashpoint" for tribal-state conflict; examining the rise of revenue sharing provisions in compacts and the development of the meaningful concession test, suggesting elimination of the compact requirement as a potential legislative solution);

Add the following to the end of the footnote before the period:

, *cert. denied, sub nom. Kickapoo Traditional Tribe of Texas v. Texas*, 555 U.S. 881 (2008)

P.553, n.222. **Add the following to line 5 of the footnote after the semicolon:**

Florida House of Representatives v. Crist, 999 So. 2d 601, 611–16 (Fla. 2008) (governor lacks authority to enter into compacts for forms of gambling otherwise prohibited under state law);

P.554, n.224. **Add the following to line 3 of the footnote after "1491,":**

1495–1500

P.555, n.230 **Add the following to the end of the footnote:**

See Cachil Dehe Band of Wintun Indians v. California, 629 F. Supp. 2d 1091, 1172, 1182 (E.D. Cal. 2009), *aff'd in part and rev'd in part*, 618 F.3d 1066 (9th Cir. 2010) (unrestricted revenue sharing directly relates to gaming within the meaning of § 2710(d)(3)(C)(vii) and, as such, is an allowable topic of compact negotiation, but also holding that if the concession offered by the state does not offer a meaningful benefit to the tribe, the requested revenue sharing may constitute a tax under IGRA).

P.556, n.231. **Add the following to line 2 of the footnote before the period:**

but see Rincon Band of Luiseno Mission Indians v. Schwarzenegger, 602 F.3d 1019, 1042 (9th Cir. 2010), *cert. denied*, ___ S. Ct. ___ (2011) (unrestricted revenue sharing provision in amended compact constituted an impermissible demand for payment of a tax and a violation of the state's duty under IGRA to negotiate in good faith, exclusivity was not meaningful concession in a negotiation for an amended compact); *Wisconsin v. Ho-Chunk Nation*, 512 F.3d 921, 932 (7th Cir. 2008) (dicta describing revenue-sharing arrangements as "arguably barred by the IGRA itself"), *cert. dismissed*, 129 S. Ct. 28, *on remand*, 564 F. Supp. 2d 856 (W.D. Wis. 2008); *Big Lagoon Rancheria v. California* 759 F. Supp. 2d 1149, 1159 (N.D. Cal. 2010) ("The State correctly asserts that, under Rincon and Coyote Valley II, it may, in good faith, bargain for some form of revenue sharing")

Add the following to line 9 of the footnote after *"see generally"*:

Virginia W. Boylan, *Reflections on IGRA 20 Years After Enactment*, 42 Ariz. St. L.J. 1, 14 (2010) (noting that at the time IGRA was enacted, "Congress did not anticipate that tribes would willingly offer to share with states revenue from gaming profits in return for 'exclusivity' of gaming"); Courtney J.A. DaCosta, Note, *When "Turnabout" Is Not "Fair Play": Tribal Immunity Under the Indian Gaming Regulatory Act*, 97 Geo. L.J. 515, 545–46 (2009) (discussing tribal immunity's effect on the enforceability of revenue-sharing arrangements and the implicit conflict between In re Indian Gaming Related Cases and *Ho-Chunk*); Ezekiel J.N. Fletcher, *supra*, note 6, at 436, 448 (2009) (discussing In re Indian Gaming Related Cases, and reasoning further that "[i]f the statements and guidance provided by the federal government are added to the equation, there is ample support to negotiate other tribal economic incentives, aside from substantial exclusivity, in exchange for revenue sharing payments to state and/or local governments" including relief from "double" taxation—e.g., "[i]f a state agrees not to tax any business or tax at a lower rate, as part of negotiating a class III gaming compact, these economic incentives in exchange for the payment of a percentage of gaming revenue may qualify as a 'valuable economic benefit' for the tribe");

P.557, n.236.   Add the following to the end of the footnote before the period:

; *Amador County, Ca., v. Salazar*, 640 F.3d 373 (D.C. Cir. 2011) (county had standing to challenge Secretary's decision to allow compact to be deemed approved and such a decision is reviewable under the Administrative Procedures Act if the decision is contrary to law)

P.558, n.240.   Add the following to line 17 of the footnote before the semicolon:

, *cert. dismissed*, 129 S. Ct. 28, *on remand*, 564 F. Supp. 2d 856 (W.D. Wis. 2008) (finding state's contract-based claims and good-faith negotiation claim under 25 U.S.C. § 2710(d)(7)(B) subject to arbitration)

P.558, n.241.   Add the following to line 1 of the footnote after the semicolon:

State ex rel. Dewberry v. Kulongoski, 210 P.3d 884, 888–90 (Or. 2009) (citizens not required to join tribe in mandamus action challenging governor's authority to enter into compact); *Mudarri v. State*, 196 P.3d 153, 162–64 (Wash Ct. App. 2008) (absent tribe indispensable to nontribal gaming operator's action seeking to invalidate compact but not indispensable to adjudicate non-compact claims);

Add the following to line 8 of the footnote after "(9th Cir. 2008)":

, *amended*, 547 F.3d 962, 969–72 (9th Cir. 2008)

Add the following to the end of the footnote before the period:

, *cert. denied*, 129 S. Ct. 1987 (2009)

P.561, n.261. **Add the following to line 2 of the footnote after "*see generally*":**

John C. Kuzenski, *The Paving Principle of Good Intentions? Calls for Reform of the Indian Gaming Regulatory Act and the Private Game Theory Equilibrium Opposing Them*, 30 N.C. Cent. L. Rev. 168 (2008) (rejecting recent calls by commentators to change IGRA, and arguing instead that, by employing classic game theory, Indian tribes and states will seek to maximize their own rational self-interest in the compact negotiation process, but will moderate their advantage-seeking through negotiation and compromise where it is believed the other side has an ability to harm or interfere with their goal; noting tribes' ability to seek secretarial procedures against states unwilling to bargain, and the states' ability to allow broader non-Indian gaming within their jurisdictions);

P.562, n.263. **Add the following to line 1 of the footnote before the period:**

, *cert. denied, sub nom. Kickapoo Traditional Tribe of Texas v. Texas*, 555 U.S. 881 (2008)

P.562, n.264. **Add the following to line 1 of the footnote after the first period:**

An Alabama federal district court expressly disagreed with the Fifth Circuit and dismissed on ripeness grounds the state's facial and as-applied challenges to regulations promulgated by the Secretary in response to *Seminole Tribe v. Florida*, 517 U.S. 44 (1996). *Alabama v. United States*, 630 F. Supp. 2d 1320, 1328–29 (S.D. Ala. 2008).

P.563, n.267. **Add the following to the end of the footnote before the period:**

; *see generally* Courtney J.A. DaCosta, Note, *When "Turnabout" Is Not "Fair Play": Tribal Immunity Under the Indian Gaming Regulatory Act*, 97 Geo. L.J. 515, 546–48 (2009), (arguing that "[c]ourts' narrow construction of the still-valid [25 U.S.C. § 2710(d)(7)](A)(ii) abrogation helps, albeit in a roundabout way, to restore the original balance: this construction curtails a state's capacity to intrude on tribal prerogatives just as *Seminole Tribe I* curtailed a tribe's ability to intrude on state prerogatives," while recognizing the same narrow construction "can preclude states from blocking illegal, uncompacted class III gaming," "can permit tribes to violate federal law with impunity," and "results in a net gain of unlawful gaming activity," particularly when "federal enforcement against admittedly unlawful gaming has at time seen ineffective"; "[t]his gives tribes greater leeway to operate illegal class III gaming, a result that may be desirable under equitable and federalism lenses but obstructs the rule of law and runs counter to IGRA's stated purpose of keeping Indian gaming free from 'organized crime and other negative externalities'")

P.565, n.283.   Add the following to the end of the footnote before the period:

; *cf. Rincon Band of Luiseno Mission Indians v. Schwarzenegger*, 602 F.3d 1019 (9th Cir. 2010), *cert. denied* 131 S. Ct. 3055 (2011) (evaluating tribe's claim that state engaged in bad faith compact negotiations in relation to an amended compact); *Big Lagoon Rancheria v. California*, 759 F. Supp. 2d 1149 (N.D. Cal. 2010) (discussing state's negotiating position that revenue sharing for the state's general fund as bad faith negotiating in light of the *Rincon* decision)

P.566, n.284.   Add the following to the end of the footnote before the period:

; *see also Big Lagoon Rancheria v. California*, 700 F. Supp. 2d 1169, 1176 (N.D. Cal 2010) (nothing in IGRA expressly limits discovery, tribe entitled to discovery regarding bad faith compact negotiation claim against state, Eleventh Amendment did not bar tribe's discovery), *recons. granted in part*, 2010 WL 2735567, at *5 (Jul. 12, 2010) (in light of *Rincon Band of Luiseno Indians v. Schwarzenegger, 602 F.3d 1019 (9th Cir. 2010)*, excluding from discovery "[e]vidence . . . that bears only on subjective intent[,]" but directing discovery as to "documents in the State's possession—beyond the bargaining positions of the parties—[that] are relevant to an objective evaluation of the good faith of the State's bargaining positions"); *Fort Independence Indian Cmty. v. California*, 679 F. Supp. 2d 1159, 1186–88 (E.D. Cal. 2009) (court denied cross motions for summary judgment in bad faith compact negotiation case because after evaluating record of negotiation and expert opinions regarding the dollar value of the state's offer of exclusivity, material question remained as to whether the state's offer of exclusivity was a meaningful concession)

P.569, n.307.   Add the following to the end of the footnote:

Cf. Guadalupe Gutierrez, Note, *Jurisdictional Ambiguities Among Sovereigns: The Impact of the Indian Gaming Regulatory Act on Criminal Jurisdiction on Tribal Lands*, 26 Ariz. J. Int'l & Comp. L. 229, 257 (2009) ("IGRA has created a jurisdictional maze in which crimes associated with Indian gaming may or may not be prosecuted under federal, state, or tribal authority depending on who committed the crime, whether the crime is a priority, and whether resources are available for adjudication").

P.570, n.314.   Add the following to the end of the footnote before the period:

; *see generally* Courtney J.A. DaCosta, Note, *When "Turnabout" Is Not "Fair Play": Tribal Immunity Under the Indian Gaming Regulatory Act*, 97 Geo. L.J. 515, 548–49, 552–53 (2009) (suggesting Congress should reform IGRA to incorporate a limited abrogation of tribal immunity in gaming-related claims by gaming establishment employees and patrons, where no viable tribal forum is available for such claims)

Chapter 13
Indian Child Welfare Act

P.572, n.12.   **Add the following to line 6 of the footnote after "*see*":**

In re Noreen G., 105 Cal. Rptr. 3d 521, 545 (Ct. App. 2010) (although "ICWA itself does not require an *inquiry,* where, as here, no evidence of an Indian child has been presented[,]" relevant state law imposes "'an affirmative and continuing duty to inquire whether a [*dependent*] child . . . is or may be an Indian child in all *dependency proceedings*"); *In re R.R.*, 103 Cal. Rptr. 3d 110, 122–24 (Ct. App. 2009) (ICWA did not preempt extension of its protections to delinquency proceedings otherwise excluded from scope of "child custody proceedings" in 25 U.S.C. § 1903(1); *In re J.B.*, 100 Cal. Rptr. 3d 679 (Ct. App. 2009) ("Indian child custody proceeding" as used in state statute refers to "child custody proceeding" as defined in ICWA and thereby does not encompass removal of custody from mother and placement with father); *In re Damian C.*, 100 Cal. Rptr. 3d 110, 112 (Ct. App. 2009) (state statutory amendments did not modify "reason to know" standard from ICWA's; "[i]nstead, the legislative history reveals an intention to standardize the interpretation of ICWA provisions and ICWA inquiry and noticing practice throughout the state and to broaden the statutory interpretation"); *In re A.A.*, 84 Cal. Rptr. 3d 841 (Ct. App. 2008) (discussing various issues with reference to both ICWA and complementary state Indian child-related custody proceeding provisions, including adequate efforts to provide remedial services, the "Indian child exception" established under California statute, and child placement);

Add the following to the eighth-to-last line of the footnote after "see *also*":

In re T.S., 96 Cal. Rptr. 3d 706, 712–13 (Ct. App. 2009) (no state law-imposed requirement to adhere to tribal placement plan without conducting independent assessment of detriment to the involved child, and agency properly declined to follow plan which failed to identify any family member not disqualified from consideration by virtue of criminal records);

Add the following to the fourth-to-last line of the footnote after *"Compare"*:

In re L.N.B.-L, Nos. 28850-2-II & 38854-5-II, 2010 WL 3075179, at *10 (Wash. Ct. App. Aug. 3, 2010) (declining to extend scope of state statute requiring notice to "'all tribes'" to encompass non-federally recognized groups); *In re M.S.*, 2010 OK 46, 2010 WL 2376323, at *9 (Okla. June 15, 2010) (Oklahoma Indian Child Welfare Act requires transfer of all child custody proceedings, not merely involuntary proceedings, to tribal court absent good cause not to do so);

P.573, n.14.   **Add the following to line 1 of the footnote after "see":**

In re C.C.M., 202 P.3d 971, 976–77 (Wash. Ct. App. 2009) (custody proceeding brought by Indian custodian and his spouse constituted a foster care proceeding since purpose was "to divest [the father] of his legal right to custody"); *In re N.B.*, 199 P.3d 16, 18–19 (Colo. Ct. App. 2007) (citing to, and agreeing with, decisions from other jurisdictions that deem step-parent adoptions "where a child will remain with one biological parent after the adoption" subject to ICWA);

P.574, n.17.   **Add the following to line 11 of the footnote after "cf.":**

In re J.S.B., 214 P.3d 827, 832 (Or. Ct. App. 2009) (new active-efforts determination required when modified permanency plan issued two months after original plan; "in light of the policies of the ICWA to afford an opportunity for reunification at every dispositional step that could result in contributing to the permanent removal of children subject to its protections, that it was incumbent on the juvenile court at the August hearing to either make new findings . . . or to find that the circumstances regarding reunification had not changed since the last hearing"); *Danielle A. v. State Dep't of Health & Soc. Servs.*, 215 P.3d 349, 354 (Alaska 2009) (extensions of child custody orders did not constitute new child custody proceeding that required compliance with 25 U.S.C. § 1912(e) because "ICWA does not address custody extensions" and "the issue [here] is extending [agency] custody so [mother and child] may reunify gradually, not removal");

P.574, n.18.   **Add the following to line 4 of the footnote after the semicolon:**

In re Esther V., 248 P.3d 863, 869 (N.M. 2011) (same);

Add the following to the end of the footnote:

Compare In re J.M., 218 P.3d 1213, 1217 (Mont. 2009) (mother's consent to agency's assuming temporary legal custody after involuntary foster care placement proceeding commenced did not convert action into voluntary proceeding subject to requirements in 25 U.S.C. § 1913(a)); and *In re Welfare of MG*, 201 P.3d 354, 358 (Wash. Ct. App. 2009) (case that commenced as an involuntary dependency proceeding, and hence a foster care placement proceeding under ICWA, was not transformed into a voluntary proceeding by mother's subsequent consent to a dependency order; "the intent of 25 U.S.C. § 1913 is to encourage parents to make appropriate placement of their children when they are not confident of their own ability to parent[,]" but such "intent would not be furthered by applying it to involuntary placements where the parents are represented by counsel"), *with In re R.S.*, 101 Cal. Rptr. 3d 910, 923 (Ct. App. 2009) (although action commenced as an involuntary dependency proceeding, after voluntary relinquishment of parental status, the adoption agency "became subject to separate provisions of ICWA relating to voluntary relinquishments by the parents of an Indian child[,]" thereby mooting mother's claimed violation of, *inter alia*, ICWA notice provisions).

P. 574, n. 20.   Add the following to line 17 of the footnote after "*with*":

In re Beach, 246 P.3d 845, 847 (Wash. App. 2011) (dispute between child's mother and mother's former boyfriend fell under ICWA because boyfriend, although a parental figure to the child, did not meet ICWA's definition of a biological or adoptive parent);

Add the following to the end of the footnote before the period:

; Jill E. Tompkins, *Finding the Indian Child Welfare Act in Unexpected Places: Applicability in Private Non-Parent Custody Actions*, 81 U. Colo. L. Rev. 1119 (Fall 2010) (same)

P.575, n.22.   Add the following to line 1 of the footnote after "*Compare*":

In re C.C.M., 202 P.3d 971, 979, 980 (Wash. Ct. App. 2009) (since "[i]n an action for foster care placement such as that herein, ICWA expresses no preference for placement of an Indian child with a parent over an Indian custodian," application of a state law-based "preference for parental custody over non-parental custody" gave effect to 25 U.S.C. § 1921 insofar as the preference "provides greater protection to the parent in this context than does ICWA");

Add the following to line 8 of the footnote after "*with*":

Guardian ad Litem v. State ex rel. C.D., 245 P.3d 724, 728–29 (Utah 2010) (once custody had been granted to children's biological fathers, grandfather was no longer an "Indian custodian" and therefore was not entitled to active efforts);

P.576, n.25.   **Add the following to the end of the footnote before the period:**

; *cf. In re R.R.*, 103 Cal. Rptr. 3d 110, 122 (Ct. App. 2009) (amendments to state statutes applying ICWA protections to delinquency proceedings not preempted; "ICWA merely established minimum protections, and does not preempt legislation that is more protective of Indian children with respect to their tribal relationships")

P.576, n.26.   **Add the following to line 1 of the footnote after "E.g.,":**

In re D.C., 928 N.E.2d 602, 605 (Ind. Ct. App. 2010) (adhering to binding state supreme court precedent, and rejecting parent's challenge to existing Indian family exception doctrine); *In re Parental Rights of N.J.*, 221 P.3d 1255, 1264 (Nev. 2009) (applying existing Indian family exception on a "case-by-case basis to avoid results that are counter to the ICWA's policy goal of protecting the best interests of a Native American child");

P.577, n.27.   **Add the following to line 1 of the footnote after "E.g.,":**

In re N.B., 199 P.3d 16, 22 (Colo. Ct. App. 2007) (reasoning in part that "[a]pplying the exception would result in each state court using its own value system to decide whether a child is 'Indian enough' for the ICWA to apply, which would limit the tribes' efforts to regain members who were lost because of earlier governmental action");

P.577, n.28.   **Add the following the fourteenth-to-last line of the footnote before the period:**

; *cf. In re N.B.*, 199 P.3d 16, 23 (Colo. Ct. App. 2007) (declining to follow *Bridget R.* in connection with a constitutional challenge on various grounds to ICWA insofar as it applies to step-parent adoption proceedings, and observing in response to a substantive due process–based claim that "[n]either the United States Supreme Court nor the Colorado Supreme Court has recognized a child's substantive due process right to a stable home")

P.579.   **Add the following to the end of the carryover paragraph:**

Indeed, the Kansas Supreme Court—the appellate court originating the exception—subsequently concluded that the doctrine is inconsistent with ICWA.[33.1]

[33.1] *In re A.J.S.*, 204 P.3d 543, 550 (Kan. 2009) (overruling *In re Adoption of Baby Boy L., 643 P.2d 168 (Kan. 1982)*, and identifying various reasons for its determination including the influence of "our sister states' and commentators' widespread and well-reasoned criticism of the doctrine"); *see generally* Dan Lewerenz & Padraic McCoy, *The End of "Existing Indian Family" Jurisprudence: Holyfield at 20, In the Matter of A.J.S., and the Last Gasps of a Dying Doctrine,*

36 Wm. Mitchell L. Rev. 684, 689–90, 718 (2010) (concluding that "state court judges and state legislatures have effectively neutered the 'existing Indian family' doctrine in most jurisdictions where it has been considered, relegating it to little more than a troublesome footnote in a handful of states[,]" and describing *A.J.S.* as a "[n]ail in the [c]offin").

P.580, n.34.   **Add the following to line 1 of the footnote after "*see*":**

In re Melisssa R., 98 Cal. Rptr. 3d 794, 801 (Ct. App. 2009) (alleged ICWA violations mooted where proceeding began when child was 16 years old but was 20 when challenged order entered); *In re E.G.*, 88 Cal. Rptr. 3d 871, 873 (Ct. App. 2009) ("[a]n alleged father may or may not have any biological connection to the child[,]" and thus "[u]ntil biological paternity is established, an alleged father's claims of Indian heritage do not trigger any ICWA notice requirement"); *People ex rel. L.O.L.*, 197 P.3d 291, 294 (Colo. Ct. App. 2008) (trial court did not err in applying clear-and-convincing-evidence standard in parental rights termination proceeding, not the beyond-a-reasonable-doubt standard required under ICWA, in light of the fact that "notice was sent to the relevant tribes, the record does not show that L.O.L. was a member of, or was eligible to be a member of, any Indian tribe");

Add the following to line 7 after the period:

In re K.P., 95 Cal. Rptr. 3d 524, 526 (Ct. App. 2009);

Add the following to line 13 of the footnote after "*see also*":

In re Interest of "A" Children, 193 P.3d 1228, 1244 (Haw. Ct. App. 2008) (ICWA inapplicable to child custody proceeding involving Native Hawaiians);

P.580, n.35.   **Add the following to line 1 of the footnote after "*E.g.,*":**

Bruce L. v. W.E., 247 P.3d 966 (Alaska 2011) (the party asserting the applicability of ICWA has the burden to produce necessary evidence to support it, but where parties do not dispute the Act's applicability it is error for the court to find that the child was not an Indian child on the basis of a lack of evidence of the child's eligibility for tribal enrollment without allowing the parties to present evidence); *In re J.J.L.*, 223 P.3d 921, 926 (Mont. 2010) ("[w]here [the biological father] could not assert that he himself was enrolled in the [the tribe], it cannot be said that the District Court had reason to believe the children qualified as Indian children under either method articulated in the statute"); *In re C.C.*, 2010 Ohio 780, 2010 WL 728535, at *2 (Ct. App. Mar. 4, 2010) ("[r]egardless of whether the great-grandmother was a member of a Cherokee tribe, the father did not establish his own membership in a tribe" and "thus failed to prove that the daughter was the biological child of a member of an Indian tribe, so she did not meet the statutory definition of an 'Indian child'"); *In re Trevor I.*, 973 A.2d 752, 759 (Me. 2009) (where "father's asserted potential affiliation with the . . . Tribe did not provide the information that the [BIA] would have needed . . . to determine the father's, or the child's, ancestry[,]" the father failed to discharge "his burden of producing sufficient information to obligate the Department or the court to make further inquiry into his ancestry beyond the steps taken");

P.580, n.36.   Add the following to the beginning of the footnote:

In re Jack C., III, 122 Cal. Rptr. 3d 6, 16 (Ct. App. 2011); *In re B.R.,* 97 Cal. Rptr. 3d 890, 896 (Ct. App. 2009); *In re Interest of R.R.,* 294 S.W.3d 213, 217–18 (Tex. Civ. App. 2009); *D.B. v. Superior Ct.,* 89 Cal. Rptr. 3d 566, 574–75 (Ct. App. 2009);

Add the following to line 10 of the footnote after *"contra"*:

Nielson v. Ketchum, 640 F.3d 1117, 1123–24 (10th Cir. 2011) (holding that the Cherokee Nation Citizenship Act—which provides that any newborn child who is a direct descendant of an original enrollee is automatically admitted as a citizen of the Cherokee Nation for 240 days following the child's birth—did not grant a child status required to define the child as an "Indian child" under ICWA because "[t]he tribe cannot expand the reach of a federal statute by a tribal provision that extends automatic citizenship to the child of a nonmember of the tribe");

P.581, n.37.   Add the following to the end of the footnote before the final period:

; *but see In re C.B.,* 117 Cal. Rptr. 3d 846, 871–75 (Ct. App. 2010) (holding that state statute required efforts to secure children's tribal enrollment to comply with ICWA's "active efforts" requirement)

P.582, n.42.   Add the following to line 4 of the footnote after "See":

Bruce L. v. W.E., 247 P.3d 966, 979 (Alaska 2011) (holding that "to qualify as an ICWA parent[,] an unwed father does not need to comply perfectly with state laws for establishing paternity, so long as he has made reasonable efforts to acknowledge paternity");

P.582, n.44.   Add the following to line 1 of the footnote after "See":

Jared P. v. Glade T., 209 P.3d 157, 161 (Ariz. Ct. App. 2009) (because ICWA "does not define how paternity can be acknowledged or otherwise detail any procedure to establish paternity[,]" state law controls, and under Arizona precedent paternity had been acknowledged by virtue of the father's admission and genetic testing);

P.583, n.46.   Add the following to line 1 of the footnote after "*E.g.,*":

In re Jeremiah G., 92 Cal. Rptr. 3d 203, 208 (Ct. App. 2009) ("both the federal regulations and [state statutes] require more than a bare suggestion that a child might be an Indian child[;]" here, "[the] father retracted his claim of Indian heritage, and . . . there was no other basis for suspecting that [the child] might be an Indian child"); *In re Shane G.*, 83 Cal. Rptr. 3d 513, 517 (Ct. App. 2008) (maternal grandmother's statement that child's great-great-great-grandmother was a "Comanche princess" inadequate showing of "reason to know" where "no one in the family ever lived on a reservation, attended an Indian school, participated in Indian ceremonies or received services from an Indian health clinic" and where, "[m]ost significantly, the evidence before the court showed the Comanche tribe requires a minimum blood quantum for membership that excludes [the child]");

P.584, n.47.   Add the following to line 1 of the footnote after "*E.g.,*":

In re M.R.P.-C., 794 N.W. 2d 373, 379 (Minn. App. 2011) (requiring an inquiry by the court into the applicability of ICWA on the basis of the child's reported Indian heritage); *In re E.W.*, 88 Cal. Rptr. 3d 338, 342 (Ct. App. 2009) (failure to give notice as to one of two siblings with common biological parents deemed harmless "since tribal investigations determined [one sibling] is not an Indian child, [the other] is also not an Indian child"); *In re A.B.*, 79 Cal. Rptr. 3d 580 (Ct. App. 2008) (any error in complying with ICWA notice harmless given both biological parents' admitted absence of Indian ancestry as indicated on form filed in another proceeding by the mother with respect to involved child's sibling; leave granted to augment appeal record with the form);

Add the following to the end of the footnote:

Whether the absence of an express determination of ICWA's non-applicability by the trial court in jurisdictions giving a broad reading to the term "reason to know" constitutes a basis for reversal appears to be fact dependent. *E.g.*, *In re E.W.*, 88 Cal. Rptr. 3d at 345 ("an implicit ruling suffices, at least as long as the reviewing court can be confident that the juvenile court considered the issue and there is no question but that an explicit ruling would conform to the implicit one").

P.585, n.49.   Add the following to line 1 of the footnote after "*E.g.,*":

People in re Interest of N.D.C., 210 P.3d 494, 500 (Colo. Ct. App. 2009) (absent evidence of Indian child status, "the [trial] court cannot make that finding and should not use the higher burdens of proof or apply the ICWA's other substantive provisions[,]" and thus, "if following remand, the tribe chooses not to intervene or again states N.D.C. is not eligible to enroll, the court should not apply the ICWA's substantive provisions"); *Justin L. v. Superior Ct.*, 81 Cal. Rptr. 3d 884, 886 (Ct. App. 2008) ("We are growing weary of appeals in which the only error is the Department's failure to comply with ICWA. . . . Remand for the limited purpose of the ICWA compliance is all too common") (citation omitted);

P.587, n.55.   **Add the following to the end of the footnote before the period:**

; *see also In re Esther V.*, 248 P.3d 863, 873 (N.M. 2011) (finding that the Guidelines, statute's legislative history, and decisions of other jurisdictions support court's holding that states may "perform an emergency removal of an Indian child without first adhering to the requirements of § 1912")

P.588, n.62.   **Add the following to line 8 of the footnote after "see":**

In re Fair Hearing of Hanna, 227 P.3d 596, 600 (Mont. 2010) (construing § 1919 to authorize agreement between federal agencies, state and tribe under which state agency possessed jurisdiction to pursue a child-abuse "substantiation" proceeding against tribal member for on-reservation acts directed at Indian child; "[t]he substantiation proceeding, which is an adjudication of [the mother's] rights, . . . arose directly from [her] 'care' of an Indian child, . . . fits within the language of § 1919(a)" and, together with investigation and verification, is a "necessary component[] of an effective foster care program" under Title IV-E of the Social Security Act);

P. 589.   **Add footnote 66.1 at the end of the next-to-last sentence on the page (ending with ". . . tribal court declination") as follows:**

[66.1]   *But see In re Breana M.*, 795 N.W.2d 660, 666 (Neb. App. 2011) (holding that ICWA controls state versus tribal court jurisdictional issues, but "[a] determination of which state juvenile court has subject matter jurisdiction over a juvenile proceeding is outside the scope of the Act").

P.589, n.64.   **Add the following to the sixth-to-last line of the footnote before the second period:**

; *but see generally* Dennis Puzz, Jr., *Untangling the Jurisdictional Web: Determining Indian Child Welfare Jurisdiction in the State of Wisconsin*, 36 Wm. Mitchell L. Rev. 724, 728, 733–34 (2010) (relying in part upon a 1981 Wisconsin Attorney General's opinion for the proposition that "reassumption of jurisdiction under the ICWA section 1918(a) is not required for the tribe to have exclusive jurisdiction" pursuant to § 1911(a) with regard to involuntary child custody proceedings and that, as to voluntary proceedings involving an Indian child domiciled on reservation, jurisdictional reassumption under § 1918 serves to "eliminate the State's concurrent jurisdiction over these actions within the reservation"—*i.e.*, to reassume exclusive jurisdiction)

P.590, n.68.   **Add the following to line 1 of the footnote after "E.g.,":**

In re Welfare of the Child of R.S., 793 N.W. 2d 752, 758–59 (Minn. App. 2011) (the Act neither requires nor forbids the transfer of pre-adoptive placement proceedings to tribal court);

P.591, n.71.   **Add the following to line 8 of the footnote after "related case law)":**

but see State v. Native Village of Tanana, 249 P.3d 734, 751 (Alaska 2011) (overruling "[w]hat remains of *Nenana*" and instead "adopt[ing] the view that P.L. 280 did not divest tribes of all jurisdiction under § 1911(a), but rather created concurrent jurisdiction with the State.")

P.592, n.75.   **Add the following to the beginning of the footnote:**

In re S.F., 230 P.3d 911, 914 (Okla. Civ. App. 2009);

P.593, n.79.   **Add the following to line 3 of the footnote after "see":**

In re G.L., 99 Cal. Rptr. 3d 356, 366 (Ct. App. 2009) (although paternal grandmother had possessed Indian custodian status, "[t]he transfer of an Indian minor's care and custody to an Indian custodian is, by definition, 'temporary,' and thus revocable[;]" mother's revocation therefore terminated such status); *Ted W. v. State Dep't of Health & Soc. Servs.*, 204 P.3d 333, 338–39 (Alaska 2009) (party who obtained "Indian custodian" status by virtue of mother's temporary transfer of custody was deprived of such status when the mother revoked her consent);

P.593, n.80.   **Add the following to line 1 of the footnote after "See, e.g.,":**

In re Z.W., 124 Cal. Rptr. 3d 419, 425 (Ct. App. 2011) (holding that there was no error in notice sent to agents listed in Federal Register despite that some named agents changed before the final ICWA compliance hearing because the notice was complete prior to the newly published list and because while the named individuals changed, the addresses for service did not); *In re Welfare of L.N.B.-L.*, 237 P.3d 944, 957 (Wash. Ct. App. 2010) (notice not required for tribe that is not federally recognized, but notice is required when identified tribe may be federally recognized [such as "Black Foot" instead of "the Blackfeet Indian Reservation of Montana"]); *People in the Interest of T.M.W.*, 208 P.3d 272, 275 (Colo. Ct. App. 2009) (even though child had sibling with the same biological parents for whom ICWA notice had been given and was determined as not eligible for membership by the tribe, failure to provide such notice constituted reversible error "because the tribe is free to change its enrollment criteria at any point");

P.595, n.83.   **Add the following to line 1 of the footnote after
"*see*":**

In re Interest of R.R., 294 S.W.3d 213, 220–21 (Tex. Civ. App. 2009) (cataloguing notice procedural requirements, and holding that "[s]ubstantial compliance with these notice provisions will not suffice");

P.595, n.84.   **Add the following to end of the footnote before the
period:**

; *see also In re J.J.C.*, 302 S.W.2d 896, 901 (Tex. App. 2009) (following "non-binding" BIA Guidelines, and concluding that notice failed to include all information specified in 25 C.F.R. § 23.11); *People in re Interest of N.D.C.*, 210 P.3d 494, 499 (Colo. Ct. App. 2009) (requiring Guidelines be followed with respect to notice, and deeming noncompliance not harmless "because all known information was not provided to the tribe in a manner that appears in the record"); *In re K.M.*, 90 Cal. Rptr. 3d 692, 695 (Ct. App. 2009) (notice's family background information sufficient given the degree of cooperation from the child's mother and grandmother)

P.595, n.85.   **Add the following to line 1 of the footnote after
"*Compare*":**

In re Z.W., 124 Cal. Rptr. 3d 419, 429–30 (Ct. App. 2011) (balancing tribes' right to notice with child's interest in permanency and stability and holding that parent had had numerous opportunities to object to ICWA notice contents on remand and had not done so, therefore parent waived appeal of accuracy of notice); *In re S.B.*, 94 Cal. Rptr. 3d 645, 648 (Ct. App. 2009) (no reversible error on the basis of agency's failure to file all return receipts in light of social worker's testimony that notice was sent to the relevant tribes and evidentiary presumption under state statute "that official duty has been regularly performed[;]" stating further that "[m]ore troubling in this case is the failure of parents' trial counsel to carefully review the record at the time of the hearing in order to raise any potential ICWA notice problem in a timely manner" and that "an attorney practicing dependency law in the juvenile court should be sufficiently familiar with ICWA notice requirements to point out a flaw in notice if the record shows that there is one—especially when specifically asked to do so");

**Add the following to line 11 of the footnote after
"*with*":**

In re D.W., 122 Cal. Rptr. 3d 460, 463 (Ct. App. 2011) ("Because the principal purpose of the ICWA is to protect and preserve Indian tribes, a parent's failure to raise an ICWA notice issue in the juvenile court does not bar consideration of the issue on appeal."); *In re B.R.*, 97 Cal. Rptr. 3d 890, 893 (Ct. App. 2009) ("parents' failure to raise the ICWA issue now before us does not prevent us from considering the issue on the merits");

P.596, n.86. **Add the following to the beginning of the footnote:**

In re G.L., 99 Cal. Rptr. 3d 356, 366 (Ct. App. 2009) ("a notice violation under ICWA is not jurisdictional in the fundamental sense, but instead is subject to a harmless error analysis");

Add the following to the end of the footnote before the period:

cf. In re J.J.C., 302 S.W.2d 896, 899 (Tex. App. 2009) ("the provisions of the ICWA [in 25 U.S.C. § 1914] allowing post-judgment challenges to involuntary termination proceedings preempt the Texas rules and statutes regarding preservation of error"); *In re C.C.M.*, 202 P.3d 971, 978 (Wash. Ct. App. 2009) (declining to find waiver of right to intervene on the basis of tribal social worker's declination absent evidence of her authority to make the waiver, and further declining to find adequate "limited intervention" rights thereafter granted tribe for purposes of curing defective notice "[b]ecause tribes have independent interests in Indian children" and therefore "'must be allowed to participate in hearings in which [the values protected by ICWA] are significantly implicated'")

P.596, n.88. **Add the following to line 1 of the footnote after "*E.g.,*":**

People ex rel. A.R.Y.-M., 230 P.3d 1259, 1262 (Colo. Ct. App. 2010) (ICWA notice deficiencies deemed harmless where "all known information was provided to the tribes[] and mother has not shown that any new information would have resulted in a different tribal determination"); *In re Z.N.*, 104 Cal. Rptr. 3d 247, 260 (Ct. App. 2009) (judicial notice taken of docket entry in separate termination proceedings involving half-siblings in determining that ICWA notice error harmless; "[t]he question for an appellate court taking judicial notice is not whether there was a finding or sufficient evidence in the half sibling's case, but whether documents from that case show lack of prejudice in the case before it—i.e., whether there is a reasonable probability of a different result absent the error . . . or, as sometimes phrased in the ICWA context, whether there is '"no basis to believe"' a different result would occur as to the child's Indian status"); *In re I.W.*, 103 Cal. Rptr. 3d 538, 548 (Ct. App. 2010) (while concurring "with the courts that have emphasized the importance of strict compliance with the ICWA notice requirements[,] . . . not all deficiencies in notice are prejudicial error[,] . . . [a]nd mother does not suggest how the supposed deficiencies she notes would have made a difference given the information that was in the notices"); *In re J.J.C.*, 302 S.W.2d 896, 902 (Tex. App. 2009) (conditionally affirming termination judgment "in the event that it is determined that [the two children] are not Indian children" after proper notice given);

P.597, n.89. **Add the following the end of the footnote:**

Another court has held that ICWA does not "except[] a transfer order from the laws and rules governing vacation of orders procured by misrepresentation."

In re Welfare of Children of R.A.J., 769 N.W.2d 297, 303 (Minn. Ct. App. 2009) (vacating order entered on the basis of agreement that tribal representative lacked authority to negotiate).

P.597, n.91.   Add the following to line 8 of the footnote after "*cf.*":

In re Jack C., III, 122 Cal. Rptr. 3d 6, 20–21 (Ct. App. 2011) (rejecting court's finding of good cause to deny transfer because although there was evidence to support that there would be hardship in presenting evidence in tribal court, there was no evidence that tribal court was unable to mitigate the hardship);

P.598, n.92.   Add the following to the beginning of the footnote:

In re Interest of M.F., 206 P.3d 57, 62 (Kan. Ct. App. 2009) (applying Guidelines, and upholding transfer denial on the basis of delay by mother in requesting transfer to Wyoming tribe);

Add the following to line 10 of the footnote before "*cf.*":

but see In re M.S., 2010 OK 46, 2010 WL 2376323, at *8 (Okla. June 15, 2010) (vacating order that found good cause not to transfer on delay basis since "it cannot be said that the Tribe's delay in requesting transfer 'was not prevented by the actions of the State'");

Add the following to line 10 of the footnote after "*cf.*":

In re Jack C., III, 122 Cal. Rptr. 3d 6, 19–20 (Ct. App. 2011) (a transfer petition was not untimely under California procedural rules, which allow for filing the petition after reunification efforts have failed and reunification services have been terminated); *In re Louis S.*, 774 N.W.2d 416, 423 (Neb. Ct. App. 2009) (no abuse of discretion in denying transfer motion under Nebraska Indian Child Welfare Act where the case had been pending before juvenile court for 2½ years "when proof of the children's membership or eligibility for membership in the Omaha Tribe was offered to the juvenile court"); *In re Leslie S.*, 770 N.W.2d 678, 683 (Neb. Ct. App. 2009) (applying provisions of Nebraska Indian Child Welfare Act, and finding no abuse of discretion when juvenile court denied transfer request on delay grounds; the father "did not file the motion to transfer until well after 2 years following the filing of the juvenile petition, during which time [he] did very little to participate in the case[,]" and "[a]t the time of the hearing on this motion to transfer, proceedings had begun to terminate both parents' parental rights");

Add the following to the end of the footnote before the period:

; *see generally* Emily Bucher, Case Comment, *Narrowed Lens, Clearer Focus: Considering the Use of De Novo Review in Indian Child Welfare Proceedings—In* re *Welfare of Child of T.T.B.*, 34 Wm. Mitchell L. Rev. 1429, 1447, 1449 (2009) (arguing that the majority opinion in *In re Welfare of Child of T.T.B.*, 724 N.W.2d 300 (Minn. 2006), which upheld a district court's denial of transfer on the basis of delay in the request, "precariously skirts the edge of presumptive tribal court jurisdiction in child protection proceedings involving Indian children not residing within or domiciled on reservations[;]" arguing that deference to trial court determinations of good-cause issues raises "[t]he peril [of] a return to the dominance of ill-suited state laws in Indian child welfare proceedings[;]" and recommending adoption of *de novo*, rather than abuse-of-discretion appellate review standard)

P.598, n.94.   **Add the following to line 1 of the footnote after "E.g.,":**

In re B.C., 786 N.W.2d 350, 351–53 (S.D. 2010) (because tribes had intervened as a matter of right, they were parties and therefore appeals were subject to dismissal because the appealing parties had failed to serve notices of appeal on the tribes);

P.598, n.95.   **Add the following to line 2 of the footnote after "cf.":**

J.P.H. v. Florida Dep't of Children & Families, 39 So.3d 560, 560 (Fl. Dist. Ct. App. 2010) (tribe has absolute right to intervene and therefore "is not required to be represented by a member of the state bar" because "state prohibitions on the unauthorized practice of law interfere with and are thus preempted in the narrow context" of ICWA proceedings); *In re Interest of Elias L.*, 767 N.W.2d 98 (Neb. 2009) (state-law requirement that non-party litigants be represented by a state-licensed attorney incompatible with tribe's right to intervene under ICWA and not otherwise justified by a state interest held preempted; tribe's "designated representative" therefore entitled "to fully participate" in trial court proceedings);

P.600, n.103.   **Add the following to the beginning of the footnote:**

In re M.S., 2010 OK 46, 2010 WL 2376323, at *4 (Okla. June 15, 2010) (adopting clear-and-convincing-evidence standard); *In re Louis S.*, 774 N.W.2d 416, 423 (Neb. Ct. App. 2009) (abuse-of-discretion standard applied under Nebraska Indian Child Welfare Act);

P.602, n.111.   **Add the following to line 1 of the footnote after "E.g.,":**

Neal M. v. State Dep't of Health & Soc. Servs., 214 P.3d 284 (Alaska 2009) ("[i]n evaluating whether the state met its active efforts burden, the court may consider 'a parent's demonstrated lack of willingness to participate in treatment'"); *Roland L. v. State Dep't of Health & Soc. Servs.*, 206 P.3d 453, 457 (Alaska 2009) (identifying several factors that militated against parent's claim that the active-efforts requirement had not been satisfied, including failure to comply "with the portion of his case plan requiring him to get a mental health evaluation when he had the opportunity to do so in jail");

P.602, n.112.   Add the following to line 1 of the footnote after "E.g.,":

Dashiell B. v. State Dep't of Health & Soc. Servs., 222 P.3d 841, 846–47 (Alaska 2009) ("[a]lthough Alaska statutes make an exception in some cases where the parent is incarcerated (in which case reasonable efforts are not required), ICWA has no exception for incarceration, and requires active efforts even when a parent is incarcerated"); *Jon S. v. State Dep't of Health & Soc. Servs.*, 212 P.3d 756, 763 (Alaska 2009) (court "look[s] 'to the state's involvement in its entirety[,]'" but a "parent's willingness to cooperate is relevant to determining whether the state has met its active efforts burden," and a parent's incarceration constitutes "a significant factor" that affects level of required active efforts); *Ben M. v. State Dep't of Health & Soc. Servs.*, 204 P.3d 1013, 1021 (Alaska 2009) ("[i]ncarceration can 'significantly affect[ ]' the scope of active efforts required, though it does not eliminate the requirement");

P.603, n.113.   Add the following to the beginning of the footnote:

Yvonne L. v. Ariz. Dep't of Econ. Sec., No. 1 CA-JV 10-0233, 2011 WL 2419857, at * 7 (Ariz. Ct. App. June 16, 2011) (holding that agency need not provide every imaginable service or program or force a parent to participate in services for a finding of active efforts); *Sandy B. v. State Dep't of Health & Soc. Servs.*, 216 P.3d 1180, 1188–89 (Alaska 2009) (identifying the "question before us" as "narrow"—*i.e.*, "[w]hen a child is born while [the agency] is involved with the family in an ongoing case, should the trial court view [the agency's] efforts toward each child in isolation rather than in the context of its efforts toward all of the children"—and answering it "'no'"); *In re JL*, 770 N.W.2d 853, 867 (Mich. 2009) (active-efforts requirement satisfied by admittedly compliant efforts made previously with respect to Indian child's siblings; "the question is whether the efforts made and the services provided in connection with the parent's other children are relevant to the parent's current situation and abilities so that they permit a current assessment of parental fitness as it pertains to the child who is the subject of the current proceeding"); *State ex rel. C.D.*, 200 P.3d 194, 205 (Utah Ct. App. 2008) (rejecting family services agency's attempt to rely on reunification services directed to mother as a basis to satisfy the active-efforts requirement as to grandfather Indian custodian since, *inter alia*, "construing the ICWA liberally and in favor of the Indians supports an interpretation that requires the State to provide more remedial services and rehabilitative programs for Indian parents and custodians, rather than fewer[,]" but concluding that such efforts would have been futile as to grandfather in light of his previous employment with, and training by, the family services agency itself);

P.603, n.114.   Add the following to line 1 of the footnote after "*E.g.,*":

In re Louis S., 774 N.W.2d 416, 425, 426 (Neb. Ct. App. 2009) ("the ICWA requirement of 'active efforts' requires more than the 'reasonable efforts' standard applicable in non-ICWA cases and that 'at least some efforts should be "culturally relevant"'" and must be determined through "a case-by-case analysis" that demands more than a showing of "passive services" where "'a plan is drawn up and the client must develop his or her own resources towards bringing it to fruition'"); *In re JL*, 770 N.W.2d 853, 865 (Mich. 2009) (citing, and concurring with, precedent from other states for the principle that "'active efforts' require more than the 'reasonable efforts' required under state law"); *In re Nicole B.*, 976 A.2d 1039, 1059–60 (Md. 2009) (deeming it unnecessary to resolve question whether ICWA's "active efforts" requirement more stringent than Maryland statute's "reasonable efforts" duty because agency's efforts satisfied ICWA standard); *In re K.B.*, 93 Cal. Rptr. 3d 751, 761, 763 (Ct. App. 2009) (where any reunification efforts would have been futile in view of father's sexual offender status, no obligation to make active efforts existed, and thus trial court's use of reasonable-efforts standard did not violate ICWA; as to mother's challenge to the parental rights termination order, the applicable standard was whether "the state caseworker takes the client through the steps of the plan rather than requiring that the plan be performed on its own" and was held to have been satisfied) (internal quotation marks omitted); *In re T.N.*, 203 P.3d 262, 263 (Colo. Ct. App. 2009) ("[t]he 'active efforts' standard is understood to impose on the agency an obligation greater than simply creating a reunification plan and requiring the client to execute it independently . . . [and] means that the agency must assist the client through the steps of a reunification"); *State ex rel. C.D.*, 200 P.3d 194, 206 (Utah Ct. App. 2008) ("[W]e join the majority of courts considering this issue that have held that the phrase active efforts connotes a more involved and less passive standard than that of reasonable efforts. We also believe this is the result Congress intended when it explicitly required 'active efforts' as part of the ICWA");

P.603, n.116.   Add the following to the beginning of the footnote:

Yvonne L. v. Ariz. Dep't of Econ. Sec., No. 1 CA-JV 10-0233, 2011 WL 2419857, at * 6, n.15 (Ariz. Ct. App. June 16, 2011) (holding that because clear and convincing evidence showed that agency had made active efforts to prevent the breakup of the Indian family, the court need not address the agency's claim that active efforts were different than "diligent efforts" required under state law); *People ex rel. J.I.H.*, 768 N.W.2d 168, 173 (S.D. 2009) (adhering to existing precedent for principle that "'active' efforts pursuant to ICWA [are] distinguished from 'reasonable' efforts, as required by the Adoption and Safe Families Act[,]" but finding it unnecessary to resolve "active efforts" issue "because there was no evidence that DSS's efforts were *unsuccessful* or that they *failed*, even though they were limited by Father's incarceration");

P.604, n.117.   **Add the following to line 1 of the footnote after "E.g.,":**

State ex rel. Children Youth & Families Dep't v. Arthur C., 251 P.3d 729, 739 (N.M. Ct. App. 2011);

P.604, n.118.   **Add the following to line 1 of the footnote after "E.g.,":**

Yvonne L. v. Ariz. Dep't of Econ. Sec., No. 1 CA-JV 10-0233, 2011 WL 2419857, at * 6 (Ariz. Ct. App. June 16, 2011) (adopting clear-and-convincing standard); *Pravat P. v. State Dep't of Health & Soc. Servs.*, 249 P.3d 264, 270 (Alaska 2011) (findings of fact are reviewed for clear error and questions of law are reviewed de novo; whether the department made active efforts as required by ICWA is a mixed question of law and fact); *Jon S. v. State Dep't of Health & Soc. Servs.*, 212 P.3d 756, 763 (Alaska 2009) (applying clear-and-convincing standard); *In re Vaughn R.*, 770 N.W.2d 795 (Wis. Ct. App. 2009) (adopting clear-and-convincing standard); *In re D.D.*, 897 N.E.2d 917, 923 (Ill. App. Ct. 2008) (adopting preponderance standard);

P.604, n.120.   **Add the following to line 6 of the footnote after "see also":**

In re C.C.M., 202 P.3d 971, 974 (Wash. Ct. App. 2009) (ICWA "explicitly does not employ a 'best interests' standard in this type of proceeding, which qualifies as an action for foster care placement[;]" standard instead supplied by § 1912(e)); *Marcia V. v. State Dep't of Health & Soc. Servs.*, 201 P.3d 496, 508 (Alaska 2009) ("The findings of a likelihood of serious emotional or physical damage [under § 1912(e)] are findings that must be made by the trial judge, not the expert witness. The expert testimony constitutes some of the evidence upon which the judge bases this finding. But it does not need to be the sole basis for that finding; it simply must support it");

Add the following to the end of the footnote before the period:

cf. In re Holly B., 92 Cal. Rptr. 3d 80, 84 (Ct. App. 2009) (although dependency proceeding constituted a foster care placement, order directing a minor to undergo psychological evaluation was unaffected by ICWA, since the statute "does not apply to related issues affecting the minor such as paternity, child support or, as in this case, a ruling on a petition for modification which affects only the information available to the department in making its decisions")

P.605, n.121.   **Add the following to line 1 of the footnote after "E.g.,":**

In re M.B., 107 Cal. Rptr. 3d 107, 115 (Ct. App. 2010) (qualified expert witness testimony itself need not be sufficient to warrant termination of parental rights but, instead, constitutes "but one factor considered by the trial court in deciding, beyond a reasonable doubt, that continued custody by the parents would result in serious physical or emotional damage to the child"); *In re T.C.*, 984 A.2d 549, 556 (Pa. Super. Ct. 2009) (affirming trial court's finding "that, although Father appears to be a good parent to his older daughter, the determinative factor regarding the subject children is the serious emotional trauma they would suffer if removed from the foster parents and returned to Father[,]" and rejecting "argument that the evidence of his recent sobriety would compel a reasonable fact finder to have reasonable doubt that returning the children to Father would cause them serious emotional harm"); *In re JL*, 770 N.W.2d 853, 870 (Mich. 2009) (although presuming parent's unfitness predicated on past conduct alone or "invocation of the doctrine of anticipatory neglect" would be improper under ICWA's reasonable doubt standard, "the evidence concerning respondent's past conduct established that she was an unfit parent in the past, and the current evidence revealed that she continued to make choices that demonstrated a lack of maturity and ability to care for a child"); *In re Vaughn R.*, 770 N.W.2d 795 (Wis. Ct. App. 2009) (§ 1912(f)'s reference to "continued custody" does negate its applicability to parental-rights-termination proceeding where the involved child has been in foster care for a significant period);

P.605, n.122.   Add the following to the beginning of the footnote:

In re Esther V., 248 P.3d 863, 872 (N.M. 2011) (holding that findings under § 1912(d) and (e) must be made at the adjudicatory hearing rather than earlier ex parte proceedings because that "is the procedural phase that affords the Indian parent and tribe the most procedural due process protection and best accommodates the requirements of § 1912");

Add the following to the end of the footnote after the period:

But see In re A.S., No. DA 10-0448, 2011 WL 1376311, at * 7–8 (Mont. April 12, 2011) (holding that parent had waived claim regarding timeliness of finding under § 1912(e) by not objecting until after the termination of her parental rights, and urging early compliance with § 1912(d) and (e)).

P.606, n.123.   Add the following to line 6 of the footnote after *"see also"*:

In re Louis S., 774 N.W.2d 416, 425, 429 (Neb. Ct. App. 2009) (applying BIA Guidelines); *In re Tamika R.*, 973 A.2d 547, 552 (R.I. 2009) (failure to offer any testimony from a qualified expert witness and to make a determination that placement with parent would likely result in serious emotional or physical damage to the child was not harmless error; *e.g.*, "[q]ualified expert testimony may well have been helpful in assessing the seriousness and cultural significance of [father's] marijuana use"); *In re T.W.F.*, 210 P.3d 174, 181 (Mont. 2009) ("[w]hile expert input is required in an ICWA case, the district court 'need not conform its decision to a particular piece of evidence or a particular expert's report or testimony as long as a reasonable person could have found, beyond a reasonable doubt, that the continued custody of the child by the parent

. . . is likely to result in serious emotional or physical damage to the child'"); *Steven H. v. Ariz. Dep't of Econ. Sec.*, 190 P.3d 180, 186 (Ariz. 2008) ("[I]n addition to any evidence establishing the state statutory grounds for dependency, ICWA requires qualified expert testimony that addresses the determination that the Indian child is at risk of future harm unless the child is removed from the parents' custody. But the statute does not require that the necessary expert testimony recite the specific language of § 1912(e); nor need such testimony be expressed in a particular way. As long as the expert testimony addresses the likelihood of future harm, it will suffice");

P.606, n.124.   Add the following to the beginning of the footnote after "*E.g.,*":

In re Emma J., 782 N.W.2d 330, 336–37 (Neb. Ct. App. 2010) (ordinarily applicable preponderance standard governed threshold determination of whether jurisdiction existed over Indian child under state statute identifying grounds for the exercise of juvenile court jurisdiction as to any child); *Timmons v. Arkansas Dep't of Human Servs.*, 2010 Ark. App. 418, 2010 WL 1904519 (May 12, 2010) (reviewing authority from other states on dual-burden-of-proof issue, and observing that "the better practice for the [trial] court would have been to employ a dual burden of proof to separate sets of findings"); *In re Parental Rights of N.J.*, 221 P.3d 1255, 1260–61 (Nev. 2009) (applying clear-and-convincing standard to state law-required findings and beyond-a-reasonable-doubt standard to ICWA-required findings in parental rights termination proceeding); *Dep't of Human Servs. v. K.C.J.*, 207 P.3d 423, 429–30 (Or. Ct. App. 2009) (rejecting agency's contention that state statute, which requires evidence beyond a reasonable doubt to support termination of parental rights when an Indian child is involved, applied only to determination of whether continued parental custody will likely result in serious emotional or physical damage; although sparse, legislative history "suggests quite strongly that the legislature understood that the effect of the law was to impose a reasonable doubt standard to all facts necessary to terminate parental rights when ICWA is applicable");

Add the following to line 7 of the footnote before the semi-colon:

, *aff'd*, 198 P.3d 1203, 1207 (Ariz. 2009) ("nearly every other state court that has considered this issue has concluded that ICWA allows states to specify the standard of proof for state-law findings distinct from the findings required by ICWA")

P.607, n.127.   Add the following to line 1 of the footnote after "*see*":

In re Interest of Ramon N., 789 N.W.2d 272, 280–81 (Neb. Ct. App. 2010) (holding that child's mother, although a member of the tribe, did not qualify as an expert witness in the absence of evidence that the tribal community recognized her as knowledgeable of Indian customs and childrearing practices, that she has substantial experience in the delivery of services to Indians, or that she is a professional person); *In re T.W.F.*, 210 P.3d 174, 180 (Mont. 2009) (Guidelines do not mean "that witness must have knowledge of the cultural standards of the particular tribe");

P.607, n.128.   Add the following to line 1 of the footnote after "E.g.,":

In re Welfare of L.N.B.-L., 237 P.3d 944, 960–61 (Wash. Ct. App. 2010) (finding a social worker qualified on the basis of ten years' experience with over 100 Indian families in an ICWA division, despite her lack of knowledge of the child's particular tribe's childrearing practices); *In re Interest of M.F.*, 225 P.3d 1177, 1185–86 (Kan. 2010) (applying BIA Guidelines, and finding two social workers failed to satisfy qualified expert witness requirements because neither possessed substantial education and experience in the area of her specialty; and declining to find noncompliance harmless because "it is difficult to conclude a procedural violation of the ICWA can be harmless in light of 25 U.S.C. § 1914" which authorizes collateral review and thereby "creates the potential of future invalidation of the foster care placement and termination of parental rights"); *In re Interest of Shayla H.*, 764 N.W.2d 119, 129 (Neb. Ct. App. 2009) (applying Guidelines; qualified-expert status not established where witness did not possess substantial experience in the delivery of child and family services to Indians, extensive knowledge of the tribe's childrearing practices, or credentials as a professional person with substantial education and experience in the area of her specialty); *Marcia V. v. State Dep't of Health & Soc. Servs.*, 201 P.3d 496, 503 (Alaska 2009) ("[w]hen the basis for termination is unrelated to Native culture and society and when any lack of familiarity with cultural mores will not influence the termination decision or implicate cultural bias in the termination proceeding, the qualifications of an expert testifying under § 1912(f) need not include familiarity with Native culture"); *Steven H. v. Ariz. Dep't of Econ. Sec.*, 190 P.3d 180, 185 (Ariz. 2008) (endorsing approach that determines need for knowledge of Indian childrearing and cultural practices, as opposed to simple possession of expertise in the relevant discipline generally, as "depending upon the basis urged for removal");

P.607, n.129.   Add the following to line 1 of the footnote after "E.g.,":

Brenda O. v. Ariz. Dep't of Econ. Sec., 244 P.3d 574, 578 (Ariz. Ct. App. 2010) (holding that psychologist was a qualified expert witness because he testified within his professional specialty regarding a parent's alcohol abuse, and cultural mores were not implicated because there was no evidence that a parent's alcoholism affects Indian children differently than any other child); *In re M.B.*, 107 Cal. Rptr. 3d 107, 114 (Ct. App. 2010) (absence of interview did not compromise qualified expert witness's testimony because, "unless interviews by the Indian expert with specific parties is relevant to the purpose of the expert's testimony—i.e., whether specific behavior patterns need to be placed in the context of Indian culture to determine whether they are likely to cause serious harm—the failure to interview the parents does not infect the trial court's judgment"); *Sandy B. v. State Dep't of Health & Soc. Servs.*, 216 P.3d 1180, 1191 (Alaska 2009) (clinical psychologist with doctorate degree "was qualified as an expert in psychology and his testimony was well within his expertise[,]" and his testimony was not "'compromised'" because it was received telephonically or otherwise improper because it was based on materials provided by agency); *Ben M. v. State Dep't of Health & Soc. Servs.*, 204 P.3d 1013, 1020 (Alaska 2009) (expert witness's opinion properly considered despite the absence of any interview with the child; "the requirement for expert testimony is that it support the ultimate conclusion[,]" and thus the "issues are whether the expert disregarded or was unaware of contrary evidence, and whether the testimony was so vague and generalized that the trial court clearly erred in according weight to it");

P.608, n.130.   Add the following to the beginning of the footnote:

Lucy J. v. State Dep't of Health & Social Servs., 244 P.3d 1099, 1118 (Alaska 2010) ("A witness can be qualified as an expert under ICWA because of her personal contact with Native cultures or experience working with such cultures."); *In re L.N.B.-L*, Nos. 28850-2-II & 38854-5-II, 2010 WL 3075179, at *20 (Wash. Ct. App. Aug. 3, 2010) (social worker with 13 years' experience, including ten years in the Indian child welfare division, qualified by her expertise despite the lack of any "particular training or education in [the involved tribe's] child-rearing practices"); *In re T.C.*, 984 A.2d 549, 555–56 (Pa. Super. Ct. 2009) (tribal welfare agency director constituted qualified expert who properly relied for her conclusions on case file prepared by agency social worker and the employee's updates); *In re Vaughn R.*, 770 N.W.2d 795 (Wis. Ct. App. 2009) (Guidelines applied in determining that social worker was not a qualified expert witness; her education background—bachelor's and masters' degrees in criminal justice—did not relate to the proof required under § 1912(f), while her employment "experience in monitoring the conditions imposed on parents for the return of their children [did] not suggest something beyond normal social work qualifications or functions");

P.609, n.131.   Add the following to line 1 of the footnote after "E.g.,":

In re L.N.B.-L, Nos. 28850-2-II & 38854-5-II, 2010 WL 3075179, at *19 (Wash. Ct. App. Aug. 3, 2010) (notwithstanding witness's difficulty describing tribe's "family unit," she qualified as qualified expert given her "official designation" by tribe as an expert—a conclusion otherwise bolstered by her long on-reservation residence and experience there in "the family services setting"); *In re D.D.*, 897 N.E.2d 917, 921 (Ill. App. Ct. 2008) (witness, although a Navajo Tribe member, was a qualified expert with respect to Cherokee Tribe child-rearing practices where he had "completed 40 hours of coursework on the history of the Cherokee Nation, possessed a bachelor's degree, . . . was currently working towards a master's degree[,]" had "attended courses conducted by the Cherokee Nation on the ICWA, and also participated in Cherokee pow-wows and holidays");

P.609, n.134.   Add the following to line 1 of the footnote before the period:

; *see In re S.L.J.*, 782 N.W.2d 549, 553 (Minn. 2010) (concluding that ICWA required appointment of counsel, and directing counties to pay fees without addressing issue of whether Secretary of the Interior should bear attorney fees under 25 U.S.C. § 1912(b)); *In re David H.*, 82 Cal. Rptr. 3d 81, 89 n.9 (Ct. App. 2008) (claim that counsel denied at two hearings subject to harmless-error-beyond-a-reasonable-doubt standard and not a *per se* reversal standard as argued by parent)

P.610, n.138.   Add the following to line 1 of the footnote after "see":

Empson-Laviolette v. Crago, 760 N.W.2d 793, 801, 802 (Mich. Ct. App. 2008) (withdrawal of consent to temporary guardianship authorized under § 1913(b), and state-law requirement that guardianship order remain in place until superseded by court order preempted under § 1921 insofar as it did not provide "a higher standard of protection to the Indian child's parent or Indian custodian[;]" any perceived conflict between definition of "foster care placement" and such withdrawal right must be resolved in favor of permitting withdrawal, since § 1901(1)(i) controls "whether the ICWA applies to a custody proceeding" but § 1913(b) "delineates the rights of the parent or Indian custodian who has consented to a 'foster care placement' of an Indian child");

Add the following to line 3 of the footnote after "cf.":

In re R.S., 101 Cal. Rptr. 3d 910, 923 (Ct. App. 2009) (although action began as involuntary dependency proceeding, "[a]fter the parents' voluntary relinquishment freed the minor for adoption through State Adoptions, the minor was effectively freed from the dependency proceedings to the extent they might result in involuntary foster care placement, guardianship, or adoptive placement following an involuntary termination of parental rights[,]" and the adoption agency "became subject to separate provisions of ICWA relating to voluntary relinquishments by the parents of an Indian child"); *In re J.M.*, 218 P.3d 1213, 1217 (Mont. 2009) (mother's consent to agency's assuming temporary legal custody after involuntary foster care placement proceeding commenced did not convert action into voluntary proceeding subject to requirements in 25 U.S.C. § 1913(a); mother "did not approach the Department voluntarily to give up custody as contemplated by § 1913" but, rather, "appeared at the hearing with her appointed counsel in light of the adversarial nature of the proceedings"); *In re Welfare of MG*, 201 P.3d 354, 358 (Wash. Ct. App. 2009) (same);

P.611, n.142.   Add the following to the end of the footnote before the period:

see also State ex rel. C.D., 200 P.3d 194, 211 (Utah Ct. App. 2008) (requiring placement preferences to be given effect, or good cause for not doing so, at the time of the initial "dispositional" determination that, under state law, could be held as early as 15 days after the "shelter hearing" required within 72 hours of the child's removal from the parent or Indian custodian; extensions of time permissible "only when [the family services agency] can demonstrate meaningful attempts to comply with the ICWA preferences along with some articulated plan for completing those preference obligations" in view of the fact that "the ICWA was adopted to prevent Indian children from spending even limited time separated from their Indian culture" and that "extending the duration of a noncompliant placement increases the risk of subsequent disruption and trauma ")

P.611, n.143.   Add the following to the beginning of the footnote:

In re M.B., 204 P.3d 1242, 1248 (Mont. 2009) (persons who adopted involved child's siblings deemed "extended family" on the basis of expert-witness testimony that "the tribe 'would consider other persons as extended family' beyond the list contained within ICWA's definition of 'extended family member'");

P.612, n.149.   Add the following to the end of the footnote:

One court has reviewed a finding regarding the diligence of an agency's search for an ICWA-preferred placement for clear error. *People ex rel. South Dakota Dep't of Soc. Servs.*, 795 N.W.2d 39, 44 (S.D. 2011).

P.612, n.150.   Add the following to line 1 of the footnote after "*E.g.,*":

In re B.B.A., 224 P.3d 1285, 1288 (Okla. Civ. App. 2009) ("[t]he persuasive language of the Guidelines authorizes reliance upon only one factor to establish the existence of good cause"); *In re M.B.*, 204 P.3d 1242, 1246 (Mont. 2009) (Guidelines deemed "persuasive" and applied; parental preference provision construed to have as its purpose protection of "the biological parents' confidentiality, if they so choose" and was given no weight where confidentiality was not at issue);

P.613, n.151.   Add the following to line 15 of the footnote after "*cf.*":

State ex rel. C.D., 200 P.3d 194, 211 n.29 (Utah Ct. App. 2008) (noting split among other states' courts, but deeming the issue "not before us today");

P.614, n.153.   Add the following to line 1 of the footnote after "*See*":

Dep't of Human Servs. v. Three Affiliated Tribes of Ft. Berthold Reservation, 238 P.3d 40, 51 (Or. Ct. App. 2010) (considering "the serious and lasting harm that will result from the removal of the children from their current home" and "the significant potential that the preferred caretakers will engage in conduct or conditions will exist in their home that would be seriously detrimental to the children"); *In re G.L.*, 99 Cal. Rptr. 3d 356, 368–69 (Ct. App. 2009) (departure from placement preferences warranted where suggested family member—the paternal grandmother—was not capable of providing requisite care; where child could not be placed "in an Indian foster home approved by the [child's] tribe because none existed[;]" and where "[i]n accordance with ICWA's third level of placement preferences, the court placed [the child] in an Indian foster home approved by a non-Indian licensing authority, where she had been living since she was taken into protective custody");

P.614, n.154.   Add the following to line 1 after *"Compare"*:

People ex rel. South Dakota Dep't of Soc. Servs., 795 N.W.2d 39, 44 (S.D. 2011) (holding that "clear and convincing" is the appropriate standard for a finding of good cause to deviate from the placement preferences);

Add the following to line 1 of the footnote after *"with"*:

In re B.B.A., 224 P.3d 1285, 1287 (Okla. Civ. App. 2009) (abuse-of-discretion standard applied); *In re N.M.*, 94 Cal. Rptr. 3d 220, 225 (Ct. App. 2009) (review of trial court's determination of good-faith issue subject to substantial-evidence standard);

P.614, n.155.   Add the following to line 1 after *"See"*:

State ex rel. Children Youth & Families Dep't v. Arthur C., 251 P.3d 729, 739 (N.M. Ct. App. 2011) (addressing parent's unpreserved ICWA claims because parent has ability under § 1914 to move to invalidate proceedings that do not comply with certain ICWA requirements); *In re Interest of Ramon N.*, 789 N.W.2d 272, 277–78 (Neb. Ct. App. 2010) (holding that adjudication order had been a final appealable order and was not subject to collateral attack in appeal from a subsequent order);

P.615, n.160.   Add the following to the beginning of the footnote:

In re Adoption of A.B., 245 P.3d 711, 720 (Utah 2010) (holding that ICWA does not preempt state-law notice of appeal requirements);

Chapter 14
State-Tribal Cooperative Agreements

P.622, n.10.   **Add the following to line 2 of the footnote after *"see also"*:**

N.M. Stat. Ann. §§ 11-18-1 to -5 (State-Tribal Collaboration Act adopted in 2009 and requiring New Mexico state agencies to establish policies and appoint tribal liaisons to promote effective communication and collaboration between that state agencies and tribes; providing for training and an annual summit);

P.624, n.16.   **Add the following to line 1 of the footnote after *"See, e.g.,"*:**

Memphis Biofuels, LLC v. Chickasaw Nation Indus., Inc., 585 F.3d 917, 920 (6th Cir. 2009) (suit against tribal corporation dismissed, despite contractual provision expressly waiving corporation's sovereign immunity, because required tribal board approval had not been obtained);

P.624, n.17.   **Add the following to the second-to-last line of the footnote after *"see generally"*:**

Brian Pierson, *Resolving A Perilous Uncertainty: The Right of Tribes to Convey Fee Simple Lands,* 57-APR Fed. Law. 49 (2010) (discussing whether Nonintercourse Act constraints on alienability apply to transfers of land held in fee by tribes);

P.632.   **Add the following new footnote 59.1 to the end of the first sentence in the first full paragraph of the text:**

[59.1] *See generally* Marren Sanders, *Ecosystem Co-Management Agreements: A Study of Nation Building or a Lesson on an Erosion of Tribal Sovereignty?,* 15 Buff. Envtl. L.J. 97, 132–163 (2007–2008) (providing case studies of the Columbia River Inter-Tribal Fish and Great Lakes Indian Fish and Wildlife Commissions and the Nez Perce gray wolf management program, together with related inter-sovereign agreements); Angelique EagleWoman, *Tribal Hunting and Fishing Lifeways and Tribal-State Relations in Idaho,* 46 Idaho L. Rev. 81,

115–16 (2009) (discussing wildlife agreements between tribes and the State of Idaho).

P.633, n. 64.   Add the following to the end of the footnote before the period:

; Amanda M. Murphy, *A Tale of Three Sovereigns: The Nebulous Boundaries of the Federal Government, New York State, and the Seneca Nation of Indians Concerning State Taxation of Indian Reservation Cigarette Sales to Non-Indians*, 79 Fordham L. Rev. 2301 (April 2011) (detailing cigarette tax disputes in New York State and advocating resolution of such disputes through negotiating government-to-government agreements, as in Washington State)

P.633, n. 66.   Add the following to the end of the footnote:

The Adam Walsh Act has given rise to discussions about tribal-state cooperative agreements. Chapter 4, part I.A.1 nn.13–16 & accompanying text; *see generally* Brian P. Dimmer, *How Tribe and State Cooperative Agreements Can Save the Adam Walsh Act From Encroaching Upon Tribal Sovereignty*, 92 Marq. L. Rev. 385 (2008) (arguing that the Adam Walsh Act should be amended to require cooperative agreements to carry out the Act's required sex offender registration and notification rather than providing for state authority—either under Public Law 280 or whether non–Public Law 280 tribes do not implement tribal programs); Virginia Davis & Kevin Washburn, *Sex Offender Registration in Indian Country*, 6 Ohio St. J. Crim. L. 3 (2008) (discussing impact of Adam Walsh Act on existing cross-deputization agreements). Another area for collaboration is developing in cooperative agreements between state and tribal courts. *See generally* Hon. Korey Wahwassuck *et al., Building a Legacy of Hope: Perspectives on Joint Tribal-State Jurisdiction*, 36 Wm. Mitchell L. Rev. 859 (2010) (describing Joint Powers Agreement between Minnesota state court and Leech Lake Band of Ojibwe Tribal Court to form DWI "Wellness Court" with joint jurisdiction over tribal members and non-Indians, and discussing other examples of tribal-state cooperation). For an argument against cross-jurisdictional law enforcement agreements, *see* Andrew G. Hill, *Another Blow to Tribal Sovereignty: A Look at Cross-Jurisdictional Law Enforcement Agreements Between Indian Tribes and Local Communities*, 34 Am. Indian L. Rev. 291 (2009–2010) (suggesting that agreements authorizing on-reservation law enforcement by non-Indians disadvantage tribes in various ways, including subjecting Indians to bias from non-Indian officers and causing confusion in tribal courts).

P.635, n.71.   Add the following to line 1 of the footnote before the period:

; *see generally* Blake R. Bertagna, *Reservations About Extending Bivens to Reservations: Seeking Monetary Relief Against Tribal Law Enforcement Officers for Constitutional Violations*, 29 Pace L. Rev. 585, 610–618 (2009) (discussing application of FTCA to tribal officers when acting under color of federal law pursuant to Bureau of Indian Affairs special law enforcement officer commission, and distinguishing the "substantive cause of action" available for constitutional violation under *Bivens v. Six Unknown Named Agents*, 403 U.S. 388 (1971))

P.635   Add the following new paragraph to the text after the paragraph ending with footnote "71":

The Tribal Law and Order Act of 2010,[71.1] became effective on July 29, 2010. Section 221 of the Act provides concurrent federal jurisdiction in Public Law 280 states to prosecute violations of 18 U.S.C., sections 1152 and 1153 at the request of an Indian tribe and after consultation with and consent by the United States Attorney General. Section 222 of the Act allows the United States Attorney General to provide technical and other assistance to state, tribal and local governments that enter into cooperative agreements relating to mutual aid, hot pursuit of suspects and cross-deputization to improve law enforcement in Indian country. Section 223 allows law enforcement personnel of an Indian tribe to satisfy training standards at a state or local government police academy.

[71.1]   Pub. L. No. 111-211, 124 Stat. 2258 (2010)

P.635, n.73.   Add the following to line 13 of the footnote after "E.g.,":

Erica Shively, Note, *The Future of Quantifying Tribal Water Rights in North Dakota*, 84 N.D. L. Rev. 455 (2008); Robert T. Anderson, *Indian Water Rights, Practical Reasoning, and Negotiated Settlements*, 98 Cal L. Rev. 1133 (August 2010) (providing overview of caselaw framework regarding Indian water rights and trend toward congressionally-approved water rights settlements; the article includes an Appendix of water rights settlements); Dena Marshall & Janet Neuman, *Seeking a Shared Understanding of the Human Right to Water: Collaborative Use Agreements in the Umatilla and Walla Walla Basins of the Pacific Northwest*, 47 Willamette L. Rev. 361 (Spring 2011) (discussing history and benefits of the regional Umatilla Basin agreement and proposed Walla Walla water basin agreements with tribal, federal state, local governments and irrigators);

P.637.   Add the following new footnote 76.1 to the end of the carryover paragraph:

[76.1]   *See generally* Mary Christina Wood & Matthew O'Brien, *Tribes as Trustees Again (Part II): Evaluating Four Models of Tribal Participation in the Conservation Trust Movement*, 27 Stan. Envtl. L.J. 477, 479 (2008) (discussing transactional paradigms, as well as negotiating and drafting considerations, for tribes to pursue land conservation through public and private partnerships in light of "the Native environmental sovereignty movement aimed at protecting environmental resources located off the reservations[] and the conservation trust movement created in response to the deficiencies of environmental law"); Joanna M. Wagner, *Improving Native American Access to Federal Funding for Economic*

Development Through Partnerships with Rural Communities, 32 Am. Indian L. Rev. 525, 551, 588 (2007–2008) (although "Indians and their non-Indian neighbors have not historically been allies, and the rift between Indian and rural communities runs deep and is not easily overcome by pointing out their common characteristics and experiences[,]" tribes and rural communities have "things to gain by working with the other" given an often overlapping set of governmental challenges caused by, *inter alia*, remoteness, small populations and relative lack of political power).

P.646. **Add the following new paragraphs after the first paragraph:**

Implementation of the settlement encountered challenges resulting in further agreement, legislation and litigation. In 1996, it became apparent that the portion of the settlement regarding the Animas and La Plata Rivers could not be implemented. Endangered Species Act issues, water quality problems, and other concerns halted the construction of Phase I of the Animas–La Plata Project. Colorado's Governor Romer and Lt. Governor Schoettler initiated a lengthy public process to bring the different interests together to discuss solutions. After additional NEPA review, a substantially scaled-down Project with reduced depletions from the Animas and La Plata Rivers was the environmentally preferred alternative. The reduced amount will be shared by the Southern Ute Tribe, Ute Mountain Ute Tribe, and Navajo Nation, and also will provide a long term municipal water supply to non-Indians in southwest Colorado and northern New Mexico. To authorize waiver of the tribes' reserved rights claims for this reduced amount of water, Congress passed the Colorado Ute Settlement Act Amendments of 2000.[88.1] Water from the reduced Project may only be used for municipal and industrial purposes.[88.2] Congress provided substitute benefits of $20 million to each Ute Tribe over a period of five years for their changed water supply.[88.3]

In August 2002, the Department of the Interior filed applications in the Colorado Water Court to amend the tribal water rights decrees to reflect the revised settlement terms. A citizens group challenged the proposed modifications, protesting both the tribal decrees and the entire Project. After extended litigation, the Colorado Water Court found against the objector and entered the amended decrees. The decision was upheld on appeal.[88.4] The Animas–La Plata Project began pumping water from the Animas River to Lake Nighthorse in April, 2009.

[88.1] Colorado Ute Settlement Act Amendments of 2000, Pub. L. No. 106-554, § 301, 114 Stat. 2763, 2763A-258 (2000).

[88.2] *Id.* § 302(a)(1)(C)(i).

[88.3] *Id.* § 303.

[88.4] *In the Matter of the Application for Water Rights of the United States of America (Bureau of Indian Affairs, Southern Ute and Ute Mountain Ute Indian Tribes) for*

Claims to the Animas River, Nos. W-1603-76F *et al.* (La Plata County Dist. Ct., Colo. Water Div. 7) (decree filed Nov. 9, 2006 and amended Feb. 8, 2007), *appeal dismissed*, No. 07SA100 (Colo. S. Ct. Oct. 2, 2008).

P.658, n.105.   Add the following to the end of the footnote:

Agreements entered into under 25 U.S.C. § 1919 of the Indian Child Welfare Act have been construed by at least one court to encompass reservation-related state administration of foster care programs under Title IV-E of the Social Security Act, 42 U.S.C. §§ 670–679c, for purposes of investigating and substantiating allegations of child abuse by a licensed foster home tribal member provider. *In re Hanna*, 227 P.3d 596, 600 (Mont. 2010) ("The substantiation proceeding, which is an adjudication of Hanna's rights, . . . arose directly from [the provider's] 'care' of an Indian child, M.S. As such, it fits within the language of § 1919(a)").

Table of Cases

Table of Codes, Public Laws, and Regulations

Bibliography

Albert, Michelle Kay, Note, *Obligations and Opportunities to Protect Native American Sacred Sites Located on Public Lands,* 40 Colum. Hum. Rts. L. Rev. 479 (2009)

Anderson, Robert T., *Indian Water Rights, Practical Reasoning, and Negotiated Settlements,* 98 Cal. L. Rev. 1133 (2010)

Anderson, Terry L. & Dominic P. Parker, *Sovereignty, Credible Commitments, and Economic Development on American Indian Reservations,* 51 J.L. & Econ. 641 (2008)

Banker, Paul A. & Christopher Grgurich, *The Plains Commerce Bank Decision and Its Further Narrowing of the Montana Exceptions as Applied to Tribal Court Jurisdiction Over Non-member Defendants,* 36 Wm. Mitchell L. Rev. 565 (2010)

Barber, Drew K., Note, *The Power of Indian Tribes to Tax the Income of Professional Athletes and Entertainers Who Perform in Indian Country,* 41 Conn. L. Rev. 1785 (2009)

Barnum, Cassandra, Note: *A Single Penny, an Inch of Land, or an Ounce of Sovereignty: The Problem of Tribal Sovereignty and Water Quality Regulation under the Maine Indian Claims Settlement Act,* 37 Ecology L. Q. 1159 (2010)

Berger, Bethany R., *Red: Racism and the American Indian,* 56 UCLA L. Rev. 591 (2009)

Bertagna, Blake R., *Reservations About Extending Bivens to Reservations: Seeking Monetary Relief Against Tribal Law Enforcement Officers for Constitutional Violations,* 29 Pace L. Rev. 585 (2009)

Blumm, Michael C. & Jane G. Steadman, *Indian Treaty Fishing Rights and Habitat Protection: The Martinez Decision Supplies a Resounding Judicial Reaffirmation,* 49 Nat. Resources J. 653 (2009)

Boylan, Virginia W., *Reflections on IGRA 20 Years After Enactment,* 42 Ariz. St. L.J. 1, (2010)

Braccio, Audrey Bryant, Special Feature: *How the Anti-Gaming Backlash is Redefining Tribal Government Functions,* 34 Am. Indian L. Rev. 171 (2009/2010)

Brand, Emily, *The Struggle to Exercise a Treaty Right: An Analysis of the Makah Tribe's Path to Whale,* 32 Environs Envtl. L. & Pol'y J. 287 (Spring 2009)

Bryar, Jeremiah A., Comment, *What Goes Around, Comes Around: How Indian Tribes Can Profit in the Aftermath of Seminole Tribe and Florida Prepaid,* 13 Marq. Intell. Prop. L. Rev. 229 (2009)

Bucher, Emily, Case Comment, *Narrowed Lens, Clearer Focus: Considering the Use of De Novo Review in Indian Child Welfare Proceedings—In re Welfare of Child of T.T.B.,* 34 Wm. Mitchell L. Rev. 1429 (2009)

Candrian, Jeff, Note & Comment: *Building With Blinders On: How Policymakers Ignored Indian Water Rights to the Colorado, Setting the Stage for the Navajo Claim*, 22 Colo. J. Int'l Envtl. L. & Pol'y 159 (2011)

Carter, John B., *Montana Groundwater Law in the Twenty-First Century*, 70 Mont. L. Rev. 221 (2009)

Carvell, Charles, *Indian Reserved Water Rights: Impending Conflict or Coming Reapprochement Between the State of North Dakota and North Dakota Indian Tribes*, 85 N.D. L. Rev. 1 (2009)

Chaffee, Eric C., *Business Organizations and Tribal Self-Determination: A Critical Reexamination of the Alaska Native Claims Settlement Act*, 25 Alaska L. Rev. 107 (2008)

Christie, Thomas W., *An Introduction to the Federal Tort Claims Act in Indian Self-Determination Act Contracting*, 71 Mont. L. Rev. 115 (2010)

Clarkson, Gavin, *Wall Street Indians: Information Asymmetry and Barriers to Tribal Capital Market Access*, 12 Lewis & Clark L. Rev. 943 (2008)

Clinton, Robert N., *Enactment of the Indian Gaming Regulatory Act of 1988: The Return of the Buffalo to Indian Country or Another Federal Usurpation of Tribal Sovereignty?*, 42 Ariz. St. L.J. 17 (2010)

Comment, *The Legacy of Solem v. Bartlett: How Courts Have Used Demographics to Bypass Congress and Erode the Basic Principles of Indian Law*, 84 Wash. L. Rev. 723 (2009)

Cordiano, Benjamin J., *Unspoken Assumptions: Examining Tribal Jurisdiction Over Nonmembers Nearly Two Decades After Duro v. Reina*, 41 Conn. L. Rev. 265 (2008)

Cornell, Stephen & Joseph P. Kalt, *Sovereignty and Nation-Building: The Development Challenge in Indian Country Today*, 22 Am. Indian Culture & Res. J. 187 (1998)

Coursen, David F., *EPA's New Tribal Strategy*, 38 Envtl. L. Rep. News & Analysis 10643 (2008)

Cowan, Antonia, *You Can't Get There from Here: IGRA Needs Reinvention into a Relevant Statute for a Mature Industry*, 17 Vill. Sports & Ent. L.J. 309 (2010)

Cryne, Julia A., Comment, *NAGPRA Revisited: A Twenty-Year Review of Repatriation Efforts*, 34 Am. Indian. L. Rev. 99 (2010)

Cushner, Quintin and Jon M. Sands, *Tribal Law and Order Act of 2010: A Primer With Reservations*, 34 Champion 38 (2010)

DaCosta, Courtney J.A., Note, *When "Turnabout" Is Not "Fair Play": Tribal Immunity Under the Indian Gaming Regulatory Act*, 97 Geo. L.J. 515 (2009)

Davidson, Michael, Comment, *United States v. Friday and the Future of Native American Religious Challenges to the Bald and Golden Eagle Protection Act*, 86 Denv. U. L. Rev. 1133 (2009)

Davies, Lincoln T., *2009 Skull Valley Crossroads: Reconciling Native Sovereignty and the Federal Trust*, 68 Md. L. Rev. 290 (2009)

Davis, Ethan, *An Administrative Trail of Tears: Indian Removal*, 50 Am. J. Legal Hist. 49 (2010)

Davis, Virginia & Kevin Washburn, *Sex Offender Registration in Indian Country*, 6 Ohio St. J. Crim. L. 3 (2008)

Dimmer, Brian P., *How Tribe and State Cooperative Agreements Can Save the Adam Walsh Act from Encroaching Upon Tribal Sovereignty*, 92 Marq. L. Rev. 385 (2008)

Dreveskracht, Ryan David, *Native Nation Economic Development via the Implementation of Solar Projects: How to Make it Work*, 68 Wash. & Lee L. Rev. 27 (2011).

Ducheneaux, Franklin, *The Indian Gaming Regulatory Act: Background and Legislative History*, 42 Ariz. St. L.J. 99 (2010)

EagleWoman, Angelique, *Tribal Hunting and Fishing Lifeways & Tribal-State Relations in Idaho*, 46 Idaho L. Rev. 81 (2009)

EagleWoman, Angelique A., *Tribal Values of Taxation Within Tribalist Economic Theory*, 18-FALL Kan. J.L. & Pub. Pol'y 1 (2008)

Endreson, Douglas B. L., *Reconciling the Sovereignty of Indian Tribes in Civil Matters with the Montana Line of Cases*, 55 Vill. L. Rev. 863 (2010)

Ennis, Samuel E., *Implicit Divestiture and the Supreme Court's (Re)Construction of the Indian Canons*, 35 Vt. L. Rev. 623 (2011)

Ennis, Samuel E., *Reaffirming Indian Tribal Court Criminal Jurisdiction Over Non-Indians: An Argument for Statutory Abrogation of Oliphant*, 57 UCLA L. Rev. 553 (2009)

Erickson, Jessica M., Comment, *Live and Letting Die: The Biopolitical Effect of Navajo Nation v. U.S. Forest Service*, 33 Seattle U. L. Rev. 463 (2010)

Ezra, David Alan, *Doe v. Kamehameha Schools: A "Discrete and Insular Minority" in Hawai'i Seventy Years After Carolene Products?*, 30 U. Haw. L. Rev. 295 (2008)

Fenner, Benjamin, *Indian Country in Cyber Space: Tribal Tax and Regulatory Jurisdiction and Online Business*, 12 No. 5 J. Internet L. 3 (2008)

Fisher, William, Note, *The Culverts Opinion and the Need for a Broader Property-Based Construct*, 23 J. Envtl. L. & Litig. 491 (2008)

Fletcher, Ezekiel J.N., *De Facto Judicial Preemption of Tribal Labor and Preemption Law*, 2008 Mich. St. L. Rev. 435

Fletcher, Ezekiel J.N., *Negotiating Meaningful Concessions from States in Gaming Compacts to Further Tribal Economic Development: Satisfying the "Economic Benefits" Test*, 54 S.D. L. Rev. 419 (2009)

Fletcher, Matthew L.M., *Indian Tribal Businesses and the Off-Reservation Market*, 12 Lewis & Clark L. Rev. 1047 (2008)

Fletcher, Matthew L.M., *Factbound and Splitless: The Certiorari Process as Barrier to Justice for Indian Tribes*, 51 Ariz. L. Rev. 933 (2009)

Florey, Katherine J., *Indian Country's Borders: Territoriality, Immunity, and the Construction of Tribal Sovereignty*, 51 B.C. L. Rev. 595, 609 (2010)

Florey, Katherine, *Sovereign Immunity's Penumbras: Common Law, "Accident," and Policy in the Development of Sovereign Immunity Doctrine*, 43 Wake Forest L. Rev. 765 (2008)

Fromherz, Nicholas A. & Joseph W. Mead, *Equal Standing with States: Tribal Sovereignty and Standing After Massachusetts v. EPA*, 29 Stan. Envtl. L.J. 130 (2010)

Garcia, Ryan William Nohea, *Who is Hawaiian, What Begets Federal Recognition, and How Much Blood Matters*, 11 Asian-Pac. L. & Policy J. 85, 162 (2008)

Gardina, Jackie, *Federal Preemption: A Roadmap for the Application of Tribal Law in State Courts*, 35 Am. Indian L. Rev. 1 (2010–2011)

Garry, Patrick M., Candice J. Spurlin, and Derek A. Nelsen, *Wind Energy in Indian Country: A Study of the Challenges and Opportunities Facing South Dakota Tribes*, 54 S.D. L. Rev. 448 (2009)

Goldsby, Aubri, Note, *The McCarran Amendment and Groundwater: Why Washington State Should Require Inclusion of Groundwater in General Stream Adjudications Involving Federal Reserved Water Rights*, 86 Wash. L. Rev. 185 (2011)

Gover, Kevin & Tom Gede, *The States as Trespassers in a Federal-Tribal Relationship: A Historical Critique of Tribal-State Compacting Under IGRA*, 42 Ariz. St. L.J. 185 (2010)

Gover, Kirsty, *Comparative Tribal Constitutionalism: Membership Governance in Australia, Canada, New Zealand, and the United States*, 35 Law &. Soc. Inquiry 689 (2010)

Gover, Kirsty, *Genealogy as Continuity: Explaining the Growing Tribal Preference for Descent Rules in Membership Governance in the United States*, 33 Am. Indian L. Rev. 243 (2008–2009)

Gregory, Liana, Note, *"Technically Open": The Debate Over Native American Reserved Groundwater Rights*, 28 J. Land Resources & Envtl. L. 361 (2008)

Grijalva, James M., *EPA's Indian Policy at Twenty-Five*, 25-SUM Nat. Resources & Env't 12 (2010)

Gunn, Steven J., *The Native American Graves Protection and Repatriation Act at Twenty: Reaching the Limits of Our National Consensus*, 36 Wm. Mitchell L. Rev. 503 (2010)

Gutierrez, Guadalupe, Note, *Jurisdictional Ambiguities Among Sovereigns: The Impact of the Indian Gaming Regulatory Act on Criminal Jurisdiction on Tribal Lands*, 26 Ariz. J. Int'l & Comp. L. 229 (2009)

Haddock, David D., *To Tax Tribes or Not to Tax Tribes? That Is the Question*, 12 Lewis & Clark L. Rev. 971 (2009)

Hagen, Alex M., *From Formal Separation to Functional Equivalence: Tribal-Federal Dual Sovereignty and the Sixth-Amendment Right to Counsel*, 54 S.D. L. Rev. 129 (2009)

Halldin, Amber, *Restoring the Victim and the Community: A Look at the Tribal Response to Sexual Violence Committed by Non-Indians in Indian Country Through Non-Criminal Approaches*, 84 N.D. L. Rev. 1 (2008)

Handler, Matthew, *Tribal Law and Disorder: A Look At a System of Broken Justice in Indian Country and the Steps Needed to Fix It*, 75 Brook L. Rev. 261 (2009)

Hart, Gideon M., *Crisis in Indian Country: An Analysis of the Tribal Law and Order Act of 2010*, 23 Regent U. L. Rev. 139 (2010–2011)

Haskins, Nathaniel T., Note, *Framing Current Jurisdiction Issues in the Self-Determination Era: Accepting the First Circuit's Analysis but Rejecting Its Application to Preserve Tribal Sovereignty*, 32 Am. Indian L. Rev. 441 (2007–2008)

Hayden, James F. *et al.*, *New Bonds Available to Tribes to Finance Hotels and Other Amenities*, 13 Gaming L. Rev. & Econ. 217 (2009)

Hill, Andrew G., *Another Blow to Tribal Sovereignty: A Look at Cross-Jurisdictional Law Enforcement Agreements Between Indian Tribes and Local Communities*, 34 Am. Indian L. Rev. 291 (2009–2010)

Hill, Sean, Note, *Sunshine in Indian Country: A Pro-FOIA View of Klamath Water Users*, 32 Am. Indian L. Rev. 463 (2007–2008)

Johnson, Aaron Drue, Comment: *Just Say No (To American Capitalism): Why American Indians Should Reject the Model Tribal Secured Transactions Act and Other Attempts to Promote Economic Assimilation*, 35 Am. Indian L. Rev. 107 (2010/2011)

Key, James E., *This Land Is My Land: The Tension Between Federal Law and the Religious Freedom Restoration Act*, 65 Air Force L. Rev. 51 (2010)

Koppelman, Carol B., *Anderson v. Evans: The Ninth Circuit Harmonizes Treaty Rights and the Marine Mammal Protection Act*, 16 Hastings W.-Nw. J. Envtl. L. & Pol'y 353 (2010)

Kowalski, Tonya, *The Forgotten Sovereigns*, 36 Fla. St. U. L. Rev. 765 (2009)

Kronk, Elizabeth Ann, *Alternative Energy Development in Indian Country: Lighting the Way for the Seventh Generation*, 46 Idaho L. Rev. 449 (2010)

Kuo, Angela (Riya), *Let Her Will Be Done: The Role of the Kamehameha Policy in Promoting Native Hawaiian Self-Determination*, 13 Asian Pac. Am. L.J. 72 (2008)

Kuzenski, John C., *The Paving Principle of Good Intentions? Calls for Reform of the Indian Gaming Regulatory Act and the Private Game Theory Equilibrium Opposing Them*, 30 N.C. Cent. L. Rev. 168 (2008)

Lane, David L., Comment, *Twice Bitten: Denial of the Right to Counsel in Successive Prosecutions by Separate Sovereigns*, 45 Hous. L. Rev. 1869 (2009)

Langridge, Ruth, *The Right to Habitat Protection*, 29 Pub. Land & Resources L. Rev. 41 (2008)

LeBeau, Tracey A., *The Green Road Ahead: Renewable Energy Takes a Stumble But Is on the Right Path, Possibly Right Through Indian Country*, 56-APR Fed. Law. 38 (2009)

Lewerenz, Dan & Padraic McCoy, *The End of "Existing Indian Family" Jurisprudence: Holyfield at 20, In the Matter of A.J.S., and the Last Gasps of a Dying Doctrine*, 36 Wm. Mitchell L. Rev. 684 (2010)

Lewis, Brian L., *A Day Late and a Dollar Short: Section 2719 of the Indian Gaming Regulatory Act, the Interpretation of its Exceptions and the Part 292 Regulations*, 12 T.M. Cooley J. Prac. & Clinical L. 147 (2010)

Lewis, Brian L., *So Close, Yet So Far Away: A Comparative Analysis of Indian Status in Canada and the United States*, 18 Willamette J. Int'l. L. & Disp. Resol. 38 (2010)

Limas, Vicki J., *The Tuscagornization of the Tribal Workforce*, 2008 Mich. St. L. Rev. 467

Long, Larry, et al., *Understanding Contextual Differences in American Indian Criminal Justice*, 32 Am. Indian Culture & Res. J. 41 (2008)

Marshall, Dena and Janet Neuman, *Seeking a Shared Understanding of the Human Right to Water: Collaborative Use Agreements in the Umatilla and Walla Walla Basins of the Pacific Northwest*, 47 Willamette L. Rev. 361 (2011)

McGee, Jack B., *Subsistence Hunting and Fishing in Alaska: Does ANILCA's Rural Subsistence Priority Really Conflict With the Alaska Constitution?*, 27 Alaska L. Rev. 221 (2010).

McMillin, Christopher, *Failure to Object: Tribal Waiver of Immunity by Participation in Arbitration*, 2009 J. Disp. Resol. 517

Meek, Aaron F.W., *The Conflict Between State Tests of Tribal Entity Immunity and the Congressional Policy of Indian Self-Determination*, 35 Am. Indian L. Rev. 141 (2010/2011)

Meister, Alan P., Kathryn R.L. Rand & Steven Andrew Light, *Indian Gaming and Beyond: Tribal Economic Development and Diversification*, 54 S.D. L. Rev. 375 (2009)

Merjian, Armen H., *An Unbroken Chain of Injustice: The Dawes Act, Native American Trusts, and Cobell v. Salazar*, 46 Gonzaga L. Rev. 609 (2010–11)

Morisset, Mason D. & Carly A. Summers, *Clear Passage: The Culvert Case Decision as a Foundation for Habitat Protection and Preservation*, 1 Bellwether: The Seattle J. Envtl. L. & Pol'y 29 (2009)

Moylan, Mary Beth, *Sovereign Rules of the Game: Requiring Campaign Finance Disclosure in the Face of Tribal Sovereign Immunity*, 20 B.U. Pub. Int. L. J. 1 (2010)

Murphy, Amanda M., Note, *A Tale of Three Sovereigns: The Nebulous Boundaries of the Federal Government, New York State, and the Seneca Nation of Indians Concerning State Taxation of Indian Reservation Cigarette Sales to Non-Indians*, 79 Fordham L. Rev. 2301 (2011).

Murphy, Matthew, Note, *Betting the Rancheria: Environmental Protections as Bargaining Chips Under the Indian Gaming Regulatory Act*, 36 B.C. Envtl. Aff. L. Rev. 171 (2009)

Oakley, Katharine C., *Defining Indian Status for the Purpose of Federal Criminal Jurisdiction*, 35 Am. Indian L. Rev. 177 (2010)

Oeser, Michael D., *Tribal Citizen Participation in State and National Politics: Welcome Wagon or Trojan Horse?*, 36 Wm. Mitchell L. Rev. 793 (2010)

Ottem, Sidney P., *The General Adjudication of the Yakima River: Tributaries for the Twenty-First Century and a Changing Climate*, 23 J. Envtl. L. & Litig. 275 (2008)

Painter-Thorne, Suzanne D., *If You Build It, They Will Come: Preserving Tribal Sovereignty in the Face of Indian Casinos and the New Premium on Tribal Membership*, 14 Lewis & Clark L. Rev. 311 (Spring 2010)

Panel discussion, *Paternalism or Protection? Federal Review of Tribal Economic Decisions in Indian Gaming*, 12 Gaming L. Rev. & Econ. 435 (2008)

Perdue, Kimberly C., Comment, *The Changing Scope of the United States' Trust Duties to American Indian Tribes: Navajo Nation v. United States*, 80 U. Colo. L. Rev. 487 (2009)

Persaud, Kyle, *A Permit to Practice Religion for Some but Not for Others: How the Federal Government Violates Religious Freedom When It Grants Eagle Feathers Only to Indian Tribe Members*, 36 Ohio N. U. L. Rev. 115 (2010)

Pierson, Brian, *Resolving a Perilous Uncertainty: The Right of Tribes to Convey Fee Simple Lands*, 57-APR Fed. Law. 49 (2010)

Plaut, Ethan, Comment, *Tribal-Agency Confidentiality: A Catch-22 for Sacred Site Management?*, 36 Ecology L.Q. 137 (2009)

Pommersheim, Frank, *At the Crossroads: A New and Unfortunate Paradigm of Tribal Sovereignty*, 55 S.D. L. Rev. 48 (2010)

Puzz, Dennis, Jr., *Untangling the Jurisdictional Web: Determining Indian Child Welfare Jurisdiction in the State of Wisconsin*, 36 Wm. Mitchell L. Rev. 724 (2010)

Quasius, Marie, Note, *Native American Rape Victims: Desperately Seeking an Oliphant-Fix*, 93 Minn. L. Rev. 1902 (2009)

Rand, Kathryn R.L., Alan P. Meister & Steven Andrew Light, *Questionable Federal "Guidance" on Off-Reservation Indian Gaming: Legal and Economic Issues*, 12 Gaming L. Rev. & Econ. 194 (2008)

Reinhard, Taylor, Comment, *Advancing Tribal Law Through "Treatment as a State" Under the Obama Administration: American Indians May Also Find Help from Their Legal Relative, Louisiana—No Blood Quantum Necessary*, 23 Tul. Envtl. L.J. 537 (2010)

Rhoan, Erick J., Comment, *What Congress Gives, Congress Takes Away: Tribal Sovereign Immunity and the Threat of Agroterrorism*, 19 San Joaquin Agric. L. Rev. 137 (2010)

Rice, G. William, *The Indian Reorganization Act, the Declaration on the Rights of Indigenous Peoples, and a Proposed Carcieri "Fix": Updating the Trust Land Acquisition Process*, 45 Idaho L. Rev. 575 (2009)

Rice, G. William, *Some Thoughts on the Future of Indian Gaming*, 42 Ariz. St. L.J. 219 (2010)

Richotte, Keith, Jr., *Legal Pluralism and Tribal Constitutions*, 36 Wm. Mitchell L. Rev. 447 (2010)

Roggensack, Patience Drake, *Plains Commerce Bank's Potential Collision with the Expansion of Tribal Court Jurisdiction by Senate Bill 3320*, 38 U. Balt. L. Rev. 29 (2008)

Rosecan, Stephen, Note, *A Meaningful Presentation: Proposing a Less Restrictive Way to Distribute Eagle Feathers*, 42 New Eng. L. Rev. 891 (2008)

Rosser, Ezra, *Ahistorical Indians and Reservation Resources*, 40 Envtl. L. 437 (2010)

Rosser, Ezra, *Protecting Non-Indians from Harm? The Property Consequences of Indians*, 87 Or. L. Rev. 175 (2008)

Royster, Judith V., *Practical Sovereignty, Political Sovereignty, and Indian Tribal Energy Development and Self-Determination Act*, 12 Lewis & Clark L. Rev. 1065 (2008)

Sai, David Keanu, *A Slippery Path Towards Hawaiian Indigeneity: An Analysis and Comparison Between Hawaiian State Sovereignty and Hawaiian Indigeneity and Its Use and Practice in Hawai'i Today*, 10 J. L. & Soc. Challenges 68 (2008)

Salamander, Nicole C., *A Half Full Circle: The Reserved Rights Doctrine and Tribal Reacquired Lands*, 12 U. Denv. Water L. Rev. 333 (2009)

Sanders, Marren, *Clean Water in Indian Country: The Risks (and Rewards) of Being Treated in the Same Manner as a State*, 36 Wm. Mitchell L. Rev. 533 (2010)

Sanders, Marren, *Ecosystem Co-Management Agreements: A Study of Nation Building or a Lesson on an Erosion of Tribal Sovereignty?*, 15 Buff. Envtl. L.J. 97 (2007–2008)

Saugee, Dean B. & Jack F. Trope, *Protection of Native American Sacred Places on Federal Lands*, 54 Rky. Mt. Min. L. Inst. 12-1 (2008)

Schnipper, Merritt, Note, *Ambiguous Abrogation: The First Circuit Strips the Narragansett Indian Tribe of Its Sovereign Immunity*, 31 W. New Eng. L. Rev. 243 (2009)

Shagen, Paul W., *Safeguarding the Integrity of Tribal Elections Through Campaign Finance Regulation*, 8 Cardozo Pub. L. Pol'y & Ethics J. 103 (2009)

Shaw, Kevin L. & Richard D. Deutsch, *Wind Power and Other Renewable Energy Projects: The New Wave of Power Project Development on Indian Lands*, 5 Rky. Mtn. Min. L. Inst 9-1 (2005)

Shipps, Thomas H., *Tribal Energy Resource Agreements: A Step Toward Self-Determination*, 22 Nat. Resources & Env't 55 (2007)

Shively, Erica, Note, *The Future of Quantifying Tribal Water Rights in North Dakota*, 84 N.D. L. Rev. 455 (2008)

Singel, Wenona T., *The Institutional Economics of Tribal Labor Relations*, 2008 Mich. St. L. Rev. 487

Sirica, Allison, *A Great Gamble: Why Compromise is the Best Bet to Resolve Florida's Indian Gaming Crisis*, 61 Fla. L. Rev. 1201 (2009)

Sixkiller, Jesse, Note, *Procedural Fairness: Ensuring Tribal Civil Jurisdiction After Plains Commerce Bank*, 26 Ariz. J. Intl' & Comp. L. 779 (2009)

Skibine, Alex Tallchief, *Culture Talk or Culture War in Federal Indian Law?*, 45 Tulsa L. Rev. 89 (2009)

Skibine, Alex Tallchief, *Indian Gaming and Cooperative Federalism*, 42 Ariz. St. L.J. 253 (2010)

Skibine, Alex Tallchief, *Tribal Sovereign Interests Beyond the Reservation Borders*, 12 Lewis & Clark L. Rev. 1003 (2008)

Slepnikoff, Lisa M., Student Article, *More Questions Than Answers: Plains Commerce Bank v. Long Family Land and Cattle Company, Inc. and the U.S. Supreme Court's Failure to Define the Extent of Tribal Civil Authority Over Nonmembers on Non-Indian Land*, 54 S.D. L. Rev. 460 (2009)

Slonim, Marc, *Indian Country, Indian Reservations, and the Importance of History in Indian Law*, 45 Gonz. L. Rev. 517 (2010)

Smith, Kaighn Jr., *Tribal Self-Determination and Judicial Restraint: The Problem of Labor and Employment Relations Within the Reservation*, 2008 Mich. St. L. Rev. 505

Smith, Mark A., *Contracting with Tribes Under 25 U.S.C. § 81: The Uncertainty Continues*, 20 Prob. & Prop. 8 (Mar/Apr 2006)

Smith, Michelle & Janet C. Neuman, *Keeping Indian Claims Commission Decisions in Their Place: Assessing the Preclusive Effect of ICC Decisions in Litigation Over Off-Reservation Treaty Fishing Rights*, 31 U. Haw. L. Rev. 475 (2009)

Spruhan, Paul, *The Canadian Indian Free Passage Right: The Last Stronghold of Explicit Race Restriction in United States Immigration Law*, 85 N.D. L. Rev 301 (2009)

Staudenmaier, Heidi McNeil & Anne W. Bishop, *The Three-Billion Dollar Question*, 57 Drake L. Rev. 323 (2009)

Struble, Matthew G., *Seminole Gaming Compact Part II: Whether Senate Bill 788 Satisfies the Compact Process Requirements as Written*, 34 Nova L. Rev. 296 (2009)

Swier, Brooke Delores, Student Article, *Gaming Goldmines Grow Green: Limited Gaming, Good Faith Negotiations, and Economic Impact of the Indian Gaming Regulatory Act in South Dakota*, 54 S.D. L. Rev. 493 (2009)

Taylor, Scott A., *Taxation in Indian Country After Carcieri v. Salazar*, 36 Wm. Mitchell L. Rev. 590 (2010)

Taylor, Scott A., *The Importance of Being Interest: Why a State Cannot Impose Its Income Tax on Tribal Bonds*, 25 Akron Tax J. 123 (2010)

Taylor, Scott A., *The Unending Onslaught of Tribal Sovereignty: State Taxation of Non-Member Indians*, 91 Marq. L. Rev. 917 (2008)

Terry, Matthew E., Note, *What's Fair Is Fair: Tribal Assertions of Jurisdiction Over Arbitration Decisions*, 2009 J. Dispute Resol. 255

Threedy, Debora L., *Claiming the Shields: Law, Anthropology, and the Role of Storytelling in a NAGPRA Repatriation Case Study*, 29 J. Land Resources & Envtl. L. 91 (2009)

Tompkins, Jill E., *Finding the Indian Child Welfare Act in Unexpected Places: Applicability in Private Non-Parent Custody Actions*, 81 U. Colo. L. Rev. 1119 (Fall 2010)

Tweedy, Ann E., *Connecting the Dots Between the Constitution, the Marshall Trilogy, and United States v. Lara: Notes Toward a Blueprint for the Next Legislative Restoration of Tribal Sovereignty*, 42 U. Mich. J.L. Reform 651 (2009)

Tweedy, Ann E., *Sex Discrimination Under Tribal Law*, 36 Wm. Mitchell L. Rev. 392 (2010)

Unger, Kathleen R., Note, *Change Is in the Wind: Self-Determination and Wind Power Through Tribal Energy Resources Agreements*, 43 Loy. L.A. L. Rev. 329 (2009)

Wagner, Joanna M., *Improving Native American Access to Federal Funding for Economic Development Through Partnerships with Rural Communities*, 32 Am. Indian L. Rev. 525 (2007–2008)

Wahwassuck, Korey, Hon. *et al.*, *Building a Legacy of Hope: Perspectives on Joint Tribal-State Jurisdiction*, 36 Wm. Mitchell L. Rev. 859 (2010)

Washburn, Kevin K., *Agency Conflict and Culture: Federal Implementation of the Indian Gaming Regulatory Act by the National Indian Gaming Commission, the Bureau of Indian Affairs, and the Department of Justice*, 42 Ariz. St. L.J. 303 (2010)

Washburn, Kevin *et al.*, Panel Discussion, *Paternalism or Protection? Federal Review of Tribal Economic Decisions in Indian Gaming*, 12 Gaming L. Rev. & Econ. 435 (2008)

Whittlesey, Dennis J., *Washington's Newest Battle: Indian Gaming v. Indian Gaming*, 12 Gaming L. Rev. & Econ. 408 (2008)

Wildenthal, Bryan H., *How the Ninth Circuit Overruled a Century of Supreme Court Indian Jurisprudence—And So Far Has Gotten Away with It*, 2008 Mich. St. L. Rev. 547

Wood, Alexander, Note & Comment, *Watering Down Federal Court Jurisdiction: What Role Do Federal Courts Play in Deciding Water Rights?*, 23 J. Envtl. L. & Litig. 241 (2008)

Wood, Mary Christina & Matthew O'Brien, *Tribes as Trustees Again (Part II): Evaluating Four Models of Tribal Participation in the Conservation Trust Movement*, 27 Stan. Envtl. L.J. 477 (2008)

Zanoni, Michelle Uberuaga, *Evaluating the Consequences of Climate Change on Indian Reserved Water Rights and the PIA: The Impracticable Irrigable Acreage Standard*, 31 Pub. Land & Resources L. Rev. 125 (2010)

Zug, Marcia A., *Dangerous Gamble: Child Support, Casino Dividends, and the Fate of the Indian Family*, 36 Wm. Mitchell L. Rev. 738 (2010)